Marginal Groups and Mainstream American Culture

Feminist Ethics

Marginal Groups and Mainstream American Culture

Edited by Yolanda Estes,
Arnold Lorenzo Farr, Patricia Smith,
and Clelia Smyth

University Press of Kansas

Published by the University Press of Kansas (Lawrence, Kansas 66045),
which was organized by the Kansas Board of Regents and is operated and
funded by Emporia State University, Fort Hays State University, Kansas State
University, Pittsburg State University, the University of Kansas, and Wichita
State University

Library of Congress Cataloging-in-Publication Data

Marginal groups and mainstream American culture / edited by
    Yolanda Estes . . . [et al.].
        p. cm. — (Feminist ethics)
Includes bibliographical references and index.
ISBN 978-0-7006-1047-1 (cloth : alk. paper)
ISBN 978-0-7006-1048-8 (pbk: alk. paper)
1. Marginality, Social—United States—Case studies. 2. Socially handicapped—
United States—Case studies. 3. Victims—United States—Case studies.
I. Estes, Yolanda. II. Series.
HN90.M26M37   2000   00-034983
305.5'6'0973—dc21

British Library Cataloguing in Publication Data is available.

Printed in the United States of America

10 9 8 7 6 5 4 3 2 1
The paper used in this publication meets the minimum requirements of the
American National Standard for Permanence of Paper for Printed Library
Materials Z39.48-1984.

Contents

Preface

Yolanda Estes and Arnold Lorenzo Farr

> *A Klee painting named "Angelus Novus" shows an angel looking as though he is about to move away from something he is fixedly contemplating. His eyes are staring, his mouth is open, his wings are spread. This is how one pictures the angel of history. His face is turned towards the past. Where we perceive a chain of events, he sees one single catastrophe which keeps piling wreckage upon wreckage and hurls it in front of his feet. The angel would like to stay, awaken the dead, and make whole what has been smashed. But a storm is blowing from paradise, it has got caught in his wings with such violence that the angel can no longer close them. This storm irresistibly propels him into the future to which his back is turned, while the pile of debris before him grows skyward. This storm is what we call progress.[1]*

Marginalization is a mode of creating and maintaining social identities and individual self-definitions affecting individuals at all levels of society, which involves constructing a dominant social identity against the background of excluded individuals and social groups. This process can become counterproductive for the dominant society as well as for alienated individuals or groups. *Marginal Groups and Mainstream American Culture* is a multidisciplinary collection of essays addressing marginalization (the problematic and relatively opaque side of identity formation) at a variety of social levels and within many different social phenomena. Essayists describe varied experiences of socially alienated individuals, providing theoretical analysis and ethical criticism of the contingent, historical mechanism of identity formation within marginalized groups.

The task of this book is to give a theoretical voice to individuals whose voices have been misinterpreted, usurped, or stifled and thus to reveal the personal, moral, and social implications of the process of marginalization by providing a critique of conventional modes of inquiry, individual critical descriptions of the experience of social alienation, and ethical criticism of marginalization. This book is intended for academics in the arts and sciences of humanities, but it should be accessible to college students and thus suitable for the classroom.

The authors fill lacunae in existing studies of marginalization. Despite the proliferation of recent academic literature addressing the topic, four defects exist in many discussions. Numerous accounts of marginalization approach the subject from an external perspective, fail to incorporate individual experience within a theoretical framework, overemphasize the pain, victimization, and powerlessness of marginalized individuals, and discourage moral self-reflection by marginalized groups.

The representation of the social margin as nothing more than a realm of degradation and impotence denies marginalized individuals any affirmation of their social identity other than a celebration of pain and diversity. Various theories of marginalization constitute another mode of derogating marginalized individuals, thereby neglecting their strength, autonomy, and virtues. Although well intentioned, many of these accounts present the social margin as a realm both alien to theory and immune to moral criticism. This approach compounds the conditions of social alienation by intimating that marginalized people are different in kind from other members of society, thus denying marginalized individuals' full rational and ethical status. Rather than initiating productive social change, this attitude encourages fatalism about social conflict and perpetuates the myth that "some incomprehensible other" is marginalized.

In order to provide accurate accounts of marginalization, it is necessary to reexamine conventional modes of inquiry and to produce critical descriptions of the personal experience of marginalization. Moreover, in order to increase theoretical comprehension of marginalization and to increase the theoretical power of marginalized individuals, it is essential to relate first-person descriptions to more general theoretical inquiries. Finally, marginalized individuals' self-affirmation degenerates into a sanctification of suffering insofar as their social groups lack opportunities to affirm their positive attributes and strengths or to articulate ethical criticism of themselves and other social groups. It is therefore crucial to articulate multidimensional moral, social, and political critiques of marginalization, which affirm the positive attributes of marginalized groups without ignoring their negative attributes or condoning the systems of oppression that give rise to both.

Despite valiant efforts to shed the external perspective, many discussions of marginalized groups remain naive because they make little effort at critical interpretation and oversimplify (or discount) firsthand descriptions of marginalization. Various theories of marginalization disregard individual experience. Other discussions assume an internal perspective but remain resistant to theory and self-reflective ethical criticism. Many works attempt to formulate emancipatory solutions to the problems of marginalized groups but fail to acknowledge the extent to which these very solutions may have an oppressive effect or may inhibit critical self-reflection.

The authors of this book compensate for these deficiencies in many contemporary discussions of marginalization. Authors examine how theoretical accounts of marginalization often exacerbate the problems they investigate or sustain myths that impose theorists' preconceptions or prejudices on marginalized groups. They explain how marginalized individuals can explicate their comprehension of their own situations and assume their rightful place within the ongoing theoretical dialogue. Finally, by considering the general implications of marginalization in the ethical realm and formulating a thorough critique of the harmful effects of this process, essayists discuss the need for expanded theoretical accounts of marginalization that do not merely comprehend the phenomenon but also initiate social change.

Note

1. Walter Benjamin, *Illuminations*, trans. Harry Zohn (New York: Shocken Books, 1968), 257–258.

Acknowledgments

The editors thank our departments (and former departments) at Baruch College, CUNY, Mississippi State University, Saint Joseph's University, the University of Colorado at Boulder, and the University of Kentucky for tangible and intangible support of our work. Our work on this anthology was partly supported by grants from Mississippi State University.

The editors acknowledge the University Press of Kansas. In particular, we thank Nancy Scott Jackson, Dorothea Anderson, and Susan Schott for their prompt, intelligent, and cheerful advice. In addition, the series editor, Claudia Card, provided a generous and very helpful review of the book proposal and the manuscript, for which we remain grateful. We thank Lucius Outlaw for reading and commenting on the entire manuscript. Our contributors deserve hearty thanks for bearing with us throughout the project and for lending us their talents.

Finally, several individuals deserve special acknowledgment. Paul Jacobs, the department head at Mississippi State University, was very supportive of the project. Others at Mississippi State University to whom we owe our thanks include Cindy Henson, who gave daily invaluable secretarial support; Jared Hutson, who provided superb editorial assistance; Erin Murphry, who helped with completing the index and assembling the final manuscript; and the office assistants, who made our task much easier: Sonia Kelly, Matt Barnes, Jared Hutson, Kayce Smith, Carolyn Keltc, Kristy Fleming, and Clint Livingston. We will not forget these individuals or their efficient and unstinting support.

Introduction

Yolanda Estes

Women live in the social margins of almost every land and culture because men represent the ideal of humanity, and women represent a poor imitation of that ideal. Women everywhere experience oppression, which ranges from subtle discrimination to flagrant abuse. Moreover, worldwide oppression of women manifests itself in similar ways, which include control over women's bodies, reproductive power, economic condition, nutrition, labor, and sexuality. Nonetheless, the marginalization of women differs according to their socioeconomic, geographical, and cultural positions. Individual values and choices also influence women's experience of oppression. Any generalization seems open to boundless counterexamples embodied by unique, individual women. In light of this, can we say that women share a common identity? Gender seems to play a role in the formation of these diverse, individual identities, but does that mean that women are bound to a feminine essence, which determines their identities and personal choices?

In Chapter 1, Diana Tietjens Meyers addresses the difficulties some feminists face in attempting to define a common identity or experience for women. Meyers reiterates contemporary feminist analyses of the interplay between socialization and individual women's lives. She argues that women have no common identity, but gender and marginalization affect individual identity. Consequently, "cultural gender, race, sexuality, class, and ethnicity conceptions are internalized, to be sure, but they are also processed psychologically. . . . However, this processing neither dissolves the individual's ties to her cultural milieu and its regnant conceptions of these identities nor endows the individual with complete control

1

over her identity insofar as it bears imprints of gender, race, class, and ethnicity." Moreover, these tensions provide an invaluable impetus for moral reflection, social criticism, and political activism. Meyers argues that many so-called essentialist gender theories are not so much inductive generalizations as literary texts, metaphors, or tropes, which support many different interpretations. She concludes that this view "advances our understanding of the epistemology of social critique" and "epistemically vindicates the project of theorizing marginalized groups."[1]

The idea of women's marginalization suggests a struggle between the "boys" and the "girls." Many theorists distinguish between sex (males and females) and gender (boys and girls). Some theorists believe the binary opposition of genders (and sexes) reflects the oppressive expectations of a sexist and heterosexist society. As a matter of fact, people are classified by gender, and people (many of them female) experience gender-based oppression. This sociopolitical fact leaves feminists wondering what to do with gender. If gender is the basis for certain types of oppression, would eliminating gender end those forms of oppression? Alternatively, should we simply reevaluate or expand concepts of gender in order to escape gender conceptions that devalue women and restrict everyone to a binary gender structure?

In Chapter 2, Christine Overall considers three feminist proposals for transforming gender: the revaluation of the feminine, the appeal to androgyny, and the endorsement of multiple genders. After discussing the strengths and weaknesses of each position, she argues that radical feminist principles entail the elimination of gender. Like many theorists, she believes gender-based oppression serves as a keystone within many other oppressive systems. She contends that a fundamental shift away from gender, in terminology, theory, and practice, could lead us closer to the feminist ideal of a world without oppression, in which the remaining margins would be more malleable than the present gender-dependent barriers.

Until we realize this ideal, marginalized people will continue to fight oppression. Sexism is one common form of marginalization, but the marginalization of particular races, ethnicities, and sexual orientations is nearly universal as well. Unlike most women, these groups are often forced into the physical margins (ghettos) of towns and cities. The geographical exclusion of groups and individuals serves as a powerful device for regulating marginalized groups. However, many such groups carve out physical spaces for themselves in which they can live authentically in relative safety. These spaces serve to consolidate resources, create sites of resistance, and establish a physical, political, and economic "presence" for marginalized groups. Ironically, and perhaps predictably, the visible concentration of marginalized groups in "safe" spaces leaves them vulnerable to pointed psychic and physical attack.

In Chapter 3, Gavin Brown uses his reflections on the April 1999 bombings in London as a springboard for a critical analysis of queer spaces and the position of gay people in contemporary British society.[2] He shows how gays and lesbians have used intangible, political, and economic resources to create city spaces where they can express their sexuality, or simply exist, without fear or pressure to pass as straight. Brown considers the social progress achieved by gays and lesbians (and the positive changes in relations between the straight and gay communities) without disguising the degree to which society and political institutions remain heterosexist. He also dismantles the simplistic conception of marginalized groups as victims by demonstrating the manner in which they can shape an adverse environment. Brown considers the troubling fact, which many theorists loathe to address, that multiple layers of marginalization exist even in marginalized communities. He suggests that straight and gay people would do well to consider the degree to which insidious racial, economic, and sexual marginalization flourishes beneath our enlightened rhetoric of equality and tolerance.

One (but not the only) reason gays and lesbians are marginalized is that their sexuality threatens heterosexual norms based on the domination of women. Historically, feminine sexuality represents passivity and receptivity whereas activity and productivity characterize masculine sexuality. Although social institutions encourage women to conform to the "feminine" model, many theorists conceive this model as an inferior, inverted, or incomplete form of sexual expression. Mainstream society and many theories of sexuality condemn any sexual practice that expresses passivity and receptivity.

In Chapter 4, Jami Weinstein and Jeffrey Bussolini use masturbation as an example of a sexual expression that originates from desire conceived as a self-fulfillment. They propose an "ontology of ethics," which allows for authentic ways of sexual being that do not depend on activity and productivity for their integrity. Weinstein and Bussolini reconsider sexual theories of philosophers such as Jean Paul Sartre and Simone de Beauvoir, who conceive sexual desire as the futile yearning for completion through the subjugation of the sexual partner. They argue for a radically open (and radically relativistic) ontological ethics, based on a reconception of sexual desire that allows for "a whole range of formerly marginalized activities," including "activities previously considered 'deviant' or 'incomplete.'" Weinstein and Bussolini maintain that they do not "desire others simply to fulfill some need but rather for the way in which we can mutually augment our joy and power through combinations of our ontological rhythms of speeds and slownesses."[3]

Despite the marginalization of many sexual practices, it might seem that contemporary society has become more receptive—if only in a voyeuristic, "experimental" manner—to sexualities that defy the ideals of activity and productivity. Although one might deplore the widespread embrace of sexual "experiments" as titillating variations from routine, one might also celebrate the fact that gays and lesbians express their sexuality openly (in some circles), that women achieve academic and economic success (in some fields), and that many ethnic and racial groups enjoy legal equality (in some countries).

Despite sustained and deep-rooted prejudice, it seems that most people espouse principles of equality, condemn "hate" crimes, and prefer a nondiscriminatory society. Nonetheless, gays and lesbians endure a disproportionate number of physical attacks, women lag behind men economically, and members of many racial groups fill the ghettos, hospitals, prisons, and morgues. These examples merely identify a few problems facing visibly marginalized groups. In the aftermath of legal reforms, social revolutions, and grassroots rebellions, fundamental social change remains a distant ideal.

In Chapter 5, Patricia Smith examines the "wind tunnel effect," which she describes as "a pervasive collection of devices by which mainstream cultures retard deviance and support the *status quo*." She uses the condition of blacks in American society as an example of how the wind tunnel operates and examines the interplay between structural and attitudinal mechanisms of marginalization. Smith argues that these mechanisms disarm potentially revolutionary movements in ways that promote stability in social institutions and practices. She acknowledges that "reform on behalf of marginalized groups will necessarily be slow, even when marginalization is recognized as illegitimate in principle, because all the social mechanisms that maintain stability and privilege maintain marginalization as well."[4]

Although discouraging, this admission contains a note of optimism: Many people recognize that marginalization is illegitimate in principle, and thus reform occurs but slowly, to be sure. People usually discern the illegitimacy of discriminatory practices, because they have the opportunity to observe the accomplishments of individual marginalized people. Indeed, reform would be impossible if not for the effort of marginalized individuals and the communities that support their endeavors. Nonetheless, transcending one's imposed status often entails leaving the marginalized community, which fostered one's dreams, and entering the dominant society, which accepts one's accomplishments grudgingly. Individuals often discover that the center views their achievements as "exceptions to the rule" or as "good for" a member of a marginalized group. These remarginalizing practices derogate the hard-earned accomplishments of marginalized people, who often accept (as the price of living their dreams) the role of outsider in the dominant as well as the marginal society.

In Chapter 6, Arnold Lorenzo Farr recalls a comment: "You're the smartest black man that I know." He calls such remarginalizing speech acts "complimentary racism." Farr proposes that "the oppressive narrative from which this speech act derives its possibility fails in its attempt to fully determine the marginalized subject. . . . due to this failure . . . the margins are a site for transformative, emancipatory political activity." He urges individuals to overcome the negative effects of marginalization by maintaining a dialectical tension between marginalization and transcendence. In other words, marginalized people must affirm their status while rejecting its power to determine their interpretation of their possibilities. Farr maintains: "Identity formation in a society is always incomplete to the extent that the dialectic between inclusion and exclusion perpetuates an ongoing process of reformulation, re-adjusting, redefining boundaries, re-excluding, remaking etc. . . . . Identity construction harbors within itself a deconstruction of the constructed identity and its own mode of self-alteration."[5]

The process of identity construction involves interpreting our limitations and freely choosing what kind of self we are to be. One problem with a marginal identity is that, however broad a person's interpretation might be, his or her possibilities are limited. Although one is free, one cannot simply interpret away the fact that one happens to be female or Jewish.[6] Nonetheless, an individual must negotiate among conflicting attitudes toward the history, values, and ideas inherited from his or her people. Everyone inherits something from the past, and thus each unique consciousness could tell a story about constructing its "self" from its history.

In Chapter 7, Sandra Bartky states that, "marginal or not, everyone is handed an identity that has somehow to be navigated." Relating how she "steered a course between the Scylla of Jewish self-hatred and the Charybdis of Jewish triumphalism," her narrative generates personal and universal appeal. Bartky delineates a pattern of identity formation, which many marginalized people could recognize in their own personal histories. She identifies three dialectical moments in this pattern: the uncritical acceptance of a marginalized identity, the rejection of that "self" in favor of a freely chosen identity, and the reconciliation of one's "selves" in a unified consciousness. Bartky's story illustrates her claim that "self-reflection, which is crucial to the construction of identity, is reflection on the variations that a subject undergoes in time; the subject is in a continual process of dispersion and retrieval in which he or she attempts to combine persistence through time with dispersion and discontinuity."[7]

Self-reflection is also necessary for groups to construct acceptable marginalized identities. Indeed, marginalized groups must construct cultural and political identities in order to survive. Many of these groups see assimilation as the key to economic and political power, and the center actually recommends this path to some marginalized groups, particularly when the social price of separation exceeds the benefits or when some greater benefit derives from integration.[8] Assimilation, however, may result in the destruction of some marginalized groups as well as loss of political identity and power. For many groups, integration means subjection to more subtle, insidious, and harmful forms of racial and economic oppression.[9] To the degree that a group technically integrates itself, it becomes practically (from a political standpoint) invisible. Marginalized groups can use their positions as powerful levers to accomplish economic, political, and social goals even as they protest the histories that brought them to the margins originally.

In Chapter 8, Rebecca Tsosie uses the struggles of the Mashpee Tribe and Native Hawaiians to illustrate the tension between indigenous sovereignty movements and the historic legacy of federal recognition policy. She shows that federal policies worked to assimilate and colonize Native Americans. Tsosie argues that this history hindered Indian groups' attempts to preserve their indigenous identities. Indeed, Native peoples' political identities depend on their ability to demonstrate their marginalization according to legal, objective criteria, and hence those groups that adapt culturally are most at risk for cultural and political extinction. She asserts that "citizenship may be inconsistent with tribalism in a society founded upon racial, social, and economic stratification and difference, where 'marginalization' is the only way to preserve the values of a different culture and political organization."[10]

Marginalized groups are often identified by objective features of their existence, but a culture's or society's experience of marginalization cannot be reduced to a set of observable criteria. The experience of marginalization generates political identities and activism. Nonetheless, acknowledging this phenomenal element raises several troubling questions. Can dominant social groups *feel* marginalized and be motivated politically by that experience? Do empirical facts of exclusion always generate an experience of marginalization?

In Chapter 9, Patrick D. Hopkins argues that the social, political, and psychological effects of marginalization are best explained by the experience of feeling marginalized rather than by some objective criterion. He claims that empirical facts of sociopolitical situation are not nearly as important in generating the experience of marginalization as facts of ideological situation, because feeling marginalized depends on ideological commitments about what counts as being respected or as being oppressed. Hopkins illustrates his claims by describing the ideological commitments that shape conservative Christians' experience of marginalization. He shows how this ideology represents "a serious altruistic and moral impulse" and that multiculturalists "cannot demand of conservative believers that they 'respect' others' beliefs without . . . failing to respect the core (evangelical) beliefs of that culture itself."[11]

The ideological commitments of social groups provide an important clue for understanding their experience and behavior. Many bigoted ideologies, such as racism and sexism, are irrational. Attempts to defeat these ideologies by exposing the irrationality of the beliefs usually have little effect, because their adherents cling dogmatically to commitments that define their identities and worldview. Moreover, these dogmatic belief systems reproduce their core values and attitudes in each generation, so the chance of converting dogmatic believers by criticizing their ideologies seems slim at best.

In Chapter 10, Wallace A. Murphree asks how dogmatic belief systems can be altered and analyzes the self-perpetuating cycle of "dogmatic evangelical exclusivism." He argues that the exclusivity of many belief systems, such as fundamentalist Christianity, is less problematic than the dogmatic evangelism. Moreover, he delineates a crucial distinction between morally motivated and selfishly motivated dogmatists. Murphree suggests that reformers draw the former into moral discussions about their metabeliefs (dogmatic evangelism) rather than ridicule their core exclusive beliefs. He applies this analysis to other forms of bigotry, suggesting that "not all dogmatism is motivated by self-interests and . . . there is no reason to believe that only members of the privileged side of the boundary embrace the dogmatism that secures it. . . . It is unfair to dutiful dogmatists to group them into the same moral category with selfish dogmatists, since they lead radically different types of ethical lives."[12]

If the marginalization, ideology, and personal choice stand in a mutually determining relationship, sorting out that relationship is a difficult task for which marginalized individuals and societies must assume responsibility. Unfortunately, time does not stand still while individuals and societies decipher these relationships. While we struggle to make sense of things, time passes, and we accumulate a past that reflects our comprehension of the world and ourselves at the time. Obviously, societies and marginalized individuals will make mistakes, and these mistakes, in turn, will be incorporated within our worldview and become part of a mutually determining dynamic of ideology and personal choice.

In Chapter 11, Yolanda Estes relays her experience as an excluded child, a rebellious adolescent, and a "renegade" youth. Attempting to walk the fine line between acknowledging one's facticity and assuming one's freedom, she considers the effects of social exclusion on children. Her narrative shows that her life as a self-marginalized social rebel, renegade, and refugee portrays a combination of poor personal decisions along with perceptions and conceptions developed as an unwillingly marginalized loner. Estes claims that social exclusion affects a child's perception, cognition, emotions, communication, and relationships. She suggests that "without caution and foresight, we may find ourselves contemplating 'statistics' rather than 'confessions.' Lest that prophecy be fulfilled (if it is not fulfilling right now), we must consider the forces that educe the attitudes, perceptions, and behaviors of loners."[13]

Marginalization imposes difficulties and restrictions on the individual, but many people usurp these mechanisms in order to initiate moral, social, and political change.[14] Many theorists, writers, and artists employ such tactics to redefine mainstream conceptions, such as beauty, humanity, and disability. These individuals set an example of how marginalized people can use their freedom to change the world.

In Chapter 12, Rosemarie Garland-Thomson analyzes the performance strategies used by two artists who identify themselves publicly and politically as physically disabled women and who, by incorporating their disabled bodies in the performance of their art, articulate a powerful political and artistic message. She argues that "we are marked not by our bodies themselves, but by responses to our bodies: by the stares that record our otherness, by the narratives that establish our inadequacy, by the barriers that keep us out, by the norms that render us abnormal." Garland-Thomson shows how these artists manipulate the "stare" to redefine mainstream conceptions of gender, beauty, and disability. She shows that the staring dynamic is a "visual interaction that can be appropriated to . . . redefine disabled female subjectivity" and that can provide the basis for a "poetics of the disabled body."[15]

The work, art, and personal example of individuals initiate

cultural change, but sociopolitical institutions often disregard or resist those changes. Consequently, the entrenchment of institutions, which intend to support individual social members and fundamental social values, often fails to reflect the needs and values of individuals. In order to achieve maximum social impact, institutional reorganization must support individual endeavors and cultural changes.

In Chapter 13, Patricia Smith claims that "institutional entrenchment . . . has had the odd effect of marginalizing the majority of family arrangements." She acknowledges that a real "crisis of caregiving" exists, which can be explained historically, and thus partially, by the influx of women into the workplace. Smith, however, argues that responsibility for this crisis is attributed to the personal choices of "abnormal" mothers, such as working mothers, single mothers, and divorced mothers, rather than to the tensions and contradictions of contemporary society itself. She analyzes some contradictory expectations of contemporary society, which encourages women to enter the workplace yet withholds institutional compensation for traditional caretaking roles. Smith admonishes that the crisis of caretaking "must be recognized as a social responsibility, not a personal problem."[16]

The notion of social responsibility must be expanded to include the care of children, elders, physically or mentally disabled individuals, and the needy. These responsibilities—once assumed by families or communities—can no longer be fulfilled without state support and intervention. In addition to providing the worst-off members of society with basic sustenance and care, small social groups traditionally provided individuals with a sense of self-esteem and membership. Social justice requires equitable obligations and rights, but these concepts reflect the cultural, economic, and technological conditions of a given society. In contemporary society, the notion of rights may include the right to self-respect, which derives from being a contributing member of one's society. All social members cannot make the same contributions, but in a just society based on the principle of equality, all members need the opportunity to contribute and participate to the best of their ability.

In Chapter 14, Sigal R. Benporath argues that traditional theories of justice make no provision for mentally disabled citizens to participate in their society. Benporath says that "functioning on the social and economic levels—working, forming social ties, and performing a variety of activities suited to the capacity of the individual—can also be a form of participation." She suggests that political theorists adopt guiding rules that promote a sense of belonging and contributing to society, because this sense is essential for the development of self-respect, which is "the most important basic good" in contemporary developed societies. Benporath sees the opportunity for meaningful work and social participation as a "first political step" toward a just society; she sees the necessary "second step" as realizing the moral obligations presupposed by her analysis "in order to act fairly and justly toward all their members, whatever their natural endowments might be."[17]

Each of these authors suggests ways to improve our theories of marginalization and draws ethical implications from their accounts. Obviously, we cannot accept every proposal, for not all of these suggestions are mutually consistent. Nonetheless, we can use these accounts as a preliminary basis for future lines of inquiry, which we hope will serve to enhance our comprehension of marginalization and to produce moral, social, and political changes in the world.

Notes

1. Diana Tietjens Meyers, Chapter 1.
2. See Gavin Brown, Chapter 3, for an overview of the bombings of Afro-Caribbean, Bangladeshi, and gay neighborhoods in London.
3. Jami Weinstein and Jeffrey Bussolini, Chapter 4.
4. Patricia Smith, Chapter 5.
5. Arnold Lorenzo Farr, Chapter 6.
6. To be sure, some individuals and groups choose to abandon the center for the margins, but these decisions are responses to *some* identity, which was originally *imposed*.
7. Sandra Bartky, Chapter 7.
8. Welfare reform is one example of how some marginalized groups (particularly single mothers) are urged to integrate themselves into the mainstream (the workplace) because the real or perceived social costs of maintaining their separation exceed the benefits. Lately, blacks, Hispanics, Native people, and some disabled people have been encouraged to assimilate for various reasons.
9. For instance, welfare reform will mean for many people, particularly single mothers, an all too familiar story of inadequate housing, underemployment, low pay, and poor child care. In the past, assimilation for some Appalachians, Hispanics, and Native people meant geographical displacement,

social alienation, and cultural loss along with more immediate problems such as disease, hunger, and homelessness. Even benignly intentioned and necessary social programs like desegregation in the South resulted in destruction of black neighborhood schools, small businesses, and recreational areas; see, for example, Farr, Chapter 6. Assimilation thus resulted in almost no significant loss or change within the dominant society but led to considerable change and destruction for the integrated groups with very little gain; see, for example, Smith, Chapter 5.

10. Rebecca Tsosie, Chapter 8.

11. Patrick D. Hopkins, Chapter 9.

12. Wallace A. Murphree, Chapter 10.

13. Yolanda Estes, Chapter 11.

14. See Farr's discussion in Chapter 6 of how complimentary racism and other speech acts can be turned against dominant social groups.

15. Rosemarie Garland-Thomson, Chapter 12.

16. Patricia Smith, Chapter 13.

17. Sigal R. Benporath, Chapter 14.

Chapter One

Marginalized Identities: Individuality, Agency, and Theory

Diana Tietjens Meyers

I must assume, not just as history but as an ongoing psychological force, that, in the eyes of white culture, irrationality, lack of control, and ugliness signify not just the whole slave personality, but me.[1]

I don't recall ever choosing to identify as a male; but being male has shaped many of my plans and actions.[2]

People do not choose their race and gender. These are thrust upon us. Nor is it within one's power as an individual to expel race or gender from one's life. That our society and the people we associate with classify us according to race and gender is not controversial. Likewise, few would dispute that access to social, economic, and political opportunities and other goods differs depending on race and gender. Yet, in recent feminist theory, a controversy has emerged about whether women have gender identities. Some feminist scholars have denied that social institutions and cultural traditions instill gender in our cognitive, emotional, and motivational infrastructures, that is, in our identities. In this chapter, I take issue with that claim. I urge that marginalization is internalized and becomes integral to individualized, marginalized identities.[3] Moreover, I explicate the epistemological contribution of individualized, marginalized identities to social critique, and I defend the epistemological feasibility of theorizing marginalized identities.

Group Membership, Identity, and Individuality

According to Iris Young, a leading exponent of the anti-identity view, women are members of a group precursor, but they do not necessarily have a gender identity.[4] To explain gender, Young invokes Jean-Paul Sartre's idea of seriality. A social series is "a social collective whose members are unified passively by the objects around which their actions are oriented or by the objectified results of the material effects of the actions of the others."[5] In other words, a series is constituted by a behavior-directing, meaning-defining environment. The lives of series members are affected by being assigned to particular social series, for serial existence is experienced as a "felt necessity" that leaves individuals feeling powerless.[6] People feel impelled to act in ways that conform to their series memberships. Yet series membership *does not define the person's identity* in the sense of forming his/her individual purposes, projects, and the sense of self in relation to others."[7] Indeed, individuals can *choose* to make none of their serial memberships important to their individual identity.[8]

Young's view is premised on a false dichotomy: Either social positioning is constitutive of individual identity, and all similarly positioned individuals share a common identity, or else social positioning is external to individual identity unless a person decides to let it in. Since it is indisputable that women do not share a common identity—the same can be said of members of racial, sexuality, class, and ethnic groups—Young opts for the voluntarist position. One is a member of this or that social series whether one likes it or not. One becomes a member of a social group only when one elects to join it. Group membership shapes one's identity only if one allows it to do so.

The alternative to this individualist voluntarism is not gender (race, sexuality, class, or ethnic) essentialism and a common feminine (racial, sexual, class, or ethnic) identity. The alternative is gendered *and* individualized identities. At one point, Young seems to concede this very point. No woman's identity "will escape the *markings of gender*," she observes, "but how gender marks her life is her own."[9] I agree—identities are individualized. But I hasten to add that how gender marks a woman's (or a man's) identity will not be entirely her (or his) own choice. Gender worms its way into identity in ways that we may not be conscious of and in ways that we may not be able to change no matter how much we try.[10] Gender is constitutive of who we are—our personalities, our capabilities and liabilities, our aspirations, and how we feel about all of these dimensions of identity. Yet, there is no feature of identity that all women or that all men share. The same is true of other marginalized and privileged identity categories. How is this possible?

Nancy Chodorow uses psychoanalytic theory to make sense of individualized, gendered identities. Psychoanalysis explains how individuals "personally animate and tint . . . the anatomic, cultural, interpersonal, and cognitive world we experience."[11] One's affective dispositions, unconscious fantasies, and interpersonal relationships filter the culturally entrenched conception of gender that one encounters. Through various psychic processes—projection and introjection together with the defense mechanisms—gender acquires a "personal meaning" that is inspired by but does not wholly replicate culturally transmitted strictures and iconography.[12] As Chodorow somewhat paradoxically puts it, each woman creates "her own personal-cultural gender."[13]

It is a mistake to picture attributes like gender as toxic capsules full of norms and interpretive schemas that individuals swallow whole and that lodge intact in their psychic structure. The diversity of individuals' experience of gender belies this view. But as the epigrams taken from Patricia Williams and Anthony Appiah attest, it is also a mistake to picture attributes like gender as systems of social and economic opportunities, constraints, rewards, and penalties that never impinge upon individual identity.[14] The seeming naturalness of enacting gendered characteristics, the passion with which people cling to their sense of their gender, and the intractability of many gendered attributes when people seek to change them testify to the embeddedness of gender in identity.

Cultural gender, race, sexuality, class, and ethnicity are internalized, to be sure, but they are also processed psychologically. This lifelong processing individualizes these socially mandated dimensions of identity. However, this processing neither dissolves the individual's ties to his or her cultural milieu and its regnant conceptions of these identities nor endows the individual with complete control over his or her identity insofar as it bears the imprint of gender, race, class, and ethnicity.

I wish to stress, however, that individuals can exert a good deal of control over their group-based identities. They can become conscious of how gender, for instance, is limiting and frustrating them; they can become estranged from these features of their identity; and they can seek out transformative practices—e.g., consciousness-raising or psychotherapy—and undertake to overcome them. Likewise, they can participate in movements that aim to redefine gender along emancipatory lines and thus seek to spare future generations of women the need to struggle against some of the pernicious strictures and meanings that they internalized as girls and had to fight as women.

Marginalized Identities, Social Critique, and Political Agency

I shall now turn to the question of why it is important to see womanhood and other marginalized social identities as dimensions of individual identity. Let us listen to Patricia Williams again:

> I think: my raciality is socially constructed, and I experience it as such. I feel my blackself as an eddy of conflicted meanings—and meaninglessness—in which my self can get lost, in which agency and consent are tumbled in constant motion. This sense of motion, the constant windy sound of manipulation whistling in my ears, is a reminder of society's constant construction of my blackness.[15]

Since Williams distinguishes between her blackself and her self and comments that her blackself threatens to eclipse her self, it might seem that she is reifying and compartmentalizing her socially imposed blackself and her imperiled own self. Thus, it is tempting to suppose that she is reviving some sort of notion of an innate, core, authentic self surrounded by layers of socially constructed, inauthentic, overpowering self-toids. I doubt, though, that she is endorsing such a simplistic and discredited view.[16] Rather I would urge that she is succinctly and poignantly accomplishing several goals: 1) she acknowledges the power of social structures and discourses to invade and inhabit individual psyches by asserting that she has a blackself; 2) she insists on the disparity between the cultural stereotype (her blackself) and the inner reality (her own self); 3) she highlights the agentic resources of individuality by affirming that her own self resists the destructive forces of social construction; and 4) she communicates the excruciating bewilderment and conflict such racialized, marginalized subjectivity inflicts. The rest of Williams's essay is a probing examination and a trenchant critique of the construction of African-American womanhood and manhood in the United States today.

I shall take my cue from Williams's text; that is, I shall focus on the interplay between group-based identities, alienation, and moral reflection. In my view, the kind of alienation Williams describes is, alas, desirable as long as we live in societies that marginalize some social groups while privileging others, for this unsettled, disquieting sense of self can spark insightful moral reflection and emancipatory social critique.

What is so awful about having a marginalized, perhaps multiply marginalized identity is that one seldom feels at ease in one's own skin. One may be plagued by layers of consciousness—one's objectives and intentions; how others, especially members of other social groups, are likely to perceive one's conduct; how others' various possible misperceptions may spoil one's undertakings; and so forth. Of course, people are never transparent to one another, and misunderstandings abound in all interpersonal relations. However, it is quite another matter when stereotyping unconsciously but systematically blocks mutual understanding.

María Lugones describes herself as an intense person, yet she knows that Anglos routinely stereotype her as an intense Latin.[17] Thus, when she is speaking or gesturing intensely, her consciousness is often split—between her desire to demonstrate the gravity of her point and to give expression to her distinctive personality traits, on the one hand, and her knowledge that her behavior will be dismissed as merely typical and that her ideas will not be accorded the weight they deserve, on the other. From one point of view, such communication blocks are tragic; they isolate us from others and impoverish our lives. But Lugones does not dwell exclusively on the misery and injustice that stem from these barriers. She also invites marginalized individuals to take delight in the absurdity of their predicament and to deliberately toy with others' bigoted preconceptions, sometimes masquerading in the stereotype and sometimes feeling intense and acting that way, but always knowing that the Other cannot tell which is which.[18]

What needs to be underscored here is that Lugones's strategy presupposes a complex understanding of who she is, an understanding that is not limited to but that incorporates her membership in social groups. She can only make a mockery of bigotry and manipulate it for her own ends if she recognizes both the potency of the social construction of her identity and the laughable megalomania of its pretensions to total control over who she is and who she can be. In a similar vein, Williams's essay documents the insidious ways in which African-American women and men are recruited into marginalized gender identities that they then inflict on one another and that whites use as excuses for despising them. But through her own simultaneous avowal and refusal of her "blackself," she marshals critical acuity that enables her to depict the pathos of this complicity and to decry the oppression that secures it.

Who one is affects the way one thinks about society—what issues will be salient, how one conceptualizes and interrelates them, what policies and practices seem benign, and what sorts of change seem urgent. One's moral outlook is not independent of one's identity, and one's identity is not independent of one's position in the world. Yet, as we have seen, one's identity is individualized. Coupled with crosscutting group allegiances, individuality often splinters marginalized groups and (lamentably) hinders mass political mobilization. Nevertheless, I would urge that the individualization of marginalized identities is indispensable to social dissidence. Each individual has peculiar talents and deficiencies, satisfactions and frustrations, fancies and antipathies, yearnings and dreads, ambitions and resignations, and the like. Not only do these attributes make people unique, but they also leverage critique. Conflicts between one's individualized, marginalized identity and dominant cultural traditions or authoritative institutions provide a vital impetus to social analysis and oppositional activism, for people care deeply about living a life that expresses who they are.

Iris Young is right, then, to stress that the specific circumstances of women's lives give rise to specific affinities around which they may choose to organize and act.[19] However, these affinities should not be severed from marginalized identities. It is the clash within the individualized, marginalized identity and between the individualized, marginalized identity and the marginalizing social context that fuels these affinities.

The Epistemic Status of "Essentialist" Theory

It might seem that my view of marginalized identity, moral reflection, and political engagement throws the whole project of theorizing marginalized groups into disrepute. And if the line of thought I have developed does not altogether dispose of this kind of theory, it might seem that it collapses it into the general project of explicating the psychological mechanism of identity consolidation. In my view, however, drawing this inference rests on a misunderstanding of the epistemic status of accounts of marginalized groups.

My argument takes off from my conviction that many of the gender theories that have been most convincingly condemned as "essentialist"—such as Chodorow's account of the perpetuation of exclusively female mothering and Catharine MacKinnon's account of women's objectified sexuality—are nevertheless insightful and illuminating. However, admitting that charges of essentialism against these theories are telling seems to contradict the latter judgment. If, contrary to Chodorow, some women are not relational and nurturant, and if, contrary to MacKinnon, some women's sexuality defies pornographic imagery and male violation, it seems to follow that these theories are false and therefore worthless.

If one regards these theories as inductive generalizations about women, they are certainly false as they stand. They couch their claims in universalist terms, and the empirical data furnish ample disconfirming evidence. However, I believe that this social scientific epistemic model is not the best one to adopt. Instead, I propose that we think of gender theories like Chodorow's and MacKinnon's on the model of interpretations of literary texts. Literary interpretations cannot ignore the texts they purport to analyze and explain. They must cite supporting passages and explain away apparent inconsistencies between the text and the interpretation being proffered. However, since the text itself may not be perfectly coherent, there may be no single interpretation that leaves nothing in it unexplained. Thus, there is a general consensus that a single text can reasonably be interpreted in more than one way and that many of these interpretations are insightful and illuminating. In other words, literary texts are rich enough to sustain a number of divergent interpretations. No text conveys just one meaning to every reader, and readers can deepen their appreciation of works of literature by familiarizing themselves with other readers' interpretations.

Similarly, social phenomena, such as gender, race, sexuality, class, and ethnicity, and psychological phenomena, such as gendered, raced, sexualized, classed, and ethnically imprinted identities, are extremely complex and variable, and they look different from different angles. Consequently, it would be foolish to expect to capture these phenomena in one comprehensive account. Nevertheless, as Marilyn Frye maintains, it is imperative that we study them and try to identify patterns in the phenomena—social forces that maintain these hierarchical social systems and motifs running through different individuals' subjective sense of their gender, race, sexuality, class, and ethnicity.[20] Frye suggests that we regard gender theory as akin to metaphors.[21] Good metaphors are apt and revealing. However, a metaphor asserts an equivalence that will prove misleading if it is taken literally and pursued too far, and no one metaphor ever expressed the complete and definitive truth about a phenomenon.

If theories of marginalized groups resemble tropes more than they resemble statistical tabulations, it is worth recalling that hyperbole numbers among the canonical figures of speech. Thus, the universalist language in which many gender theories are articulated can be understood as an instance of the rhetorical device of exaggeration. But here it might be objected that the trouble with hyperbole is that it is all too similar to yelling. The practical effect of relatively privileged feminists' hyperbolic theorizing may be to drown out the voices of other women and to enshrine their interpretations of gender as authoritative. Worse, perhaps, when relatively privileged feminists base their political activism on a gender theory that makes sense of their experience while neglecting the experience of many other women, these gender tropes may get translated into exclusionary institutions and policies. Thus, it is necessary to consider whether these unacceptable consequences can be averted without repudiating such theories.

I would like to propose several ways of mitigating the adverse impact of theories of gender. First, theorists can tone down the rhetoric in which they couch accounts of gender without shutting down the project of theorizing gender—the restraint of classical style is no less stirring than the flamboyance of the baroque. By adopting less flashy, more tentative and reflexive rhetoric, theorists can acknowledge their own social location and the need for multiple interpretations. Second, many relatively privileged feminists are educators, and as teachers we function as sales agents for publishers. Through our reading assignments, we can and should expand the market for diverse feminist theorizing, pressure book publishers and journals to meet this demand, and ensure that these "other" voices reach as wide an audience as possible. Finally, I would emphasize that activists would be far less likely to advocate privilege-perpetuating initiatives were they to recognize that the theories guiding their politics are analogous to literary interpretations and therefore are partial in both senses of the term—i.e., incomplete and perspectival.

Although African-American feminists sometimes focus on experiences quite unlike my own, my thinking about gender has been immeasurably enriched by studying their theorizing. For example, I find their analysis of intersectionality—i.e., the consequences of converging vectors of social stratification—widely applicable.[22] Instead of complacently generating counterexamples, then, I would urge readers to scrutinize this language to see what literary effects it is designed to achieve and to assess whether this language successfully achieves these aims. If gender theories are epistemic relatives of literary interpretations, ostensibly essentialist gender theories are not defeated by the discovery of disconfirming data. Moreover, such theories can be suggestive and helpful even though none conveys the Truth about gender. I would urge, then, that my view of individualized, marginalized identities not only advances our understanding of the epistemology of social critique, but it also epistemically vindicates the project of theorizing internally diverse, marginalized social groups.[23]

Notes

1. Patricia Williams, *The Alchemy of Race and Rights* (Cambridge: Harvard University Press, 1991), 11.

2. Anthony K. Appiah and Amy Gutman, *Color Consciousness: The Political Morality of Race* (Princeton: Princeton University Press, 1996), 80.

3. Marginalization of social groups is not a uniform phenomenon. Different marginalized groups are assigned to different social positions, and the prejudices against different marginalized groups vary in form and content. Women, for example, are not an isolated minority. Yet, manhood is the cultural norm of humanity, whereas womanhood is culturally coded as a defective form of manhood. Moreover, gender segmentation persists in labor markets worldwide, and women wield little political power compared to men of similar backgrounds. Likewise, minority groups may be more or less isolated—in the United States, Jews are more socially and economically integrated than African Americans. Prejudices against different groups are not uniform—homophobia is significantly different from racial bigotry. These variations notwithstanding, we may ask whether there are continuities with respect to the relationship between membership in a marginalized social group and the constitution of individual identities, and that question will be the focus of this chapter.

4. Iris Marion Young, "Gender As Seriality: Thinking About Women As a Social Collective," *Signs* 19 (1994): 713–738. Young suggests that sexual orientation, class, race, and nationality are also amenable to analysis as seriality (731–732). For related discussion, see Linda Alcoff, "Cultural Feminism Versus Post-Structuralism: The Identity Crisis in Feminist Theory," in *Culture/Power/History: A Reader in Contemporary Social Theory*, ed. Nicholas Dirks, Geoffrey Eley, and Sherry Ortner (Princeton: Princeton University Press, 1994).

5. Young, "Gender As Seriality," 724.

6. Ibid., 726.

7. Ibid., 727; emphasis added.

8. Ibid., 733.

9. Ibid., 734.

10. Sandra Lee Bartky's discussion of women's masochistic sexual fantasies provides a poignant and convincing demonstration of this point; see *Femininity and Domination: Studies in the Phenomenology of Oppression* (New York: Routledge, 1990), chap. 4.

11. Nancy J. Chodorow, "Gender As Personal and Cultural Construction," *Signs* 20 (1995): 520.

12. Ibid., 517.

13. Ibid., 518. Elizabeth Abel develops a parallel line of thought with respect to race and class in "Race, Class, and Psychoanalysis? Opening Questions," in *Conflicts in Feminism*, ed. Marianne Hirsch and Evelyn Fox Keller (New York: Routledge, 1990).

14. For related discussion, see Bartky, *Femininity and Domination*, chap. 5.

15. Williams, *The Alchemy of Race and Rights*, 168.

16. For a critique of this view, see Jean Grimshaw, "Autonomy and Identity in Feminist Thinking," in *Feminist Perspectives in Philosophy*, ed. Morwenna Griffiths and Margaret Whitford (Bloomington: Indiana University Press, 1988), 95–96, and Diana Tietjens Meyers, *Self, Society, and Personal Choice* (New York: Columbia University Press, 1989), 19–21.

17. María C. Lugones, "Playfulness, 'World'-Traveling, and Loving Perception," in *Feminist Social Thought: A Reader*, ed. Diana T. Meyers (New York: Routledge, 1997), 156.

18. Lugones, "Playfulness," 156; also see Patricia Mann's remarks about women's identification with eroticized beauty ideals in "Glancing at Pornography: Recognizing Men," in *Feminist Social Thought: A Reader*, ed. Diana Tietjens Meyers (New York: Routledge, 1997), 434.

19. Young, "Gender As Seriality," 737.

20. Marilyn Frye, "The Possibility of a Feminist Theory," in *Theoretical Perspectives on Sexual Difference,* ed. Deborah L. Rhode (New Haven: Yale University Press, 1990), 180.

21. Ibid., 181–183. For readings of Chodorow's theory and of MacKinnon's as extended tropes, see Diana Tietjens Meyers, *Subjection and Subjectivity: Psychoanalytic Feminism and Moral Philosophy* (New York: Routledge, 1994), 78–83, 106–107.

22. Diana Tietjens Meyers, "Intersectional Identity and the Authentic Self? Opposites Attract!" in *Relational Autonomy,* ed. Catriona Mackenzie and Natalie Stoljar (New York: Oxford University Press, forthcoming).

23. I am grateful to the editors of this book and to many participants at the 1999 Feminist Ethics Revisited Conference sponsored by the Ethics Center at South Florida State University for valuable comments on an earlier draft of this chapter.

Chapter Two

Return to Gender, Address Unknown: Reflections on the Past, Present, and Future of the Concept of Gender in Feminist Theory and Practice

Christine Overall

> *There are but two countries—Masculinity, rich with oil wells and skyscrapers and expensive four-star restaurants; and Femininity, a poorer land, but like many poor nations greener and prettier. In our day, there is plenty of travel between the two. Women cross the border, like migrants, to work for low wages, while men sojourn briefly and cautiously on the female side and return to where their best interests lie. But those who attempt to put down roots in the other place do so at the cost of severe alienation and under constant threat of punishment. Gender allows a person citizenship in only one country.*[1]

Within feminist theorizing and practice, gender is a key concept. Yet feminists have often disagreed about what gender is, how it is related to other fundamental ideas like the concept of biological sex, and what the value, if any, of gender is. In this chapter I briefly examine some key stages in the feminist history of the concept of gender. I then show that the next step in the evolution of feminist theorizing about gender is to advocate its disappearance. After presenting arguments for the demise of gender, I reply to several objections. By remaining committed to the feminist tradition of radicalism with respect to gender, feminists can avoid deferring, however unwittingly, either to conservative views or to people's anxieties about gender.

The inspiration for the first phrase in this chapter's title comes from Jane Caputi and Gordene O. MacKenzie, "Pumping Iron John," in *Women Respond to the Men's Movement*, ed. Kay Leigh Hagan (San Francisco: Harper Collins, 1992), 71.

Prisoners of Gender: Historical Background

A distinction between sex and gender is commonplace today.[2] One's sex is taken to be one's femaleness or one's maleness, an ordinarily fixed biological identity constituted partly or entirely by external genitalia, secondary sexual characteristics, the presence of ovaries or testes, and chromosomal and hormonal makeup.[3] By contrast, gender is usually regarded as socially rather than biologically constituted; it includes the roles, behaviors, appearances, attitudes, values, traits, and tendencies associated with each sex.

Gender is often understood as the cultural interpretation of sex, or "the social organization of sexual difference."[4] Gayle Rubin notes that there is "a taboo against the sameness of men and women, a taboo dividing the sexes into two mutually exclusive categories, a taboo which exacerbates the biological differences between the sexes and thereby *creates* gender."[5]

Within virtually all cultures, one's sex, male or female, is standardly and normatively associated with a specific gender, called, respectively, masculinity and femininity, as well as with a specific sexual orientation, heterosexuality, toward members of the other sex. Hence, feminists have recognized a large element of conventionalism with respect to gender. Whereas biological sex seems fixed and given, gender can be modified.[6]

Feminists have developed elaborate and illuminating analyses of what used to be termed the process of gender socialization and is now more often called the construction of gender, that is, the ways in which cultures create, elaborate, and maintain specific forms of femininity and masculinity assigned to women and to men.[7] In the work of some feminists, this analysis is premised on a form of social determinism; for others there remains a commitment to a voluntaristic understanding of the individual agency of the sexed person. Feminists have also shown how cultural forms of gender are sculpted by class, race, age, ability, and sexual orientation differences.

Along with nonfeminist sociologists and psychologists, feminists originally assumed that sex affects gender but that gender does not affect sex. More recently, however, some feminists have argued that since forms of gender vary so enormously from one culture to another, there can be no direct causal dependence of gender upon sex.[8] Although almost every culture prescribes certain behaviors, attitudes, duties and values to each sex, sex itself does not determine what those behaviors, attitudes, duties, and values will be; so gender is not, after all, directly dependent on sex.

On the other hand, and apparently paradoxically, sex is, to some extent, dependent on gender, for cultural notions about appropriate gender appearance and behavior create and shape people as physical beings of one sex or the other.[9] Marilyn Frye says: "Socialization molds our bodies; enculturation forms our skeletons, our musculature, our central nervous systems. By the time we are gendered adults, masculinity and femininity *are* 'biological.' They are structural and material features of how our bodies are."[10] Thus, malleable and mutable culturally constructed genders come to have the apparent fixity that biology is usually thought to have; through socialization processes, femininity or masculinity becomes part of the physical constitution of each one of us.

How do gender conventions construct sex identities? Feminists have identified three ways: first, by shaping individual bodies, through exercise, fashion, and even surgery to make them conform to certain ideas of womanliness or manliness;[11] second, by shaping entire groups of people, for example, through selective, gender-differentiated nutrition customs;[12] and third, by identifying and recognizing certain bodily differences and configurations as significant of one's identity or essence.

John Stoltenberg argues that sex is constructed, not just in Frye's sense of physically rebuilding bodies but also in the sense of putting together a package of physical characteristics (which ordinarily vary much more than we usually recognize) and calling that package meaningful: "Penises and ejaculate and prostate glands occur in nature, but the notion that these anatomical traits comprise a sex—a discrete class, separate and distinct, metaphysically divisible from some other sex, *the* 'other sex'—is simply that: a notion, an idea."[13] Differences between "the sexes" and the category itself of biological sex are in this way created, not discovered; that is, culture picks out certain features of the human being and claims that they constitute a meaningful whole. As Monique Wittig puts it, "The category 'woman' as well as the category 'man' are political and economic categories not eternal ones."[14]

As a result of these claims, the familiar feminist sex/gender distinction no longer seems clear, unambiguous, or perhaps even viable. Judith Butler suggests:

> If the immutable character of sex is contested, perhaps this construct called "sex" is as culturally constructed as gender; indeed, perhaps it was always already gender, with the consequence that the distinction between sex and gender turns out to be no distinction at all. . . . Gender ought not to be conceived merely as the cultural inscription of meaning on a pregiven sex (a juridical conception); gender must also designate the very apparatus of production whereby the sexes themselves are established.[15]

Judging Gender: Three Formulas for Transformation

Gender conventions are prescriptions for behavior, appearance, and values, prescriptions that, whatever their content might be, are founded upon a conceptualization of humanity as divided into two significant biological groups. Although there is considerable variation in what traits are taken to constitute masculinity and femininity, these concepts almost always incorporate the domination and superiority of those beings coded masculine over those beings coded feminine. Hence, virtually all feminists over the last quarter century have advocated that gender must in some way be reconstructed and transformed.

Feminists have, however, held very different opinions as to how gender should be transformed. These opinions fall into three broad categories: the revaluation of the feminine; the appeal to androgyny; and the endorsement of multiple genders.[16] The discussion that follows assesses each of these proposals.

The Revaluation of the Feminine

Some feminists have advocated that the transformation of gender must take place through a greater appreciation of those traits and behaviors associated with femininity.[17] For example, self-described "skeptical feminist" Janet Radcliffe Richards asserts that she is "proud of being female." Some women, she says, including some feminists, "want what is female to be recognizably different from what is male; they may want to cling determinedly to some existing traditions, and as well as that perhaps resuscitate old ones or even half-invent new ones, in order to keep by their own choice a separate identity for women."[18]

Revaluing the feminine is part of the program of cultural feminism.[19] Other famous examples come from Carol Gilligan's work, which urges us to value the moral thinking most characteristic of women (although it is also found in some men), and from the ethics of care interpreted as a "feminine approach to ethics."[20]

Some advocates of the revaluation of the feminine insist that femininity and masculinity are social products.[21] Others, however, resist the prevailing feminist tendency to see gender as a social product, instead construing femininity, or at least the positive aspects of femininity, as innate, essential biological epiphenomena.[22] Janice Raymond, for example, refers to "the power that women have by virtue of female biology and the fact that this power, symbolized in giving birth, is not only procreative but multidimensionally creative."[23] She says that women's power involves "culture, harmony, and true inventiveness."[24]

To revalue the feminine is certainly preferable to merely accepting the male norm and trying to assimilate all women (and men) to it. The strength of this general approach to the transformation of gender is that it encourages us to see what is good about traits and values historically associated with persons coded as women and facilitates the rethinking of ethical norms in such diverse fields as education, health care, and business.

Yet this approach to gender is, avowedly, deeply dualistic. It presupposes two distinct genders, retains their association with biological characteristics, and reinforces gender essentialism and determinism, whether biological or social. As Richard Wasserstrom points out, "even in the unlikely event that substantial sexual differentiation could be maintained without one sex or the other becoming dominant and developing oppressive institutions," the commitment to gender differentiation, however positive the genders, still imposes restraints on individual persons, based on the biological characteristics with which they are born.[25]

Revaluing femininity does not necessarily transform it; in fact, by keeping women doing the things they are allegedly good at, it is quite compatible with conservative and classist moral and political systems:[26] "Re-valuations of feminine attributes *accept* the results of an exploitative situation by endorsing its concepts."[27] Joan Williams makes the point that this approach conveniently forgets half the message of conventional femininity—the negative half—while valuing the positive half.[28] She also shows how this approach can be and has been used against women when, for example, women's supposed positive feminine traits and behavior are taken as evidence that women do not want men's jobs and prefer relationships over competition.

And what exactly would Richards's notion of "pride in being female" mean? Are we to be proud of our genitalia or chromosomes? And if so, why? Or, more plausibly, is she urging us to be proud of certain character traits typically associated with women? There is nothing wrong with such a recommendation, but there is no need to link such traits to a gendered conception of selfhood. If certain characteristics are valuable, then surely they are valuable regardless of how one's genitalia may happen to be configured.

The Appeal to Androgyny

While advocates of androgyny assume that there are biological "facts" about differences between human beings with respect to reproduction, physical strength, and so on,[29] they also recognize that certain characteristics are valuable irrespective of the biology of the persons with whom they are conventionally associated. Androgynism thus retains the concepts of two genders but recommends that they both be incarnated in each person, that persons be both feminine and masculine: "An androgynous person would combine some of each of the characteristic traits, skills, and interests that we now associate with the stereotypes of masculinity and femininity."[30] Joyce Trebilcot usefully distinguishes between monoandrogynism and polyandrogynism: according to the former, every individual should cultivate both feminine and masculine traits;[31] according to the latter, there should be a variety of gender options and combinations available to every individual, ranging from "pure" femininity or masculinity to any proportionate mixture of the two.[32] As a human ideal, androgyny has a long history. It has been adopted by some feminists during much of this century; for example, Virginia Woolf recommends it explicitly.[33] It was especially popular during the 1970s when feminists, wrestling with debates about sex and gender differences and distrustful of conventional notions of gender, were trying to envision the ideal person, free of conventional gender-bound limitations. Androgynism's strength is that it imagines and respects varieties of different combined aspects of the self and urges tolerance of personal diversity.[34] It appears to provide a liberating route out of some of the usual gender-bound expectations. Like the feminist project of revaluing the feminine, the ideal of androgyny holds out the prospect of creating social change by way of individual psychological transformation.[35]

Nonetheless, despite its potential, the concept of androgyny has deservedly generated extensive feminist criticism. As Susan Bordo has observed, femininity and masculinity are conventionally defined "through a process of mutual exclusion"; hence, the ideal of androgyny, which advocates maintaining and combining the two, is a formula for conflict and incoherence.[36] Ann Ferguson points out that insofar as androgyny assumes that femininity is completed by masculinity, the concept is also heterosexist.[37]

Androgynism fails to provide a deeper critique of femininity and masculinity beyond that of calling into question their conventional connections to persons' genitals. Thus, Arleen Dallery complains:

> Most doctrines of androgyny posit some sort of synthesis of masculine-identified and feminine-identified traits or gender characteristics. Yet, the so-called masculine traits—for example, rationality, objectivity, autonomy—are precisely those historically based on the suppression of woman's body, desire and difference. On the other side, the so-called feminine or nurturing traits—for example, empathy, caring, emotional responsiveness—are the epiphenomenon of structures of male domination and suppression, the virtues of the oppressed.[38]

Forms of and traits associated with femininity and masculinity have been defined, constituted, and enacted within oppressive contexts that severely limit the revolutionary potential of the proposal to combine femininity and masculinity.

Other feminists have, for different reasons, been critical of the ways in which androgynism, while apparently promising change, retains old gender concepts under a new guise. Mary Anne Warren argues that the concept of androgyny is "self-defeating": "While it suggests the elimination of the sexual stereotyping of human character, it is in itself formulated in terms of the very concepts of 'femininity' and 'masculinity' which it urges us to abandon."[39] Patricia Elliott asks, "If the goal of a nonsexist society is to have both sexes incorporate qualities that in a sexist society have been separated into feminine and masculine categories in order to enforce different norms for each sex, then why maintain these categorizations at all?"[40]

The notion that there is/can/should be a masculine part of women or that men have/should have a "woman within" simply assumes what it ought to be trying to show: the permanence and verity of sex distinctions. The heart of the problem with androgynism is, therefore, not just that it is usually uncritical of existing concepts of gender, but that it retains concepts of gender at all.

Multiple Genders

Some feminists have believed, with good reason, that neither revaluing the feminine nor combining masculinity and femininity goes far enough. Instead they envision a more radical approach to the transformation of gender that creates and endorses not two but many genders. For example, Marilyn Frye remarks that cultural and economic structures "construct two classes of animals, the masculine and the feminine, where another constellation of forces might have constructed three or five categories, and not necessarily hierarchically related. Or such a spectrum of sorts that we would not experience them as 'sorts' at all."[41]

A more sophisticated version of Frye's multiplicity of genders is Judith Butler's notion of a multiplicity of ways of "doing gender," gender as "repeated stylization of the body."[42] Construing gender not as a state or condition but rather as an activity, Butler advocates a "carnival of gender confusion," "a proliferation of genders freed from the substantializing nomenclature of 'woman' and 'man.'"[43] She says that her proposal can be understood "either as an internal expansion of existing gender categories or as a proliferation of gender itself beyond the usual two," in which discriminations are no longer made between right and wrong genders, right and wrong sexes.[44] The resulting "loss of gender norms would have the effect of proliferating gender configurations, destabilizing substantive identity, and depriving the naturalizing narratives of compulsory heterosexuality of their central protagonists: 'man' and 'woman.'"[45]

In this view, whatever a person with male or female genitals happens to do *is* what is masculine or feminine.[46] Extending the promise of polyandrogynism to its logical limit, the strength of this proposal is that it so powerfully validates variation, recognizing that there are and need be no behavioral limits placed on those beings conventionally called women and men.

Nevertheless, this apparently bold approach turns out to be little different from or better than the appeal to androgyny, for, like the advocates of androgyny, both Frye and Butler retain notions of gender and/or sex and thereby run the risk of preserving, at least implicitly, the invidious conventional value associations with these concepts. As she herself sometimes recognizes, Butler's "subversive resignification and proliferation [of gender and sex] beyond the binary frame" presupposes that *some* concepts of gender and sex will remain.[47] Even if each sex is said to "permit" a number of different genders, and genders are "attributed" indifferently to "either biological sex," the proposed practices would still recognize and validate concepts of biological sex, of woman and man, of femininity and masculinity.[48] Hence, "doing gender" à la Butler enacts a commitment to ideas that, even if redefined, have a history that is oppressive to women.

The question then is why it would be desirable to continue to deploy the terms "sex" and "gender" at all. Either Frye's proposal for multiple genders and Butler's for multiple ways of doing gender are potentially reformist, hence ineffective, recommendations for greater tolerance of behavioral variations, or, if they are genuinely radical and consistent, they should not continue to appeal to gender or sex at all. As Butler herself says, "The limitless proliferation of sexes . . . logically entails the negation of sex as such. If the number of sexes corresponds to the number of existing individuals, sex would no longer have any general application as a term."[49] Similarly, if the term "gender" is truly expanded in the radical fashion that Butler implies, it becomes empty of any distinct content and simply means, in the most general fashion possible, "a way of being." Thus, as a multiplication of ways of being detached from any particular body configuration, gender would, like sex, lose its "general application as a term" and be negated. The concepts of gender and sex would be rendered otiose.

Junking Gender

Despite surface differences, the three formulas for transforming gender—revaluing the feminine, androgyny, and multiple genders—are similar. They are for the most part reformist rather than radical; they merely "renovat[e] the master's house while continuing to inhabit it."[50] They retain as a key concept the very idea of gender, with its implied analytic dualism of masculinity and femininity and its historically situated tie to biological characteristics construed as sex. The notion of femininity, which in the West encompasses such dubious characteristics as passivity, submissiveness, meekness, and so on, derives its *meaning* from the tie to biological womanness: to be (gendered) feminine is to be or to act like a woman. Moreover, the second and third formulas are self-contradictory, insofar as they purport both to end and to retain gender. If gender is truly to be abandoned, then it is inconsistent to continue to advocate being, becoming, or doing (a) gender, or to deploy the term "gender" in describing one's vision of the future.

Nevertheless, the three alternatives are crucial historical stages in feminist assessments of gender. In both theorizing about them and enacting them, feminists and other gender dissidents have contributed to the creation of an environment in which characteristics traditionally considered feminine are being reevaluated, and the cultural commitment to traditional gendered formations is diminished. The three alternatives also point the way to the next step. Joyce Trebilcot glimpses this when she remarks, of her own favored ideal of polyandrogynism:

> In the long run [it] may lead to an integrating of femininity and masculinity that will yield new attributes, new kinds of personalities. The androgyne at this extreme would perhaps be

not part feminine and part masculine, but neither feminine nor masculine, a person in whom the genders disappear.[51]

I propose that the next step in radical feminist thinking about gender is to advocate its demise: the end of woman and man, femininity and masculinity, the end of all prescriptions couched in terms of gender and/or sex. What is left if one is consistently radical in criticism of gender is not its transformation but rather nothing that could be called gender at all.

With the demise of gender, there no longer would be a tie between gender and sex, not because genders become free-floating, as Butler's proposal implies, but because there is nothing left—no unified sets of behaviors, appearances, attitudes, and so on—to free-float, and no special significance accorded to particular configurations of genitalia. Clothes, work, education, relationships with children, sports, leisure activities—none of these would conventionally or inevitably be associated with femaleness and femininity or maleness and masculinity. We would not routinely speak of women and men, for being a woman or a man would not be a central fact of one's identity; "woman" and "man" as viable categories would disappear.[52] We would recognize that human beings have various physical characteristics, including genitalia and so-called secondary sex characteristics, but declare that these characteristics have and should have no inevitable or inherent meaning or association with other physical characteristics. One's genitalia would have the status that eye color has now: there are many gradations of eye color, and humanity cannot be straightforwardly divided up on that basis; it has no significance in terms of persons' meaning or value.[53]

To advocate the end of gender in this way is not particularly new. Some of the first radical feminists called for making gender "irrelevant,"[54] and Alison Jaggar claims that it is an ideal associated with socialist feminism.[55] Monique Wittig says:

A new personal and subjective definition for all humankind can only be found beyond the categories of sex (woman and man) and . . . the advent of individual subjects demands first destroying the categories of sex, ending the use of them, and rejecting all sciences which still use these categories as their fundamentals.[56]

To work toward the end of gender is the way of transforming gender that is most consistent with feminism; it fully embodies Wittig's compelling definition of "feminist" as "someone who fights for women as a class and for the disappearance of this class."[57] There are many good reasons why feminists should be calling for the demise of gender; I shall now outline five that are closely interconnected.

(1) To retain gender conventions is to continue to endorse gender distinctions. But gender is the metaphysical basis of sexism, a system of oppression particularly harmful to those defined as women. For that reason, programs that call for merely changing or "playing with" gender are inadequate. Because gender conventions are not so much founded on sex distinctions as create them, the demise of gender would mean the end of at least some invidious and discriminatory distinctions founded on body classifications. Without its metaphysical basis, there would be no sexism.

(2) Gender is constraining. For example, even the apparently daring and nonconformist conventions of drag illustrate gender's failure of imagination. Although women who cross-dress have often been severely punished when their "deception" is discovered, nonetheless to dress like a man is to dress like a person, and forms of once-"masculine" attire are (becoming) standard for females as well as males. On the other hand, to dress like a woman is to take on a role as other-than-person; hence, it is often reckless, titillating, and dangerous for persons who are male. Yet the conventions of male drag tie the performer to a caricature, a stereotype of feminine custom, and they presuppose the invidious value distinctions lodged within the feminine/masculine dichotomy. Whatever form gender conventions take, they inevitably, by definition, set limits on what certain kinds of human beings should do and are allowed to do—even when human beings set out to defy those conventions.

(3) The demise of gender would contribute to ending false universalizations about persons, universalizations that overlook both the cultural effects of other constructed categories such as race, sexual orientation, class, ability, age, and so forth, and individual variations. Commitment to the end of gender provides a political

program that enables us to finesse the debates about gender identity politics and the critique of essentializing, totalizing theories of women. Such a program would recognize existing gender formations as creating certain kinds of commonalties among certain groups of people, while at the same time it would not be committed in any way either to the idea that gender conventions reflect what people are "really" like or to their perpetuation.

(4) The demise of gender would promote individual freedom; without gender, differences would flourish more readily. The demise of gender would also mean an end to "gender dysphoria," evidenced most obviously in transsexuals but also in many others who feel and believe that their designated sex and/or gender are personally inappropriate for them.[58] Richard Wasserstrom puts this argument in terms of "sex roles":

Any set of sex roles . . . necessarily impair[s] and retard[s] an individual's ability to develop his or her own characteristics, talents, capacities, and potential life-plans to the extent to which he or she might desire and from which he or she might derive genuine satisfaction. Sex roles, by definition, constitute empirical and normative limits of varying degrees of strength—restrictions on what it is that one can expect to do, be, or become.[59]

(5) Because of the conceptual and normative baggage that gender bears, the demise of gender would have epistemological advantages: we would have much less reason to see and interpret our worlds in terms of active/passive, culture/nature, mind/body, reason/emotion, and all the other restrictive binarisms so readily associated with gender in Western culture. Thus, while gender distinctions function as "cognitive organizers,"[60] they also serve as cognitive *limiters, the absence of which could liberate our thinking and knowing.*

Rejuvenating Gender? Some Rejoinders

Because there is considerable resistance to, perhaps even fear of, ending gender, these five arguments may not be entirely convincing. There seem to be two kinds of opposition to the demise of gender, conservative and feminist (although the two may partially overlap). Examples of conservative arguments include the protest that gender is entirely biologically determined and that ending gender would be unnatural, as well as the claim that the universality of gender differentiation shows that it serves purposes that must not or cannot be abandoned.[61] I shall not deal with these arguments here, both because they have been adequately criticized elsewhere and because my topic in this chapter is feminist views on gender. Instead I will present four arguments that feminists put forward against the demise of gender, including some that seem conservative at heart.

(a) Essentialists committed to the existence of inherent gender characteristics argue that each of us *is* our gender, that there cannot be human beings who are not gendered. Thus, Julie A. Nelson claims:

You can lead a girl to Hot Wheels but you can't make her play. Either children are much more malleable than we thought— sexist influences enter so early and so very, very subtly that feminist adults cannot prevent their molding—or much less malleable, with some sex-typed proclivities (oh dear) often built in.[62]

Response: It is not clear what the justification for this claim is or could be. The evidence for sex and gender differences is highly variable and even contradictory; it does not, in any case, show that any particular characteristic (including the avoidance of Hot Wheels) is innate. However, even if it were true that some gendered characteristics are innate, the essentialist surely would not want to claim that every characteristic traditionally associated with a particular gender in this culture is in fact characteristic of and essential to women or men. There is at least room for experimentation to find out what is inherent and what is not.

I argue against any notion of gender as prescription. This approach does not mean preventing people from being a certain way if they choose (remembering that the notion of choice is itself highly contested). It does not mean compelling them to subscribe to some nongendered form of life. But it does mean refraining from setting up expectations based on body parts. And it means regarding with suspicion current research, undertaken within sexist societies, which purports to show that gender differences are inherent and inevitable. Instead, without the imposition of categories of compulsory gender, inherent characteristics, if any, would be free to emerge, without any nonessential characteristics being compelled through social pressure.[63] Thus, if large numbers of people with vulvas turn out, after the demise of gender, to have certain characteristics and abilities in common, that would be surprising and interesting—but not the basis for the re-reification of genders, which include *prescriptions* for *all* persons with vulvas.

(b) Some feminists seem to be afraid that the end of gender means a condition called "unisex" or "gender neutrality": a state in which, it is alleged, human beings would all be the same, drab and undifferentiated.[64] Gender, it is asserted, has a cultural value as a tradition. Richards, for example, assumes that the aim of feminists like me is to destroy differences between women and men, in a way comparable to the suppressing of national differences.[65] Similarly, Lynda Ashley plaintively asks:

Since when do we have to give up our femininity to gain equality? Since when do we achieve fairness for all humanity by denying the differences between men and women? When did the goal of the women's movement become sameness, instead of recognizing the value, and equal importance of, our differences?[66]

The proposal for the demise of gender might therefore be opposed on the grounds that it is too broad and too monolithic; that it appears to prescribe a single way of being for all persons and all cultures, without tolerating and indeed encouraging the diversity that is a source of strength for women and for feminism. In fact, the proposal, it might be argued, is guilty of cultural imperialism—an arrogant assumption about the supposed superiority of a gender-free form of living—particularly with respect to those social traditions in which notions of gender (for example, ideas about feminine and masculine life forces) are deeply embedded within religious and spiritual practices and beliefs.

Response: At this point in human history gender is real and woman is real; they are real social constructions, with some commonalties produced through social subordination. And, as Joan Wallach Scott puts it, gender is (and I would add, will remain) "a useful category of historical analysis."[67] But feminists should not be uncritical with respect to gender categories: culture or tradition for its own sake does not have a claim on our forbearance. With good reason, feminists of the "second wave" have never accepted genders and gender systems as they are. That these conventions exist does not make them morally acceptable; indeed, their harmful effects make them morally questionable.

As Warren observes, the absurdity of the "unisex" objection is that of supposing that an increase in freedom would lead to greater uniformity.[68] As I have already argued, difference and diversity would not be diminished but rather enhanced if gender and its conventions were to disappear. Of course, if Richards and others are right in claiming that there are feminist pressures on women not to be feminine (as distinguished from feminist critiques of conventions of femininity), then, minimally effective though these may be, they are probably inappropriate. Human beings should be self-determining, and *if* their choices include ways of being that are gendered in some historical sense, they are entitled to them. (Feminist advocates of the retention of gender traditions should, however, be prepared to show that individuals' and groups' preservation of gendered ways of being and behaving does not involve self-deception, internalized oppression, or harm to others.)

What lies behind the fear of sameness that ending gender inspires is the assumption that if there are not two types of human beings there can be only one. But to argue for the demise of gender is not to argue that everyone look and be the same, nor to require that individuals give up behaviors and patterns now associated with a particular gender. Nor does it imply that the retention of some traditions invoking genders is necessarily less advanced or less moral than their abandonment.

To advocate the end of gender is, rather, to give up seeing the genitals as symbols of a desired congruency of behavior. The elimination of gender difference is not the elimination of differences, including differences formerly associated with specific genders. It does not mean the elimination or even the regulation of choice; it is, rather, the elimination of gender as a compulsory mode of behavior. Hence, there could well be, for example, persons with vulvas who happen to be feminine in the historical sense of the term. Moreover, there could well be groups of people who structure some aspects of their lives around historically sanctioned notions of gender differences. But there would be lots of other kinds of persons and groups, too, including many that we cannot even now imagine. Gender itself does not have a positive value; it is, rather, some of the practices, attitudes, traditions, beliefs, and values that are commonly associated with one gender or the other that may be worth perpetuating.

(c) The next objection comes from the "vive la différence" school of thought and practice. It is the idea that gender differentiation enriches people's lives, particularly their sexual lives. Thus, Richards emphasizes that a component of gender conformity is the endeavor to be attractive to members of the other sex.[69] The demise of gender, it is claimed, would threaten sexuality, compromise sexual excitement, and make sexual orientation irrelevant.[70] And, lest this objection sound entirely heterosexist, lesbian feminist Jacquelyn Zita adds: "Perhaps the desire to keep this binarism [of two sexes and two genders] intensifies a desire to transgress constructed barriers, an erotic risk of transcategorical pleasure, rather than the risk of nonidentity in an in/different world of many genders and many sexes."[71]

Some feminists also fear that, given that the distinction between sex and gender no longer seems clear, the demise of gender would entail losing sight of the physical component of human existence. Thus, Zita worries, "has the body all but disappeared in the wash of multivalences and multivocalities?"[72] Nelson claims, without qualification, that what she calls "gender-neutrality" would "require the active suppression of sexual difference as a salient aspect of human experience, especially the experience of children."[73] And Prudence Allen argues that "human materiality ought to be considered as an ontological starting point in a theory of human identity."[74]

Response: I entirely agree that we should see ourselves as material beings, but I reject the indefinite perpetuation of commitment to and reproduction of the categories of "man" and "woman," since this practice forecloses on some of our possibilities as material beings.

The objection assumes that genitalia should continue to be of great importance to human beings. It assumes that sexual preferences are monolithic, that those who are engaged in sexual activity with persons of particular genitalia see all those persons as belonging to one category rather than as individuals with personal differences. This approach both presumes and validates an undesirable uniformity of individuals, based only on the sort of genitals they possess. Moreover, there is little reason to suppose that sexual activity is so fragile that its continuation is dependent upon institutionalized gender.[75] In the absence of gender conventions there would likely be less coercion, less stereotyping, and more variety within sexual practices.[76]

Maybe the point of the vive-la-différence objection is to claim that in many or most human interactions one's genitals inevitably have more significance than eye or hair color, so that a system that identifies persons by their genitals is essential to sexual activity: "The functional difference that being the reproducer makes in sex/affective social relations will make sex a more important social distinction than skin color, hair, and other physical characteristics," says Ferguson.[77] But even with the demise of gender, there is no reason why people could not choose what significance in their lives their bodily features and those of others have. For example, *if* some persons choose to run their sex lives on the basis of the presence or absence of a vulva in their partners, there would be nothing to prevent them from doing so.[78]

(d) Teresa de Lauretis says, "*If the deconstruction of gender inevitably effects its (re)construction, the question is, in which terms and in whose interest is the de-re-construction being effected?*"[79] Feminists often worry about the political consequences of deconstructing gender systems. Joan Williams argues that so-called gender-neutrality "mandates a blindness to gender that has left women in a worse position than they were before the mid-twentieth-century challenge to gender roles."[80] Thus, some feminists are worried that the end of gender would mean a lack of protections for human beings now coded as female.[81] The assumption that "underneath we are all the same" is just a version of the old song men have been singing for centuries: neutrality turns out to mean "men's way."[82] As Alison Jaggar states:

We live in a society divided deeply by gender, in which differences between the sexes, whatever their cause, are pronounced and inescapable. When these differences are ignored in the name of formal equality between the sexes, continuing substantive inequalities between women and men may be either obscured or rationalized and legitimized.[83]

Response: This worry about the alleged harm of ending gender partly reflects the grip that gender has on us now. As I have already stated, I am not proposing something called "gender-neutrality"; the demise of gender requires neither suppression of differences nor ignoring of the body. Nor does it require a premature pretense (sometimes adopted by liberal feminists) that gender does not "really" matter; or that we are not already all marked by gender, often in ways that both hurt us and constitute commonalties for political alliances. At this point in our history, there may continue to be reasons to "privilege genital anatomies in defining the truth of our sex," even while we aim for a time when we will not.[84] Hence, forms of feminist separatism may continue to be appropriate for some political actions.

Advocating the end of gender certainly does not mean that we stop working to end gender- and sex-based oppression. The claim that woman is a fiction or that there are no women undermines feminist action if it is used to rationalize nonopposition to sexist policies and behaviors.[85] My proposal is, rather, that there ought not to be women, or, more accurately, that the category "woman" ought not to be reproduced. While feminist strategy has required and may continue to require the affirmation of womanhood, one of the goals of feminism should nonetheless be its demise. Insofar as woman is constructed as an object of oppression, and we need to obviate that condition, action by the prisoners of gender to end gender is entirely consistent with, and indeed requires, paying scrupulous attention to gender categories in both feminist theory and practice.

Williams captures what I have in mind very neatly: "The core feminist goal is not one of pretending gender does not exist. Instead, it is to deinstitutionalize the gendered structure of our society. . . . The deconstruction of gender allows us to protect [people] by reference to their social roles instead of their genitals."[86] The deinstitutionalization and demise of gender require reducing as far as possible the cultural elaboration of sex, in the sense of a set of social meanings associated with a particular kind of body, and instead responding to the various needs of various individuals—including individuals who may be pregnant, or elderly, or parents of young children, or lactating, or very young.

On Beyond Gender

Having responded to a variety of objections to the project of junking gender, I wish I could paint a detailed picture of its practical implications and outcomes. What would a future without gender be like? So far we can scarcely imagine a situation in which our primary identities are not as women or as men, "in which oppositional gender categories are not fundamental to [our] self-concept."[87]

At this point all I can offer is some conjectures. Once convinced of the harms of sex/gender systems, both in concept and in practice, we need to be willing to try the experiment/take the risk of aiming for human flourishing without them. To adopt some words of Frye: "To think [the end of gender] thinkable shortcuts no work and shields one from no responsibility. Quite the contrary, it may be a necessary prerequisite to assuming responsibility, and it invites the honorable work of radical imagination."[88] Indeed, imagining a future without gender is the topic for a much longer project, including perhaps speculative feminist fiction, drama, cinema, and other art forms.

Selfhood

I do not assume that each one of us either could or should choose now to cease entirely to live our given gender. Contrary to Nelson's worries, we should neither censure women who "wear skirts and brightly colored earrings" nor compel little girls to play with Hot Wheels.[89] To call for the end of gender is not to advocate compulsory relinquishment of femininity and masculinity. But if Judith Butler is right, that "gender is not passively received, and the process of acculturation cannot be likened to the passive process of being molded or inscribed by cultural conventions," then we do have some ability to do things differently, to actively work, both individually and collectively, toward a gender-free world, if we so choose.[90] What Frye calls "disaffiliation," not only from conventional femininity but from conventional masculinity, is possible.[91] Just as women can reject femininity, men can "set themselves against masculinity," or in Stoltenberg's terms, "refuse to be a man."[92] Gender hurts those who are designated female more than those designated male, but all who are hurt by gender or who recognize the hurts caused by it can be committed to ending it.

Part of the attraction of the three feminist reforms of gender described earlier may be due to the tendency to think of ourselves as harboring one or more different selves that are essential to who we are. Theories of a revalued feminine self, or an androgynous pairing of feminine and masculine selves, or a carnival of gendered selves, all respond to our predilection for believing in the "real me(s)."

But gendered selves, in any combination or guise, have no special claim to being either real or valuable components of persons. The end of gender need not mean the end of personal authenticity, which needs to be seen primarily as a moral rather than a metaphysical concept, with an emphasis on what we choose to be and become rather than only what we discover ourselves to be.

I agree with Jane Flax in calling for "a rethinking of our ideas about what is humanly excellent, worthy of praise, or moral."[93] And I recommend, as an ethical alternative to essentialist thinking about selfhood, María Lugones's antiessentialist concept of world-traveling.[94] In practice, Lugones's idea of world-traveling encourages everyone to cultivate the capacity to shift, playfully and even lovingly, from one construction of life to another and then to another in the effort to understand and identify with those who seem different from us.

Some Generalizations

A gender-free culture is easier to describe in terms of what would likely disappear than in terms of what might develop: No more condemnations for walking, running, sitting, talking, or throwing like a girl. No more mandatory dressing like/as a woman, in fact, no more compulsory female impersonation, whether by persons without vulvas or those with them. No more "M" and "F" boxes on application forms.[95] No more obligatory categorizations by sex/gender of jobs, leisure and recreation activities, sports, clothes and other adornments, child care, art forms, educational practices, knowledge, law, ritual, patterns of consumption, housing, food and eating, artifacts, religious/spiritual practices, political activities, friendships, social life, family constitution and practice, struggle and conflict, emotions, or sexualities.

Within a gender-free culture there would be no more women or men—or at least there need not be; any women or men who exist would exist by choice, not by compulsion or construction. With the disappearance of women and men there would develop the possibility that new kinds of persons might emerge—as well, perhaps, as a resistance toward hasty categorization and more emphasis on the specialness of individuals. Perhaps, indeed, we would not adhere so commitedly to adult/child distinctions, to racial and racialized categories, or even to the supposedly self-evident human/nonhuman distinction. We might evince more interest in bonds/networks/friendships among individuals and beings who are now considered very different as well as among those who seem similar.

I predict that a gender-free culture would be a more curious, more creative culture: it would generate more possibilities for original human activities that are not bound either by gender concepts or by notions of sex identity. This flowering/flourishing would include the opening up of scientific investigation, both formal and informal. For example, while standard research programs dedicated to the investigation of gender differences would be rendered nugatory, extensive practical observations of whether having a vulva or having a penis is a difference that makes a difference would for the first time in human history be genuinely possible.

Let us therefore be suspicious of and resistant to any requirement that we return to gender—whatever its forms or manifestations may be.

Notes

1. Judith Levine, *My Enemy My Love: Women, Men, and the Dilemmas of Gender* (New York: Doubleday, 1992), 394.
2. Despite its familiarity (which is not to say its accuracy or its usefulness), the distinction between sex and gender is a relatively recent one. While they acknowledged cultural influences on women's lives, feminists prior to the seventies did not distinguish sex from gender. For example, when Virginia Woolf wrote, in *A Room of One's Own*, of current social limitations on women writers, she spoke of "the effect of *sex* upon the novelist," where later writers might instead say "gender." See Woolf, *A Room of One's Own* (Harmondsworth, England: Penguin Books, 1928), 71 (emphasis added).
3. Mary Vetterling-Braggin, "Introduction to Notions of Sex and Gender," in *"Femininity," "Masculinity," and Androgyny": A Modern Philosophical Discussion*, ed. M. Vetterling-Braggin (Totowa, NJ: Littlefield Adams, 1982), 4–5.
4. Joan Wallach Scott, *Gender and the Politics of History* (New York: Columbia University Press, 1988), 2.
5. Gayle Rubin, "The Traffic in Women: Notes on the 'Political Economy' of Sex," in *Toward an Anthropology of Women*, ed. Rayna R. Rapp (New York: Monthly Review Press, 1975), 178 (emphasis in original).
6. Rubin, "Traffic in Women," 185.
7. The distinction between sex and gender was originally derived from the fields of sociology and social psychology, within which the normative implications of femininity and masculinity were accepted as representing desirable states for women and men respectively. See Hester Eisenstein, *Contemporary Feminist Thought* (Boston: G. K. Hall, 1983), 7, 10. Considerable research effort has subsequently been devoted to trying to determine sex and gender differences. Some feminists share this concern; see, for example, Deborah L. Rhode, ed., *Theoretical Perspectives on Sexual Difference* (New Haven: Yale University Press, 1990). What interests me, however, are not supposed sex and gender differences themselves, but rather the differences and interconnections *between* sex and gender, and the role of gender as concept and ideal. For extensive descriptions and analyses of the creation and maintenance of femininity in North American culture, see Sandra Lee Bartky, *Femininity and Domination: Studies in the Phenomenology of Oppression* (New York: Routledge, 1990).
8. Judith Butler, *Gender Trouble: Feminism and the Subversion of Identity* (New York: Routledge, 1990), 6.
9. Alison M. Jaggar, "Human Biology in Feminist Theory: Sexual Equality," in *Beyond Domination: New Perspectives on Women and Philosophy*, ed. Carol C. Gould (Totowa, NJ: Rowman and Allanheld, 1983), 36.
10. Marilyn Frye, *The Politics of Reality: Essays in Feminist Theory* (Freedom, CA: Crossing Press, 1983), 37 (emphasis in original).

11. See Jaggar, "Sexual Equality," 36–37; Frye, *Politics of Reality*, 19-38; and Susan R. Bordo, "The Body and the Reproduction of Femininity: A Feminist Appropriation of Foucault," in *Gender/Body/Knowledge: Feminist Reconstructions of Being and Knowledge*, ed. Alison M. Jaggar and Susan R. Bordo (New Brunswick, NJ: Rutgers University Press, 1989), 14.

12. Jaggar, "Sexual Equality," 37.

13. John Stoltenberg, *Refusing to Be a Man: Essays on Sex and Justice* (New York: Penguin Books, 1989), 30 (emphasis in original).

14. Monique Wittig, *The Straight Mind and Other Essays* (New York: Harvester, 1992), 9, 15.

15. Butler, *Gender Trouble*, 7.

16. For a different way of carving up some of the theoretical differences about gender (into feminist rationalism, feminine antirationalism, and feminist postrationalism), which takes into account both feminist and nonfeminist approaches, see Christine Di Stefano, "Dilemmas of Difference: Feminism, Modernity, and Postmodernism," in *Feminism/Postmodernism*, ed. Linda J. Nicholson (New York: Routledge, 1990).

17. See, for example, Carolyn G. Heilbrun, *Toward a Recognition of Androgyny* (New York: Harper and Row, 1973), xvi, and Christina Sommers, "Philosophers Against the Family," in *Vice and Virtue in Everyday Life: Introductory Readings in Ethics*, ed. Christina Sommers and Fred Sommers (Fort Worth, TX: Harcourt Brace Jovanovich, 1993), 815.

18. Janet Radcliffe Richards, *The Sceptical Feminist: A Philosophical Inquiry* (Harmondsworth, England: Penguin Books, 1980), 190.

19. Alice Echols, *Daring to Be Bad: Radical Feminism in America, 1967–1975* (Minneapolis: University of Minnesota Press, 1989), 6.

20. Nel Noddings, *Caring: A Feminine Approach to Ethics and Moral Education* (Berkeley: University of California Press, 1984).

21. Nancy Chodorow, *The Reproduction of Mothering: Psychoanalysis and the Sociology of Gender* (Berkeley: University of California Press, 1978); Carol Gilligan, *In a Different Voice: Psychological Theory and Women's Development* (Cambridge: Harvard University Press, 1982).

22. Mary Daly, *Gyn/Ecology: The Metaethics of Radical Feminism* (Boston: Beacon Press, 1978); Janice Raymond, *The Transsexual Empire* (London: Women's Press, 1979); Mary O'Brien, *The Politics of Reproduction* (Boston: Routledge and Kegan Paul, 1981).

23. Raymond, *Transsexual Empire*, 28–29.

24. Ibid., 107.

25. Richard Wasserstrom, "Sex Roles and the Ideal Society," in *Vice and Virtue in Everyday Life: Introductory Readings in Ethics*, ed. Christine Sommers and Fred Sommers (Fort Worth, TX: Harcourt Brace Jovanovich, 1993), 793.

26. Julia Penelope, *Call Me Lesbian: Lesbian Lives, Lesbian Theory* (Freedom, CA: Crossing Press, 1992), 108.

27. Juliet Mitchell and Rosalind Delmar, quoted in Echols, *Daring to Be Bad*, 244 (emphasis in original).

28. Joan C. Williams, "Deconstructing Gender," in *Feminist Legal Theory: Readings in Law and Gender*, ed. Katharine T. Bartlett and Rosanne Kennedy (Boulder, CO: Westview Press, 1991), 99, 103.

29. Ann Ferguson, *Sexual Democracy: Women, Oppression, and Revolution* (Boulder, CO: Westview Press, 1991), 190.

30. Ann Ferguson, "A Feminist Aspect Theory of the Self," in *Women,*

Knowledge, and Reality: Explorations in Feminist Philosophy, ed. Ann Garry and Marilyn Pearsall (Boston: Unwin Hyman, 1989), 189.

31. A recent example of monoandrogynism is the theory put forward by Julie A. Nelson, "More Thinking About Gender: Reply," *Hypatia* 9 (1994): 199–205.

32. Joyce Trebilcot, "Two Forms of Androgynism," in *"Femininity," "Masculinity," and "Androgyny": A Modern Philosophical Discussion*, ed. Mary Vetterling-Braggin (Totowa, NJ: Littlefield Adams, 1982), 162–163.

33. Woolf, *A Room of One's Own*, 95ff.

34. Ferguson, "A Feminist Aspect Theory of the Self."

35. Eisenstein, *Contemporary Feminist Thought*, 63.

36. Bordo, "Body," 19. The doomed nature of the androgyny ideal is represented, suggests Bordo, by the anorexic woman, whose project of self-deprivation represents a paradoxical attempt to become both feminine and masculine.

37. Ferguson, *Sexual Democracy*, 213.

38. Arleen B. Dallery, "The Politics of Writing (the) Body: Écriture Feminine," in *Gender/Body/Knowledge: Feminist Reconstructions of Being and Knowledge*, ed. Alison M. Jaggar and Susan R. Bordo (New Brunswick, NJ: Rutgers University Press, 1989), 65.

39. Mary Anne Warren, "Is Androgyny the Answer to Sexual Stereotyping?" in *"Femininity," "Masculinity," and "Androgyny": A Modern Philosophical Discussion*, ed. Mary Vetterling-Braggin (Totowa, NJ: Littlefield Adams, 1982), 181.

40. Patricia Elliott, "More Thinking About Gender: A Response to Julie A. Nelson," *Hypatia* 9 (1994): 197.

41. Frye, *Politics of Reality*, 38.

42. Butler, *Gender Trouble*, 33.

43. Judith Butler, "Gendering the Body: Beauvoir's Philosophical Contribution," in *Women, Knowledge, and Reality: Explorations in Feminist Philosophy*, ed. Ann Garry and Marilyn Pearsall (Boston: Unwin Hyman, 1989), 260.

44. Ibid. Of course, as Butler recognizes, there is often a heavy price to be paid for nonconformity to standard gender expectations (256).

45. Butler, *Gender Trouble*, 146.

46. Butler, "Gendering the Body," 260.

47. Butler, *Gender Trouble*, x.

48. Butler, "Gendering the Body," 261.

49. Butler, *Gender Trouble*, 118.

50. Elliott, "Response," 198.

51. Trebilcot, "Two Forms of Androgynism," 164.

52. Wassertrom, "Sex Roles," 786. Yet Wasserstrom himself also refers, inconsistently, to "the ineradicable, naturally occurring differences between males and females" (787). His words suggest that commitment to the end of gender is difficult to sustain with consistency.

53. Ibid., 785.

54. Shulamith Firestone, *The Dialectic of Sex: The Case for Feminist Revolution* (New York: Bantam Books, 1970), 11; Ti-Grace Atkinson, *Amazon Odyssey* (New York: Links Books, 1974), 49; Echols, *Daring to Be Bad*, 6.

55. Alison M. Jaggar, *Feminist Politics and Human Nature* (Totowa, NJ: Rowman and Allanheld, 1983), 317, 340.

56. Wittig, *Straight Mind*, 19–20.

57. Ibid., 14.

58. Raymond, *Transsexual Empire*, xv.

59. Wasserstrom, "Sex Roles," 792.

60. Nelson, "Reply," 200.

61. Wasserstrom provides strong counterarguments to both of these claims.

62. Nelson, "Reply," 203.

63. Janet Radcliffe Richards, "Separate Spheres," in *Applied Ethics,* ed. Peter Singer (Oxford: Oxford University Press, 1986).

64. This criticism often was also leveled against androgynism in general, but it is certainly not applicable to polyandrogynism, which explicitly advocates a continuum of possible instantiations of combined genders.

65. Richards, *Sceptical Feminist,* 185–189.

66. Lynda Ashley, "A Case for Feminism with Femininity," *Globe and Mail,* 23 February 1993, A22.

67. Scott, *Gender,* 28.

68. Warren, "Sexual Stereotyping," 177.

69. Richards, *Sceptical Feminist,* 167–168.

70. Robert G. Pielke, "Are Androgyny and Sexuality Compatible?" in *"Femininity," "Masculinity," and "Androgyny": A Modern Philosophical Discussion,* ed. Mary Vetterling-Braggin (Totowa, NJ: Littlefield Adams, 1982).

71. Jacquelyn N. Zita, "Male Lesbians and the Postmodernist Body," *Hypatia* 7 (1992): 122.

72. Ibid., 124.

73. Nelson, "Reply," 201.

74. Prudence Allen, "Sex or Gender? Some Philosophical Implications" (paper presented at the annual meeting of the Canadian Philosophical Association, Queen's University, Kingston, Ontario, May 1991), 14.

75. Since a commitment to the existing gender system is also a commitment to the existing sexual orientation system, the end of gender would likely mean the end of sexual orientations as we know them now and the end of identities expressed in terms of sexualities. Although some of us may continue to be drawn only to a certain kind of body, that focus would no longer be identified, implausibly, in terms of a global attraction to all persons having one kind of genitalia. As Stoltenberg explains: "To be 'oriented' toward a particular sex as the object of one's sexual expressivity means, in effect, having a sexuality that is like target practice—keeping it aimed at bodies who display a particular sexual definition above all else, picking out which one to want, which one to get, which one to have. Self-consciousness about one's 'sexual orientation' keeps the issue of gender central at precisely the moment in human experience when gender needs to become profoundly peripheral. Insistence on having a sexual orientation in sex is about defending the status quo, maintaining sex differences and the sexual hierarchy, whereas *resistance* to sexual-orientation regimentation is more about where we need to be going" (*Refusing to Be a Man,* 106) (emphasis in original). However, the demise of gender would not mean, as Wasserstrom claims, that bisexuality would be the "typical intimate sexual relationship in the ideal society" ("Sex Roles," 786), for the concept of bisexuality itself presupposes gender distinctions.

76. Pielke, "Androgyny and Sexuality," 194.

77. Ferguson, *Sexual Democracy,* 211.

78. This argument in no way assumes that contemporary or historical

practices of lesbianism are always or exclusively explicable in terms of an attraction by women to other women's genitals. For example, while some lesbians define themselves in terms of sexual attraction to women, others, often called political lesbians, understand their identity in terms of personal, social, and political commitment to women. See Ruth Ginzberg, "Audre Lorde's (nonessentialist) Lesbian Eros," *Hypatia* 7 1992: 73–90.

79. Teresa de Lauretis, *Technologies of Gender: Essays on Theory, Film, and Fiction* (Bloomington: Indiana University Press, 1987), 24 (emphasis in original).

80. Williams, "Deconstructing Gender," 110.

81. Nelson, "Reply," 202.

82. Linda Alcoff, "Cultural Feminism Versus Post-Structuralism: The Identity Crisis in Feminist Theory," *Signs* 13 (1988): 421. Thus, many feminists have been suspicious of the use of the term "gender studies" rather than "women's studies." They suggest that it is a strategy by which the study of women is made to seem more scholarly and neutral, or that it is a cover for furthering the study of men or for pretending that men have suffered as much under patriarchy as women. (See Scott, *Gender,* 31.)

83. Jaggar, "Sexual Equality," 242.

84. Zita, "Male Lesbians," 107.

85. This claim is cited in Alcoff, "Cultural Feminism," 417; see also Di Stefano, "Dilemmas of Difference," 65.

86. Williams, "Deconstructing Gender," 112.

87. Alcoff, "Cultural Feminism," 435.

88. Frye, *Politics of Reality,* 127.

89. Nelson, "Reply," 204.

90. Butler, "Gendering the Body," 255. Those who have experimented with crossing gender, androgyny, and "gender-bending" provide evidence of some of the possibilities.

91. Frye, *Politics of Reality,* 118, 127.

92. Stoltenberg, *Refusing to Be a Man,* 4.

93. Jane Flax, "Postmodernism and Gender Relations in Feminist Theory," *Signs* 12 (1987): 641.

94. María Lugones, "Playfulness, 'World'-Traveling, and Loving Perception," in *Women, Knowledge, and Reality: Explorations in Feminist Philosophy,* ed. Ann Garry and Marilyn Pearsall (Boston: Unwin Hyman, 1989), 275–290.

95. I derive this example from Teresa de Lauretis, who remarks, with respect to contemporary gender practices, "while we thought that we were marking the *F* on the form, in fact the *F* was marking itself on us" (*Technologies of Gender,* 11–12).

Chapter Three

The Night They Bombed Old Compton Street: Reflections on the Position of Gay People in Blair's "New Britain"

Gavin Brown

At 6:37 P.M. on Friday, 30 April 1999, a nail bomb ripped through the Admiral Duncan, a gay pub in London's Old Compton Street, the symbolic heart of the capital's gay playground. The attack on the Admiral Duncan was the third nail bomb attack in London to target the city's minority populations in under a fortnight. On Saturday, 17 April, the first bomb exploded in Brixton, a predominantly Afro-Caribbean area in South London, injuring nearly forty people. A week later (and almost to the minute), a second nail bomb caused further devastation, though far fewer injuries, in Brick Lane, the center of East London's large Bangladeshi population. The following Friday, 30 April, was a bright, sunny spring evening, and the local gay bars were teeming with gay men and their friends relaxing after a hard week at work and warming up for the long bank holiday weekend.[1] Witnesses say that in a split second the bar disappeared in a cloud of smoke and flames. The bomb killed two people instantly, a third person died two days later, and a further sixty people were injured, one-third of them seriously. Several of the injured suffered traumatic amputations as a result of the force of the blast and the hundreds of nails and shards of glass that it hurled through the enclosed space of the packed bar and out into the busy street.

Initially, the White Wolves, a small neofascist group, claimed responsibility for all three attacks. The Brixton and Brick Lane bombings were also claimed by another far right group, Combat 18. Within forty-eight hours of the third attack, however, the police had arrested and charged Stephen Copeland, a twenty-two-year-old engineer, with all three bombings. The authorities claim that

51

Copeland worked alone and had no known links with organized neofascist groups. (Despite rumors among antifascist activists to the contrary, as yet I know of no conclusive evidence to suggest otherwise.)

I have been motivated to write this chapter by the anger and hurt that I, as a gay man living in London, felt in the days following the Old Compton Street bombing. For that, I make no apologies.[2] But in the wake of the bombing, these emotions have quickly transformed into a critical reflection on the position of lesbians and gay men in contemporary Britain. To this end, I will examine the emotional response to the attack felt by myself and other queer folk; the organized response to the bombing by the "gay community" and antifascist campaigners; and the official response of the police, the press, and politicians from across the political spectrum.[3]

The bomber could not so easily have targeted the gay population if gay men and women had not constructed enclaves in major cities where they can openly meet each other and express their sexuality. Similarly, without such spaces that are of symbolic importance to gay people across the globe, the emotional and organized response to the attack would have been far more muted, and politicians would have not felt the imperative to express their solidarity with the "gay community." I will, therefore, examine the development of Old Compton Street as a material and symbolic "queer space" and explore the complex relationship between such enclaves and the position of queer people in Blair's "New Britain."

The spatial organization of sexual relations and particular sexualized constructions of place have developed in the space between attempts to suppress and regulate gay culture and the struggle for gay empowerment. Similarly, reactions to the Admiral Duncan bombing have straddled and exposed the tensions between these two processes. This chapter will explore some of these contradictions and their possible implications for the future.

Although there was very little visible reaction to the first two bombings by white gay men (other than those already active in antiracist and socialist political activism), some straight people have reacted to the Old Compton Street attack with equal measures of outrage and generosity. In part, these positive responses have simply been a reaction to the horror of the worst terrorist attack in London since the IRA cease-fire. But on another level, it is a measure of the fact that the greater visibility of gay people at every level in society has meant that many more straight people in every walk of life can now say that they know a friend or family member who is gay. To the extent that this visibility has led to greater tolerance and understanding of the diversity of queer lives, we are beginning to move away from a situation in which it is enough to say that lesbians and gay men are marginalized within society.

However, it is important to restate that the increasing integration of gay people into straight society does not represent a linear movement toward a more just, tolerant, and equal society. For two weeks after the attack, a temporary "garden of remembrance" existed in Soho Square close to Old Compton Street. Throughout this time the flowers were guarded by a team of gay volunteers to ensure that the site was not desecrated. J. J., one of the volunteers, asserted that if their guard had not been there, some kind of vandalism would have occurred: "We received abuse from neonazis, drunkards, thieves—you name it, we heard it. We even had people spit at the flowers and say that more should have died."[4]

The taunts received by J. J. and the other volunteers were not just isolated incidents. In a piece originally published in the *Guardian,* the comedian and broadcaster Simon Fanshawe told of the calls received at the lesbian and gay lobbying group Stonewall on the morning after the bombing: "Some were sympathetic, but a greater number weren't: 'I've got a box of nails here, shall I send it to you?' asked one. 'They should have bombed every pub in the street,' said another. 'Gas the queers . . . fuck off nancies.' And on and on."[5]

It is all too easy in these days of increasing tolerance to think of incidents like the recent nail bomb attack as isolated and exceptional examples of outdated prejudice. Sadly, that is not the case. A survey carried out just three years ago revealed that one in three gay men and a quarter of lesbians had experienced a violent attack in the previous five years.[6] That many of these attacks took place near gay venues demonstrates that although queer spaces can afford gay people some level of collective security, they also provide would-be attackers with viable and easily identified targets.

In the wake of the April bombings, there have been calls for a campaign to tackle prejudice and promote greater tolerance of diversity. However, there is a significant level of legal inequality and institutional prejudice that must also be challenged. Tony Blair and the majority of his cabinet may have voted to equalize the age of consent for gay men, but they have never embraced that cause as government policy, allowing their MPs a free vote on the issue while eccentric dinosaurs from the House of Lords and the Archbishop of Canterbury captured the headlines in their campaign to block equality.[7] The Metropolitan Police were certainly swift in detaining their prime suspect after the third nail bomb attack, but there are still about twenty unsolved murders of gay men in the London area from the last ten years, and many police forces seem to prioritize arresting gay men for consensual group sex or sadomasochism rather than pursuing the queer bashers.[8] The failure of leading politicians and the police to seriously tackle prejudice and inequality gives a clear message (to those who want to hear it) that gay people are still second-class citizens as we move into the twenty-first century.

A Whirlwind of Emotions

I would not have written this chapter if it were not for the intense and, at times, confusing emotions that the nail bomb in the Admiral Duncan triggered for me. It therefore seems appropriate to chart my own experience the night the bomb exploded and in the subsequent few days. I hope readers will appreciate that this is not just an exercise in self-indulgence but a strand integral to my commentary. Working from an epistemological perspective that considers all knowledge to be socially constructed, my position as a gay man living in London has clearly influenced the writing of this chapter, and it seems infinitely better that this position is acknowledged and explicitly addressed rather than ignored.[9]

I heard about the bombing about an hour after the attack had taken place. I had just met up with a group of straight friends in an unassuming bar near my home in the East End of London. My initial response was one of disgust and muted anger, but these emotions intensified over the following hour and a half as I watched news flash after news flash on the silenced television in the corner of the bar. As it became apparent that the bomber had now killed and that this third bomb had maimed far more people than either of the previous attacks, my anger turned to rage while disgust mutated into helplessness and hurt.

I do not mean to suggest that any of my straight friends felt anything less than revulsion at the bombing, but at the time, I could not accept that after muttering a few perfunctory comments about the "fascist bastards" who committed the attack, they could just resume another Friday night of drinking. I felt a desperate need to do something, and in the absence of anything tangible that I could do, I knew that, if nothing else, I had to be around other gay people and in a queer space. In part, I needed the collective support of other sexual dissidents; in part, I needed to demonstrate that I would not be intimidated from going to gay bars. So, accompanied by a straight Jewish friend who herself was feeling a tumult of emotions in the wake of the attack, I spent the rest of the evening in the local gay bar fuming with rage, hurting because my "community" had been so cruelly attacked and fearing the worst for friends who might have been in the Admiral Duncan when the bomb went off.[10]

I also felt a fourth emotion—guilt. For days after the nail bombing, I felt an incredible sense of guilt for not having been more enraged by the attacks in Brixton and Brick Lane. After all, I reasoned, I did not really frequent the Old Compton Street bars; in fact, I actively disliked them and often dismissed their patrons as pretentious and cliquey. Why should I feel so much anger at a bomb in Old Compton Street compared to the earlier attack in Brick Lane, an area I visit far more frequently that is a fifteen-minute walk from my flat?

Since the Old Compton Street attack, however, I have read and heard stories by a number of men whose words echo elements of each of the emotions I experienced, from anger and defiance— "This is a message to all those fascist gits: we won't be bombed back into the closet"[11]—to guilt and a realization of how important the image of Old Compton Street has become:

I too felt more personally affected by the Friday bomb, than I did by the Brixton or Brick Lane bombings. . . . I found the first two bombs abhorrent and horrific, but my individual identity as a gay man, and my personal attachments (however real or perceived) with the places and people of the "gay community" really hit home on Friday. . . . I too felt immense subsequent guilt that I hadn't been similarly affected by the other two bombs. I had been angry, and I had been shocked, but not scared, or whatever. I cannot exactly word what I did feel on Friday. I live in Sheffield, and as such, all three of the bombings are geographically distant from me. Friday's bomb seemed closer. The footage of places I've been to, pubs I drink in when visiting London (I drank in the Admiral Duncan last time I was down in March) brought it all very close. . . . But two people died. Not my friends. I never met them. But the locality of the bomb, my experiences in London and my positioning as a young gay man, who does (sometimes begrudgingly!) frequent the scene made me feel like I did.[12]

Habitually, we denigrate all the shallow OCS [Old Compton Street] culture, the muscle, the mobile phones, the designer carrier bags. And now the Muscle Marys have had limbs blown off. In all the denigration, we forgot how up-front it was, Old Compton Street, how visible. More than a fashion statement, a queer statement. Who are the shallow ones now?[13]

These accounts illustrate the symbolic importance of Old Compton Street for many gay men, even those whose lives are spatially and socially distanced from it. Don Mitchell has suggested:

[Public spaces are] very importantly *space for representation.* That is, public space is a place within which a political movement can stake out the space that allows it to be *seen.* In public space, political organizations can represent themselves to a larger population. By claiming space in public, by creating public spaces, social groups themselves become public.[14]

The Admiral Duncan bombing seems to have led many men to realize how important the bars, boutiques, and open street culture of Old Compton Street have been in creating a "space" for them to feel more positive about their sexuality and potentially lead more openly gay lives. And, as the quote from Howard Bradshaw and my own experience demonstrate, the aftermath of the explosion has forced some men to reevaluate their understanding of and relationship to the "gay community."

Under Attack, We Fight Back!

Within hours of the bomb exploding, the Anti-Nazi League called a demonstration for the following afternoon and were touring London's gay venues to mobilize for it. This demonstration was the first of several events held in the week following the attack, which I want to describe briefly here along with other organized responses to the bombings.

The Anti-Nazi League demonstration that was held the afternoon following the carnage in Old Compton Street was about two hundred strong and was almost entirely made up of queer members of the Socialist Workers Party and others on the Left.[15] The protesters made the short journey from Leicester Square to Trafalgar Square where they met up with a demonstration from Brixton protesting against the first nail bomb attack and the North London May Day March. The gay contingent later reformed and marched up to Soho where they stopped for a minute's silence at the edge of the police cordon around Old Compton Street.

On the Sunday of that weekend, a vigil organized by the London Gay Men's Chorus, the London Lesbian and Gay Switchboard, and the owners and promoters of various West End venues was held in Soho Square, near the site of the bombing. This was a very different event compared to the Anti-Nazi League's, far more grassroots in feel and with a very diverse crowd of several thousand people. It was part political rally, part a demonstration of solidarity and pride, and part an opportunity for collective grief and support. It combined impassioned speeches calling for full legal equality and antihate crime legislation from Peter Tatchell of Outrage! and the club promoter Jeremy Joseph. Yet, there were also curious statements from politicians of all main parties contrasting the white supremacist and bigoted views of those behind the bombings with what they described, in various ways, as the "true British virtues of tolerance, diversity and respect." In contrast, there were also personal statements by friends of those injured and killed in the bombing as well as moving songs of mourning and defiance from the Gay Men's Chorus.

Over the course of that weekend and the days that followed, vast piles of floral tributes were placed at the edge of the police cordon around the bomb site and then, once the cordon was removed, outside the boarded-up shell of the Admiral Duncan. Eventually these were moved by members of the Gay Men's Chorus and other volunteers to be displayed in Soho Square. There the flowers and messages of support and sympathy continued to accumulate until the blooms were finally mulched to be used as compost on the square's gardens a fortnight later.

On a more practical level, a number of gay businesses and community organizations quickly came together to launch an appeal for the nail bomber's victims, and a number of gay venues across London held collections for the fund. Significantly, the fund has been named the April Bombings Appeal and, although the initiative came from gay quarters, representatives of all targeted communities are represented on the board of trustees. Not only did the fund provide material aid to those injured in the attacks, but it also was intended that monies be used to tackle prejudice and promote greater tolerance of diversity.

A Flood of Crocodile Tears

In the aftermath of the Soho bombing, politicians of all shades queued up to give the press sympathetic sound bites. But, with one exception, none called for the repeal of existing laws that treat gay people unequally or for the enactment of new legislation to outlaw homophobic hate crimes.[16] For many gay people, the election of Tony Blair's "New Labour" government in May 1997, with its battle cry of "things can only get better," unleashed an enormous sense of hope. Ahead of the 1997 election, Labour politicians promised the repeal of some of the worst pieces of Thatcherite antigay legislation, including section 28 of the Local Government Act, which attempted to curtail the "intentional promotion of homosexuality" in schools. In the two years since the election, the only significant gain made for gay civil rights has been the partial relaxation of the immigration rules to recognize gay relationships in certain situations. Having promised real change as part of his vision for a "New Britain," Blair's failure to push the equality agenda forward has engendered a mounting sense of betrayal.

In a speech to Sikh religious leaders the day after the Soho bombing, Tony Blair stated: "The only good that can come out of these nail bombs is that they spur all of us, whatever our age, creed, or sexuality, to work harder to build the one nation Britain that we want and to bring our community together." To attempt to reconstruct British nationalism, however inclusive a model is being proposed, in the wake of three bombings by a self-declared "British patriot" seems more than a little suspect. It is also telling that despite the sentiments quoted above, Blair and his ministers have chosen only to pursue new antiracist legislation. Indeed, one Home Office minister, Alun Michael, even went so far as to state that legislation on racial crime was "more appropriate" than laws against homophobic violence, because "racially motivated crime harms not only the victim, but the wider community."

It must be stated that this prioritization of anti-racism did not arise out of a vacuum. The spate of nail bombs occurred shortly after the publication of the Macpherson Report on the bungled police investigation of the murder of a black teenager, Stephen Lawrence, at the hands of a gang of white youths in southeast London in 1993. The report accused the Metropolitan Police of institutionalized racism, and its publication prompted many politicians and journalists to affirm their commitment to a "tolerant" society and their respect for "diversity." Nonetheless, even the handful of out lesbian and gay Labour MPs have not made any public pronouncements on the need to advance lesbian and gay civil rights since the bombing, and none attended the vigil in Soho Square. In the light of these ignorant proclamations, comments, and conspicuous silences, one has to question how inclusive Blair's "New Britain" really is.

The failure of the government to push through measures to combat antigay hate crimes and to hasten full legal equality for lesbians and gay men must be condemned. While there remains an unequal age of consent for gay men, while lesbians and gay men are still hounded out of the armed forces and queer relationships are not recognized in law, bigots of every shade will continue to find official sanction for their prejudice, and the violence and hatred will continue.

The response of London's Metropolitan Police has also been somewhat contradictory. At the vigil in Soho Square, two days after the attack, Chief Superintendent Jo Kaye spoke of his deep respect for the "dignity and strength of the gay community" and announced that a mobile police station staffed by lesbian and gay officers would be stationed near the site of the bombing throughout the investigation. While there is no reason to doubt the sincerity of Chief Superintendent Kaye, his views are clearly not shared by some of his officers, as within a fortnight of his statement it was reported that a number of gay officers under his command were pursuing allegations of antigay harassment against some of their colleagues.[17] It also seems that the Met are only comfortable with the more respectable face of Soho's gay enclave, as in the weeks surrounding the attack local officers have been enforcing a "clean up" campaign by Westminster City Council in which a number of gay sex shops have been targeted.

Many national newspapers echoed the "one nation" rhetoric espoused by leading politicians. It seems many editors conveniently forgot the years of antigay tirades that their papers have published. Most startlingly, the popular tabloid the *Sun*, which has been responsible for some of the most blatant antigay prejudice in the press in recent decades, commented: "There is a huge tide of sympathy towards the minorities. An attack on THEM is an attack on each and every one of US. And as we saw in Soho, the victims were certainly not all gay anyway."[18] The fact that one of the people killed in the bombing, Andrea Dykes, was a straight woman whose husband also was horrifically injured in the explosion was picked up by many papers, including the *Daily Telegraph*, which referred to them as the "innocent victims" of the attack. Some sections of the press clearly found it difficult to believe that a heterosexual, married couple would choose to drink in a gay bar, and some went so far as to claim that Andrea and Julian Dykes were there by accident. All this despite the fact that they were there with three gay friends (two of whom also died in the blast), including the best man from their wedding, and that the party was on its way to see *Mama Mia*, the ABBA musical!

The Development of Old Compton Street
As Symbolic Queer Space

One wonders whether or not those who planned and planted the bomb in the Admiral Duncan could have struck so spectacularly against gay people if space such as Old Compton Street did not exist. Although there has been a gay presence in Soho for many decades, it is only in the last ten years or so that such a focused gay enclave has developed there. Gay people are far from powerless victims of prejudice, and this section explores how we have created urban spaces in which to celebrate our sexualities. In this section I will look first at the general trends that led to the development of such spaces and then specifically at the growth of Old Compton Street.

The material and psychological impact of "gay liberation" in the early 1970s afforded a growing number of men and women the opportunity to lead openly gay lives and to construct a lifestyle based on more than just sexual adventure, although this is not to ignore the fact that for many gay men, the new openness of the period was also marked by frequent casual sex. While certain neighborhoods and cities had sustained concentrations of gay venues prior to this political shift, "gay liberation" accelerated the development of a distinctly gay ambience to these areas. Inspired by the new politics but also aware of the realities of life in a heterosexist society, many gay men and women gathered together for mutual protection, support, and indulgence. Of course, the development of urban gay enclaves also provided unparalleled opportunities for gay entrepreneurs to capitalize on the thirst for such venues and consequently shape the future development of these spaces.

The new politics of the "gay liberation" era and the development of more stable gay areas in the urban landscape reflected a reinterpretation of the public/private dyad. After all, like the women's movement of the period, the Gay Liberation Front (GLF) claimed that "the personal is political." It is common currency now to assume that one effect of the politics of the GLF and their ilk was to raise the visibility of gay men and women in everyday life. However, Chauncey asserts that this effect is only part of the story.[19] Although "gay liberation" did create a more rounded "gay community" and increase lesbian and gay visibility, this change represented a shift from the partial visibility of various social networks and sexual undergrounds, which were to some extent an open secret, rather than from a position of absolute invisibility. It is perhaps an indication of the power of the contemporary commercial gay scene that it has come to dominate our understanding of "community" so much that few people under forty (who have experienced the scene) can conceive of the possibility of leading any kind of visible gay life without the presence of that infrastructure. This domination, in part, explains the emotional impact that the attack on the Admiral Duncan produced in so many people.

The growth of gay ghettos in the early 1970s paved the way for gay men and women to participate in the gentrification of city-center and inner-city neighborhoods in many major cities in North America, Western Europe, and Australasia. This gentrification, however, has taken different forms in different cities, and there are well-documented, but contested, claims that gentrification by lesbians has taken place at a different pace and in differing ways from the construction of gay male enclaves.[20]

In Britain, gay gentrification has taken place mostly as a result of the social action of gay people themselves, although, as I will argue later, capital is increasingly beginning to play a more explicit role in the process. Gay male gentrification has often taken place in close proximity to the sexual marketplace, although this has not always been a straightforward association. Frank Mort has charted how, from the mid-1960s onward, the nodal point of the London gay scene shifted from Soho to areas of West London, such as Chelsea, Kensington, and Earls Court, as a more affluent section of the gay population attempted to distance themselves from the sexual outlaws and the theatrical demimonde of the West End.[21] However, inspired by the partial decriminalization of homosexuality in 1967 and the radical politics of gay liberation, the bars and clubs in these areas increasingly celebrated the new mood of sexual freedom with gay abandon, and once again the most desirable gay neighborhoods became aligned with the sexual marketplace.

The increasing importance of service sector employment since the 1980s has created many more opportunities for lesbians and gay men to find work in relatively tolerant environments where they can be open about their sexuality; since these jobs are largely found in major urban centers, this trend is one factor that has encouraged lesbians and gay men to migrate to the city to live and work. This process, however, also works the other way around—gay people are attracted to urban centers by the presence of a viable gay subculture and look for employment opportunities in the city that offer the possibility of reduced discrimination.[22]

The growth of the service sector is not the only way that

changes in the international political economy have had an impact on urban gay life. Lawrence Knopp argues that overaccumulation in a variety of sectors has led to increasing levels of what David Harvey calls "speculative place construction"—a series of large-scale and high-risk investments in the development of physical and social infrastructures.[23] As a result, the politics of place construction is now more dependent on exchange relations than previously. In this context, capital seeks out the "diversity of human capabilities and experience" in an attempt to find new and more profitable forms of investment. This "otherness" is spatially constructed and takes the form of place-based identities, which themselves form part of the material basis of social and political struggles.

Harvey and Knopp have both emphasized the connection between culture (and sexuality) and class interests, arguing that the cultural and sexual coding of a neighborhood can be an important element in defining an area's image.[24] This coding plays a central role in the process of capital accumulation, the reproduction of social relations, and the very way in which space is produced and transformed.

Aside from residential developments, capital has played a significant role in shaping the city center "playgrounds" of the fashionable gay consumer. It is pertinent to remember here that while the multinational brewery chain Bass Taverns has made a considerable investment in gay venues, to the point where it owns a large number of the most successful locations in London, Manchester, and Birmingham, gay-controlled capital has also played a significant role in shaping these areas. In Manchester, local gay entrepreneurs worked with the city council to consolidate and promote the Gay Village, centered on Canal Street, as part of the wider property-led regeneration of the city center and marketing of the city as a tourist destination.[25]

Frank Mort has charted the development of Old Compton Street in Soho as the symbolic "high street" of London's more spatially dispersed gay village. Although Soho has long sustained a number of gay venues, Mort explains that the revitalization of the area in the last decade has in part been fueled by market research commissioned by gay businesses in the area that "pointed to the growing demand for a distinctly gay milieu in the center of London, especially among younger men," and carefully targeted advertising promoting the new breed of "continental-style" café-bars favored by the market research respondents.[26]

The example of the development of these urban gay "playgrounds" illustrates well how the shifting social position of gay men, the various advances and disappointments of progressive gay politics, and the changing political economy over the course of this century have helped shape queer spaces in the urban landscape: from the anonymous bars of the pre-Wolfenden era that were hidden behind blacked out windows through the super-discos of the 1970s to the open and airy café-bars that have emerged in the 1990s.

James Polchin has argued that if it was the rise of industrial capitalism that created the opportunity for men and women to live independently outside of traditional family structures and experience or explore their homosexual erotic desires, then it was the rise of consumerism and through it the "ability to create, and recreate oneself [that] has played a significant role in the development of gay communities in the urban landscape."[27]

Of course, it must be remembered that these cultural shifts are not without their contradictions and do not represent a linear movement toward equality for gay men and women. Frank Mort echoes the dissenting voice of the activist and journalist Keith Alcorn on the growth of gay consumerism as typified by the queering of Old Compton Street:

> And yet, as he [Alcorn] puzzled, gay consumption was doubled-edged. If the growth of shopping and other services seemed to shift the community away from activism and politics, it also stimulated a self-confidence in urban, public space. The consumerist ethos was encouraging homosexual men to stake a greater claim in the ownership of the city.[28]

The developments outlined above are pertinent examples of what Larry Knopp has called the "fuzzy boundary between cultural politics and the more straightforward politics of market relations."[29] It should be remembered, however, that capital's turn to "speculative place construction" in the pursuit of new opportunities for profit has not always had a positive impact on urban queer spaces: new zoning regulations introduced in New York City in the autumn of 1995 "cleansed" Times Square and Forty-second Street of many public sex environments that have been replaced by more family-oriented entertainment venues.[30] In short, the spatial organization of sexual relations and particular sexualized constructions of place have developed in the space between attempts to suppress and regulate gay culture and the struggle for gay empowerment.

Through this section I have attempted to clarify what is meant by the term "queer spaces" and to demonstrate the various processes by which often mundane, everyday sites in the urban landscape can become materially or symbolically important to the lives of sexual dissidents and can, potentially, undermine the heteronormative constraints of contemporary society. In the final section of this chapter, I will attempt to draw together the various disparate strands already discussed to examine our place, as queer folk, in Britain after the bombings.

Conclusion: Smudging the Margins

The volunteers who guarded the temporary "garden of remembrance" in Soho Square that I have already mentioned witnessed a startling phenomenon: "The vast majority of people to pay their respects—and I would say about 80 percent—were heterosexual couples, although it's nice that the straights took the trouble to bring flowers, it makes you wonder where all those gays that regularly visit Soho have got to."[31]

There are several possible explanations for the strength of the response to the Soho bombing among individual straight people. Most significantly, it indicates the extent to which out gay men and women are increasingly integrated into (at least) sections of metropolitan society, particularly the media and cultural industries based around Soho. However, there is also an extent to which the deaths in the Admiral Duncan acted as a catalyst that encouraged white liberals to demonstrate their commitment to diversity and a tolerant society in a way that the previous two bombings did not. It is, of course, ironic and worrying that, despite the political and media response to the accusations of institutionalized racism in the wake of the Stephen Lawrence inquiry, it still took the death of three *white* people in a fascist attack to provoke such levels of public anger and grief.

Even if civil society *is* becoming more open and tolerant, in the face of such high levels of antigay violence, prejudice, and institutional indifference, it is hardly surprising that gay men continue to find and create spaces in the city where they can relax with (gay) friends and (potential) lovers and where they can express their sexuality in whatever way seems important at the time. In the wake of the Old Compton Street bombing, there has been an increase in the level of antigay assaults and harassment reported to the Metropolitan Police. I would suggest that this represents an increased confidence in a sympathetic response from the police rather than an actual increase in antigay violence.

Nonetheless, many gay people still experience fear of violence in public places. This fear can be personally debilitating and impact on an individual's quality of life, but given that it often leads queer folk to "edit" their behavior in public, it also perpetuates the invisibility of queer lives and bolsters the heterosexist power relations that unleash antigay violence in the first place.[32] The importance of most queer spaces, therefore, aside from the sexual opportunities they can present, is that they are perceived to be safe spaces. At best, this means the creation of positive spaces in which the rich diversity of queer sexuality is affirmed; at worst, it leads to the fostering of a "ghetto mentality" in which the presence of straight people is seen as a threat.

In this context, of course, it was significant that Andrea and Julian Dykes felt comfortable and able to join their gay friends in the Admiral Duncan for a pretheater drink on 30 April. However, the fact that heterosexuals no longer feel that gay venues are off-limits to them can in some circumstances become problematic. As whole sections of the media promote Old Compton Street and similar gay playgrounds as trendy and cutting-edge leisure zones (the city of Manchester has in recent years promoted Canal Street as an alternative tourist attraction), these spaces are increasingly being degayed by the voyeuristic curiosity of young straight couples.[33] For many, the center of Manchester's gay village has become "Banal Street." It seems that the café-bar, which not so long ago represented the self-confidence of a section of young urban gay men, has become a victim of its own chic success. Equally, the question must be asked, to what extent has the more open organization of queer space, and its concomitant strengthening of the binary opposition of homosexuality and heterosexuality, actually restricted the options of those men who cannot or do not want to define themselves and their lives on the basis of queer desire?

The irony of the increasingly contested city-center queer spaces is that, in some ways, those bars that are rougher around the edges (and which are often located in more peripheral areas of major cities) remain the most "gay." There is also an extent to which these "rougher" venues can be more accessible to those without the opportunities or the inclination to lead the "Old Compton Street lifestyle." Equally, the recent "clean up" campaign in Central London reveals the extent to which visible city-center queer space is only acceptable in a stylish and sanitized form. This is not to say that the police and local government authorities do not tolerate raunchier queer sites, but to recognize that they are more likely to be tolerated in inner-city areas that are less visible to the tourists' gaze. Indeed, the last five years have seen a growth of the gay sauna and sex club scene in areas of London such as Kings Cross, Tower Hamlets, and Streatham.

The apparent lack of a visible gay response to the first two nail bombs in Brixton and Brick Lane underscores the unwritten "white" in "gay community" and ignores the fact that black and South Asian queers have been doubly targeted by the attacks. The April Bombings Appeal has committed itself to promoting tolerance and diversity in society, and it must be hoped that these efforts will be aimed as much at the "gay community" as at white heterosexuals. While the Soho bombing spurred some gay men to realize how important the existence of Old Compton Street had been (at least symbolically) for the direction and development of their lives, the Old Compton Street lifestyle must not be conflated with the reality of most queer lives in Britain at the end of the millennium.

Hans Almgren has argued that discussions of community (like subculture) tend to reduce complex identities to the lowest common denominator and define the community under discussion in relation to whatever is outside it: "The effect is that communities tend, by their static conceptualization, to be defined at their centres and viewed in isolation."[34] This presents a false unity that marginalizes difference and diversity within the community and denigrates multiple, overlapping identities and those whose identities are in flux.

I hope that in reflecting on the various responses to the bombing of the Admiral Duncan I have illustrated the complex relationship of queers in contemporary Britain to the margins. The visibility of strategic city-center queer sites like Old Compton Street and Canal Street in Manchester has created a degree of social space in which gay people across the country (but particularly in large cities to which so many queers still migrate) can be more open about their sexuality. On another level, Britain currently has a government that is officially committed to lesbian and gay equality and has promised, but as yet failed to deliver, a "New Britain" for all.

The anger provoked by the three nail bomb attacks must be harnessed and channeled into the struggle for civil rights and full legal equality. While the nail bombings starkly illustrated that there is a small, violent neofascist fringe in Britain, the real obstacle to equality and civil rights is a political establishment that, for all its talk of a "one nation" Britain, continues to govern a country in which the law treats people differently on the basis of their ethnicity, gender, and sexuality. However, in challenging the legitimacy of those laws, we must also look inward and address the extent to which the "gay community" marginalizes and devalues the lives of many queer people.

Notes

1. The first Monday in May is a public holiday in Britain—a kind of depoliticized May Day.

2. Michael Keith, "Angry Writing: (Re)presenting the Unethical World of the Ethnographer," *Environment and Planning D: Society and Space* 10 (1992): 551–568.

3. I am very skeptical of the extent to which there is *a* lesbian and gay community, but it is a useful shorthand term at times. At best, I think we have a myriad of shifting and overlapping communities located in both space and time.

4. Quoted by David Northmore in "Flower Power in the Heart of Soho," *Pink Paper*, 21 May 1999.

5. Quoted by Terry Sanderson in "Mediawatch," *Gay Times*, June 1999.

6. Angela Mason and Anya Palmer, *Queer Bashing: A National Survey of Hate Crimes Against Lesbians and Gay Men* (London: Stonewall, 1996).

7. At the time of writing (June 1999), there remains an unequal age of consent for male homosex in the United Kingdom. Although Labour Party policy favors equalizing the age of consent at sixteen, during the two parliamentary debates on this issue in the last eighteen months, Labour MPs have been allowed to vote according to their conscience rather than in line with party policy. Nonetheless, the elected House of Commons has voted in favor of equality

in recent debates, but the unelected House of Lords has consistently utilized parliamentary maneuvering and its inherent conservatism to block equality at every turn.

8. Colin Richardson, "Police Hate," *Gay Times,* May 1999.

9. Sasha Roseneil, "Greenham Revisited: Researching Myself and My Sisters," in *Interpreting the Field: Accounts of Ethnography,* ed. Dick Hobbs and Tim May (Oxford: Oxford University Press, 1993).

10. Like many people, my friend had feared that London's Jewish population would be the bombers' third target. Alerted to this threat, community defense patrols had been set up in at least one Jewish neighborhood earlier that week. In contrast, most gay people were blissfully complacent about the threat to their safety. Although the edition of the *Pink Paper* published on the day of the bombing did carry a warning on its front page that gay people could be targeted by the bombers, this warning (through no fault of the editors) was too late to impact on many people's consciousness before the blast occurred.

11. Anonymous message, published in *Boyz,* 8 May 1999.

12. Stuart, correspondence with author.

13. Howard Bradshaw, "The Bottom Line," *axiom news,* 20 May 1999.

14. Don Mitchell, "The End of Public Space? People's Park, Definitions of the Public, and Democracy," *Annals of the Association of American Geographers* 1, no. 85 (1995): 108–133; quoted by Gill Valentine, "(Re)negotiating the 'Heterosexual Street': Lesbian Production of Space," in *Bodyspace,* ed. Nancy Duncan (London: Routledge, 1996), 152.

15. The Socialist Workers Party is the largest revolutionary socialist organization in the United Kingdom today, claiming 10,000–12,000 members. The British party is at the center of the International Socialist tendency. Uncharacteristically, the press and the police overestimated the size of this demonstration almost fivefold.

16. Ken Livingstone has been a long-term supporter of lesbian and gay equality, and in the 1980s there was much press speculation about his own sexuality. In recent years, he has tamed many of his more "controversial" opinions in the hope of accommodating himself to the Labour leadership. It seems unlikely that his decision to speak out at this time is entirely unconnected to his candidacy in the forthcoming elections for the mayor of London.

17. Colin Richardson, "Police Under Pressure to Review Michael Booth Murder," *Gay Times,* June 1999.

18. Quoted by Sanderson, "Mediawatch. Although the *Sun* has been responsible for promoting antigay prejudice for many decades, it has begun to reinvent itself as a "gay-tolerant" (if still not "gay-friendly") voice since the autumn of 1998. At that time, its editorial policy changed, quite literally, overnight with a call for toleration after the outing of three government ministers (Ron Davies, Nick Brown, and Peter Mandelson).

19. George Chauncey, Jr., *Gay New York: Gender, Urban Culture, and the Making of the Gay Male World, 1890–1940* (New York: Basic Books, 1994).

20. Sy Adler and Johanna Brenner, "Gender and Space: Lesbians and Gay Men in the City," *International Journal of Urban and Regional Research* 16 (1992): 24–34; Tamar Rothenburg, "'And She Told Two Friends': Lesbians Creating Urban Social Space," in *Mapping Desire: Geographies of Sexualities,* ed. David Bell and Gill Valentine (London: Routledge, 1995); Gill Valentine, "Out and About: Geographies of Lesbian Landscapes," *International Journal of Urban and Regional Research* 19 (1995): 96–111.

21. Frank Mort, *Cultures of Consumption: Masculinities and Social Space in Late Twentieth Century Britain* (London: Routledge, 1996).

22. Kath Weston, "Get Thee to a Big City: Sexual Imaginary and the Great Gay Migration," *GLQ: A Journal of Lesbian and Gay Studies* 2 (1995): 253–277.

23. Lawrence Knopp, "Sexuality and the Spatial Dynamics of Capitalism," *Environment and Planning D: Society and Space* 10 (1992): 651–669; David Harvey, *The Conditions of Postmodernity: An Enquiry in the Origins of Cultural Change* (Oxford: Basil Blackwell, 1989).

24. Harvey, *Conditions of Postmodernity;* Knopp, "Sexuality and Spacial Dynamics."

25. Stephen Whittle, "Consuming Differences: The Collaboration of the Gay Body with the Cultural State," in *The Margins of the City: Gay Men's Urban Lives,* ed. S. Whittle (Aldershot, England: Ashgate Publishing, 1994); Stephen Quilley, "Constructing Manchester's 'New Urban Village': Gay Space in the Entrepreneurial City," in *Queers in Space: Communities/Public Spaces/Sites of Resistance,* ed. Gordon Brent Ingram, Anne-Marie Bouthillette, and Yolanda Retter (Seattle: Bay Press, 1997).

26. Mort, *Cultures of Consumption,* 165.

27. James Polchin, "Having Something to Wear: The Landscape of Identity on Christopher Street," in *Queers in Space: Communities/Public Spaces/Sites of Resistance,* ed. Gordon Brent Ingram, Anne-Marie Bouthillette, and Yolanda Retter (Seattle: Bay Press, 1997). See also John D'Emilio, "Capitalism and the Gay Identity," in *The Lesbian and Gay Studies Reader,* ed. Henry Abelove, Michèle Aina Barale, and David M. Halperin (London: Routledge, 1993); Jeffrey Escoffier, "The Political Economy of the Closet: Notes Toward an Economic History of Gay and Lesbian Life Before Stonewall," in *Homo Economics: Capitalism, Community, and Lesbian and Gay Life,* ed. Amy Gluckman and Betsy Reed (London: Routledge, 1997); and Steven Maxwell Kates, *Twenty Million New Customers! Understanding Gay Men's Consumer Behavior* (London: Haworth Press, 1998).

28. Mort, *Cultures of Consumption,* 166.

29. Knopp, "Sexuality and Spatial Dynamics," 664.

30. David Serlin, "The Twilight (Zone) of Commercial Sex," in *Policing Public Sex,* ed. Dangerous Bedfellows (Boston: South End Press, 1996).

31. J. J. quoted by Northmore, "Flower Power."

32. Wayne D. Myslik, "Renegotiating the Social/Sexual Identities of Places: Gay Communities As Safe Havens or Sites of Resistance?" in *Bodyspace: Destabilizing Geographies of Gender and Sexuality,* ed. Nancy Duncan (London: Routledge, 1996).

33. See Wayne Clews, "As Not Seen on TV," *Gay Times,* June 1999; Quilley, "Manchester's 'New Urban Village'"; and Whittle, "Consuming Differences."

34. Hans Almgren, "Community With/Out Pro-Pink-Unity," in *The Margins of the City: Gay Men's Urban Lives,* ed. Stephen Whittle (Aldershot, England: Ashgate Publishing, 1994), 49.

Chapter Four

Comblement/Fulfillment: Toward an Ontological Ethics of Sex

Jami Weinstein and Jeffrey Bussolini

comblement/fulfillment:
The subject insistently posits the desire and the possibility of a complete satis-
faction of the desire implicated in the amorous relation and of a perfect and vir-
tually eternal success of this relation: paradisiac image of the Sovereign Good,
to be given and to be received.[1]

Contemporary experience is rife with instances of the marginalization of certain sexual activities, behaviors, and identities. Jocelyn
Elders was removed from her position as surgeon general merely
for openly and frankly discussing masturbation. Singer George
Michael was stigmatized when it was divulged that he had participated in public gay sex. Yet the constant and overbearing presence
of heterosexual sex and erotics in the U.S. media and popular culture indicates that what is at issue here is not a wholesale injunc-
tion on sexual activity and desire. Rather, there seem to be certain
normalized and socially ingrained roles and practices, which are
encouraged and sanctioned, while another range of activities is dis-
couraged, pathologized, and even banned. What is it that makes
certain practices legitimate and proper while others are invalid and
suspect? Where can we look to understand the marginalization that
takes place in and around sexuality, and, looking there, can we
move toward a praxis that will critically engage and render impo-
tent this marginalization?

In this chapter, we shall attempt to develop and explain an ontology of ethics, which we think should replace the more traditional metaphysics of morals and ultimately resituate the discourse
and practice of marginalizing sexualities. Certainly, we agree that

in the moral sense it is wrong to marginalize, for instance, queers and masturbators, but knowing that does not provide us with an understanding of how to live as marginalized subjects or to de-marginalize those behaviors or identities. We continue to wonder where we should look to reconceptualize our lived experience and quotidian existence. What is the source of the new space and grounding for behaviors that have been suppressed?

Developing an ontology of ethics casts new perspectives on thinking about marginalization. However, being ontological and process-oriented, it also bears directly on being or existing as marginalized. We take marginalization as a process that is ongoing and that therefore incorporates continual performance by the actors involved. We take process in the durative sense in which it is unceasing activity and therefore is informed by an underlying motif of change and flux. In fact, that is the key difference between what we call ethics and morality: ethics is an ongoing activity of continuous practice, whereas morality is a search for abstract, static, and almost formal ideals and principles. Thus, it is hoped that this interactive and process-oriented performative ethics will have transformative potential in everyday life and understanding.

Another feature of our ontological ethics is a consideration of the fundamental relations to being and to nothingness as experienced in sexual relationships. Changes in the conceptions of being and nothingness have dramatic influence upon attunement and a mode of existing in the world. It is our position that marginalization of certain sexualities can be read as the consequence of an underlying misconception about the relation of being and nothingness in sexual relations. This misconception is rooted in the view that desire is some form of lack rather than the further expression of an existential fulfillment always already at hand. A related element of this ethical ontology is that it involves a rethinking of the dialectic of society and the individual.

Our ethic starts from the premise of an individuality that is constituted by its myriad relations with things and people in the world but that is, in another respect, alone in terms of its being toward death and toward the nothing. Although unsettling and unclear to talk about initially, we will consider in this chapter different conceptions of nothing and different relations to it. We suggest that prevailing paradigms of general practice and marginalization in sexuality involve deficient modes of individual being and therefore present troubling conclusions about social and sexual relations. In fact, in these models, it seems that erotic or social relations are presented as fulfillments for the frantic individual search for actualization that should exist on a quite different level: that of the relationship to being itself. We hope that by starting from the individual in a more primordial way a more robust concept of sociality can be developed, which moves away from seeing the nothing as lack. We see the figure of the masturbator as a powerful and compelling example of a radical self-grounding, which offers a counterpoint to the troublesome assumptions that bring us to emphasize binary sexual relationships as the mode of self-completion.

So, the two primary ontological elements of the ethics that we will be taking up here are the underlying metaphysics of change or flux, as opposed to stasis or linear infinity, and the relation to the nothing, often coming across in terms of conceptions about desire as a lack. Prior to advancing our positive theory, we will spend a few moments tracing the emergence of the morality and concomitant marginalization of sexualities that we are opposing. Following the genealogy of the paradigm that still largely holds sway for us, we will provide the linkage between our ontology and a potentially transformative set of liberating responses and inhabitations of sexually marginalized identities.

Genealogy

In *The History of Sexuality*, Michel Foucault suggests that the distinction between and ranking of different sexual behaviors came to light against a certain norm of familial and sexual relations, which was taking shape already during the classical period of ancient Athens. In *The Use of Pleasure*, part two of *The History of Sexuality*, Foucault describes the emergence of the cultural emphasis on the binary, monogamous heterosexual pairing.[2] Practices that contravene this norm become subject to increasing disapproval. Treatises on masturbation begin to emerge, the assumption of the right of citizen men to see prostitutes, concubines, and young boys is questioned, and sex starts to be seen increasingly in terms of procreation, on the one hand, and in terms of danger and death, on the other.

Foucault also points out that a profound split between public and private society was put in place by the classical Athenians, and that there was a pronounced and rigid gendered division of labor. During the Christian period in Europe, this emphasis intensifies all the more in the mortification of the flesh and the casting as sinful any use of the flesh for purposes other than heterosexual and procreative. Sexual pleasure, a valid and important pursuit for the Greeks, becomes a sin to be avoided. Women are excluded from the priesthood for most of this Christian period (and even until quite recently in a few instances), and this exclusion relegates and encloses most women in private social space.

This moral set of judgments and regulations that comes to bear on sex and sexuality is significant for Foucault in the respect that it takes the form of the static pronouncement of right or wrong according to form of behavior; clearly, it is a profound example of social control in terms of shaping ideas and actions. He contrasts this morality with an ethics that he finds to have preceded it in which emphasis was placed on regimen (as in a routine and schedule of activities), the use of pleasure, and an ongoing practice of care of the self. Foucault reiterates throughout this volume that the conceptual framework and very understanding of sexuality in ancient Greece was so stunningly divergent from contemporary discourses that we can scarcely understand them.

A difficult interpretive task is set up in that the only way we could hope to understand the Greeks is to read them through the filter of the many currents and traditions intervening between us and them. Although we strive of course for the most attentive type of hearkening to Greek experience and texts, it is also pertinent to keep in mind Foucault's dictum of writing history of the present. In other words, he did not see history as a dry or decrepit matter closed off to us by time, but as a dynamic process that continues, has its existence in the present, and interacts in myriad ways with contemporary life. So, let us be clear here that in looking at this historical period and formation, we are not seeking to glorify the notion of a Greek golden age to which we would return. We have already pointed out that Greek sexual experience was hardly free of marginalization. Rather, we look at the Greeks to explore the possibility of a different notion of human relationship to the world and to other humans that could have salient implications for thinking about contemporary sexual marginalization—especially if Foucault is right that the general structure of norms with which we still live emerged at that juncture.

We continue to live with the marginalization that takes shape around the moral norm of the binary heterosexual relationship (especially that culminating in marriage). What sexual behaviors and regimens does this norm stigmatize? Certainly lesbian and gay sex are looked down upon as nonprocreative and as an inversion of proper desire. Consider the drastic difference in controversy between Ellen Degeneres's coming out (a static identity declaration) versus her actual lived lesbian practice both in the fictional world of her sitcom and her public life in the media.[3]

Transsexuality and transvestism also trouble the gendered assumptions behind the formation of the binary heterosexual norm in an unsettling way. It is interesting to note that there is a link between the ridicule directed at effeminate men today and Plato's dialogue *Ion* in which Socrates makes fun of Ion for his supposedly effeminate and dandylike apparel. Also interfering with this norm, masturbation is deemed as a wasteful expenditure of energy both in terms of lost opportunity for procreation and lost personal vitality. It is seen as solipsistic and immature. In many cases it has been pronounced detrimental to the health and possibly even deadly—as it did indeed prove fatal to the careers of Jocelyn Elders and Paul Reubens (Pee Wee Herman).[4]

Since this norm also has economic dimensions for Foucault, a dual register of economics and sexuality emerges. On the one hand, there is the economy of the procreation of the species and the production of further humans. Such procreation and restocking of the ranks of society is a major focus, for instance, in both Plato's *Republic* and Aldous Huxley's *Brave New World*. This propagation is often spoken about in the language of "the survival of the human species."[5] We leave aside for the moment the wisdom of Silenus divulged in Sophocles' *Oedipus at Colonus* that, for the human race, "what is best of all is utterly beyond your reach: not to be born, not to be, to be nothing. But the second best is—to die soon."[6]

On the other hand, there is the way in which the sexual norm is part of a broader set of economic structures. The Athenian model of the public sphere of men's work and the agora of democratic discourse and citizenship was constituted alongside the ideal of the home as the domain of the wife, who was to manage the household. The wife's management of the affairs of the house would guarantee the time and freedom for the male citizen's participation in public life. This gendered division of labor and public-private split is remarkably similar to Betty Friedan's description of the experience of the suburban housewife in *The Feminine Mystique*.[7]

The troubling delineation of such gender roles is related to another crucial aspect of sexual marginalization, which is the discourse of activity and passivity in sex and the values attributed to them. With the public-private split criticized by both Friedan and Foucault in situations some two thousand years apart, privileged, citizen men are the actors of the public sphere. In fact, the idea and etymology of "actor" are traceable back to the role of the stage actor of Greek theater, which for some time was a privilege open only to men. But there is also a whole host of connotations about activity and passivity in sexual activity itself that informed Greek sexual discourse and still haunt our own. Women and young boys (the sexual partners of older men) were degraded in status by virtue of their being penetrated and "passive." The idea of the adult man consecrating his activity by the passive sacrifice of the love object remains eerily close to Jean-Paul Sartre's thinking about erotic relationships as a lack, which we will soon examine and then seek to step back from. But before we do so, it is germane here to draw upon two other thinkers who noticed a peculiar coming together of erotic and economic concerns during this Greek period that is so influential on unfolding European history.

Gilles Deleuze and Felix Guattari, in their two-volume work *Capitalism and Schizophrenia*, note that around the time of Plato and embodied in his work there is a decisive shift toward an experience of desire as lack.[8] According to this model, the individual feels a sense of emptiness and incompleteness for which an external remedy is desired, for our purposes here a sexual partner who is supposed to fill a certain void in personal experience. Part of Deleuze's and Guattari's importance is that they notice it is the same lack and emptiness that capitalism is able to set upon in the sense of encouraging consumption as a way to try to gain completeness. Hence, perhaps it is no accident that so much of modern product advertising involves sexual imagery and innuendo.

A prominent example of the problem that Guattari and

Deleuze raise is found in the Aristophanes myth in Plato's *Symposium*, where Aristophanes explains an earlier stage of the world in which people did not take the shape that they currently do but instead were rotund creatures consisting of two of what we would now call individual people. These protohumans had four arms and four legs as well as two heads. As the myth would have it, these creatures were eventually split in two, which sets up a very nice and urgent dynamic in which each of us is always searching for our other part in order to become whole. This is an original lack, which we can only hope to surmount by finding the "right one," a form of discourse that is very much alive and kicking in contemporary society. So it seems that, according to Foucault, Guattari, and Deleuze, there is a problem with fundamental relation to nothingness that plays into sexual normalization and capitalistic desire. We will try to discern more about this lack and what type of relation to the nothing it entails.

Steps Toward an Ontological Ethics of Sex

Simone de Beauvoir and Jean-Paul Sartre are two existentialist thinkers who paid considerable attention in their works to the dynamics of erotic relationships and their implications for subjectivity. However, as existentialists they are also concerned with ontology and the nothing. After all, Sartre's major philosophical work is called *Being and Nothingness*.[9] So, if we are inquiring into the influence of the relationship to the nothing on sexual normalization and sexual marginalization, we would do well to consider these formidable figures.

Sartre holds a view that is ultimately pessimistic about the influence of the nothing on erotic relationships. His theory does not offer the potential for interpersonal relations of a sexual sort to remain immutable and effective. For Sartre, there is another factor that dooms erotic relations to fail in the long term. His theory is mainly ontological or existential, and it is this area of his inquiry that is the most basic and essential and, hence, most worthy of attention.

Broadly speaking, Sartre's project strives to provide an ontological basis for the phenomenology of absolute human freedom, which offers a general motive for his description of human being as possibility or nothingness. If he allowed that being could even be slightly determined, fixed, in-itself, or necessary, he would have been unable to achieve his desired result: human being as nothing other than free subjectivity, compelled by the burden of choice to define his or her essence. Because of this overarching aim, Sartre's theory of sexuality becomes tainted with a seemingly irresolvable conflict between what we, in some sense, are and what we wish we could be.

This is the notion of lack that Deleuze and Guattari have described as a yearning for another world almost akin to a Platonic backworld—an alternate existence for ourselves.[10] In other words, our desire to be fixed and determined is at odds with what is our absurd reality: that we are nothing save what we have constructed ourselves to be. In this respect, Sartre is caught between the ontology of ethics and the metaphysics of morals. He does emphasize becoming and does try to refute any notion of essence (as in his famous idea that existence precedes essence), yet he does not fully hold to a view of continual dynamism; there is still the longing to achieve a static position.

In technical terms borrowed from Hegel, Sartre refers to these two modes of being as the in-itself *(en-soi)* and the for-itself *(pour-soi)*, the former relating mainly to objects and the latter to humans. The latter can be more explicitly understood as the "nihilation of the in-itself . . . because the for-itself is *nothing* and is separated from the in-itself by *nothing*. The for-itself is the foundation of all negativity and of all relation. The for-itself is relation."[11] Here Sartre seems very much in line with the ontological disposition we are trying to approach, as he is placing a strong emphasis on the fundamental role of relation. However, as he clarifies the nature of this relation, he moves away from the dynamic ontology of ethics: "Consciousness [is] conceived as a lack of Being, a desire for Being, a relation to Being. . . . Each for-itself is the nihilation of a particular being."[12]

What this means is that the for-itself is nothingness; it is not a being in that it is something determinate, but rather it is a relational being, a becoming. It is a relational being, but according to Sartre it feels that it lacks being and therefore manifests itself in a desire for being. In contrast, the in-itself can be described as "non-conscious Being. It is the being of the phenomenon and overflows the knowledge which we have of it. It is a plenitude, and strictly speaking we can say of it only that it is."[13] This brand of being belongs to particular things/objects, to the physicality of people, and most interestingly to people's pasts. Another term that Sartre employs is facticity, which can be understood as "the For-itself's necessary connection with the In-itself, hence the world and its own past. It is what allows us to say that the For-itself *is* or *exists*."[14] It is "our existence as body in the midst of the world."[15]

In addition to the aforementioned modes of being and the relationship between them, what also must be held in mind is the notion of being-for-others. This concept articulates the connection between self and other. What is attempted by the for-itself is to become an in-itself for some other, yet this "involves a perpetual conflict as each For-itself seeks to recover its own Being by directly or indirectly making an object out of the other."[16] The attempt to attain this goal is exactly why Sartre's view of sex is doomed to fail.

Thus, it is inside this metaphysical shell, which consists in a relationship between the for-itself and the in-itself, that Sartre made the first move toward the ontology we are proposing to adopt. Although Sartre sees an unbridgeable gulf between the for-itself and the in-itself, we try to reveal a primordial unification already present prior to the binary split. By utilizing this dichotomy, he still remains rooted in the subject-object distinction we are trying to surmount. The fundamental problem for Sartre is that consciousness wants to ground its self as a for-itself in-itself through other people. He thinks we use others to attempt the allegedly impossible task of filling the void of the nothingness of our for-itself being. Thus, Sartre's pessimism about human relations is more crucially an issue of relation to emptiness and nothingness.

One of the main obstacles in accepting Sartre's theory of sexual behavior is its conclusion. According to Sartre, sexual activity of the binary type is doomed to utter failure on the grounds that we are always looking for something that by the nature of the act is impossible, one might even dare to say logically impossible. Briefly, his theory regards sexual activity as "one form of the perpetual attempt of an embodied consciousness to come to terms with the existence of others."[17] However, because "coming to terms with the existence of others" in the manner Sartre deems as our ultimate goal is psychologically impossible in a logical sense, our effort to maintain a metaphysically, ontologically, or categorically stable sexual relation is inherently ill-fated. Intuitively, this argument seems flawed, for how can it be that sex by its very nature cannot succeed? And further, where is the physical drive/urge manifested in this search to understand the existential nature of others; is sex purely cognitive? It appears almost as if the body drops out for Sartre's subject.

Though Sartre does not explicitly state it, his analysis has been undermined by his apparent traditional morality about sex. His categories of sexual behavior produce "failed attempts" when they result in sadism or masochism. This phrasing implies a moral judgment about certain types of sexual activity. In other words, not only is Sartre's theory inherently unsuccessful, but it also contains an implicit judgment about certain forms of sexuality by claiming that if we end up with those forms, sexuality is unsuccessful. There is also a bias toward having a static definition. Perhaps inherent to the essence of sex is an element of vacillation/change between these different attitudes. In that case, the interpersonal activity would not need repair; it would simply be reinterpreted as serving a purpose other than the grounding of projection as facticity. The linear model, though adequate in some instances, may be too narrow to account for the range and complexity of this particular type of behavior.

The basis of his inquiry rests on the notion that the fundamental human project is the existential grounding of ourselves as a for-itself in-itself, which is connected to our nothingness since what it suggests about us is that we are a becoming, not a being or static entity. Moreover, to Sartre, consciousness still desires this fixed nature. On his account, the unique method of acquiring this essential unity is through being-for-others. What precisely is Sartre's theory of the nothing, and why does it play such a primary motivating force in our social behavior on his account? Although he has already defined the for-itself as nothing, we have not yet seen in a deeper ontological sense what this nothing means for Sartre.

Sartre has a strong and specific stance on the nothing—it is derivative of being. For instance, in this passage from *Being and Nothingness*, he states that "man is the being through whom nothingness comes to the world. But this question immediately provokes another: what must man be in his being in order that through him nothingness may come into being?"[18] Nothingness is derivative of human being, and in this respect Sartre agrees with Hegel: "That does not mean only that we should refuse to put being and non-being on the same plane, but also that we must be careful never to posit nothingness as an original abyss from which being arose."[19] For Hegel and for Sartre, the nothing and non-being lack any positive existential qualities, which sets up a conception in which being is presence and nothing is lack of being.

Simone de Beauvoir's reflections on being and the nothing parallel Sartre's in many ways. For the epigraph of her novel *She Came to Stay*, she chooses a portentous sentence from Hegel: "Each consciousness seeks the death of the other."[20] This statement seems very much in line with Sartre's description of doomed interpersonal relations in which one is always trying to objectify another. Indeed, the characters in the novel carry out precisely this process unceasingly. All relations in the book are focused especially around binary heterosexual relations. The main protagonists are the heterosexual couple, Francoise and Pierre, who have a bond that predates the novel by at least ten years and seems still projected toward some indeterminate future. There are triangles and other variations around the strict binary coupling, but they still seem to hover very much within the binary coupling orbit.

Xaviere, a young country girl, comes to Paris at the invitation of Francoise, who hopes she will benefit from life in the urban artistic center. The relationship between the women becomes highly charged and almost lesbian, yet it cannot actually become a performative possibility for them, as they both remain locked in a competition over Pierre. In this existentialist text emphasizing radical choice, choosing outside of the heterosexual norm does not seem to be an option. A notion of existential lack to be filled by a heterosexual partner is strong in the characters of this novel. Francoise and Pierre have a long and deep relationship, which is nonetheless subject to a stipulation of openness and freedom for both parties. No character seems able to stand alone sexually, to remain aloof. Instead, it seems that all the characters are seeking existential fulfillment through sexual means—a fundamentally untenable solution.

Even Francoise and Pierre, who pride themselves on their independence, their choice, and their strength, absolutely depend on each other and are horrified at the prospect of being sexually isolated. At the end of the novel, Francoise exercises her existential choice in the decisive action of killing Xaviere, whom she had originally invited from the tiny town of Rouen and who had since come to threaten Francoise's relationship to Pierre and Francoise herself. Thus, Francoise made good on precisely Hegel's idea: each consciousness seeks the death of the other. In the face of the nothing, the radical existential action that Francoise takes to ground her being and regain her solitude is to kill (and render in-itself) another.

The Ontological Ethics of Sex

Although they undoubtedly are starting to criticize these categories and both emphasize pure becoming and choice, Sartre and de Beauvoir are within the horizon of the Hegel epigraph (which also entails the Cartesian subject-object split) in their thinking on human relationships: each consciousness seeks to objectify or kill the other. The consciousness is still there as subject over and against the sexual partner who is object. In a recent book on Buddhist philosophy fostering fascinating dialogue between Eastern and Western traditions, Joan Stambaugh helps us to portray some of the crucial dimensions of the ontology of ethics we wish to enact. In contrast to the selves portrayed in de Beauvoir and Sartre, who are still to some extent the isolated cogito and the consciousness, "the Self of Zen or the Formless Self cannot be defined or taught. We cannot look for it outside of ourselves or, for that matter, inside of ourselves either. For inside of ourselves is still differentiated from outside."[21]

De Beauvoir and Sartre, still to some degree within the throw of Hegel and Descartes, operate with the notion of a distinctly internal mental state. Hisamatsu, a Buddhist thinker, shows how this notion still fits within the dynamic of the subject and the object as "he begins to show that what we ordinarily consider 'mind' is already something objectified, thus possessing form. What the psychology, science, or philosophy of self-consciousness studies is precisely not true self-consciousness, but an objectified self."[22] Even the posits of mind and consciousness of these figures we have been examining remain part of the static metaphysics that we are trying to repudiate in favor of the process-focused materialism that we are developing as an ontology.

What we are moving toward here is a more primordial unity rather than the frozen and unrelational notion of subject and object. Stambaugh elaborates: "In this sense, the Zen experience does not coincide with the 'turning within' of Western philosophy which began with Plotinus and was followed by a few isolated thinkers."[23] We might also add that the Zen experience, here in parallel with the ontology of ethics, does not coincide with the "turning without" of Western culture whether it be in terms of erotic lack, desire for consumer products, or anxiety of nothingness. Either move would be to retain the split rather than allow the productive contradiction. The search would not be satisfied in either direction, because the unity we are seeking is of an entirely different order. It is about plenitude whereas the others are about lack.

Another significant implication of the analyses of relationships in Sartre and de Beauvoir is the way in which desire has been fused with an existential lack as a foundational incompleteness or absence in being requiring amelioration, hence the interminable pursuit of heterosexual pairings operative in their works. With a more radical ontology of ethics, by contrast, there is a significant reconceptualization of desire that allows us to step back from this lack:

> Freedom from attachment means not being bound by things, habits, or rules. People with many possessions are bound and fettered to these things: they take care of them, worry about their being lost, damaged or stolen, and insure them. But, of course, one cannot "insure" anything, least of all ones life. . . . In unattachment . . . I can very well care about the thing—or person—and take care of it—or him or her—but I am not bound by it. I can let go of it if that is what is called for.[24]

Here Stambaugh highlights several of the important dynamics of an ontology of ethics. There is, of course, the profound absence of desire as lack; instead there is a positive relationality engaging things and people. Also here, however, is the key motif that ethics and freedom from attachment involve not being bound by habits or rules. The empty ought of the metaphysics of morality and the binary heterosexual monogamous discursive formation, which Foucault described, take the form of the rule and the habit that we strive to take leave of via ontological performativity. Not being bound by things or habits or rules returns focus to the body and ongoing lived experience. Without set habits and rules, the ethic of behavior is much more fluid, and emphasis is on individual experimentation and fulfillment rather than compliance with an overarching configuration of amorous relations.

The perspective of an ontological ethics has even further bearing on the practice and conceptualization of sex. Stambaugh makes an interesting comparison between Baruch Spinoza and strains of Buddhism that bears on our consideration here:

> Spinoza, who in some ways did not have much in common with Buddhism, nevertheless is very Buddhist in his understanding of perfection. He states that the most common way of speaking about perfection is analogous to the way men talk about good and evil. They have an ideal standard in mind, say of a house, and according to how something does or does not measure up to this standard it is judged perfect or imperfect, good or evil.[25]

Certainly, this thinking applies readily to sexual marginalization. Foucault has meticulously described just what kind of ideal "house" our society holds in mind when it comes to sex, and by that standard many other sexualities are judged perfect or imperfect, good or evil. This description might evoke the image of the Greek *oikos,* or home, which in its perfect form served as the mechanism by which women were marginalized and relegated to the private social sphere. Further, we may see a link to the house of Francoise and Pierre, which in many ways prohibited and regulated the performative possibility of sexual relations between Francoise and Xaviere. In contemporary society, troubling practices such as masturbation, lesbian and gay sex, sadomasochism, transvestism, and transgenderism have been cast as imperfect and incomplete houses indeed. Just as Spinoza points out, the ways of talking about perfection are fundamentally analogous to the ways of talking about good and evil, and it is little coincidence that various sexual practices and roles have been decried as evil.

However, Spinoza's idea of perfection unfolds even another level that is relevant for us here. His conception of perfection does not hold to the formal ideal or empty ought that his discussion criticized above. Rather, as Stambaugh explicates, "Spinoza's own use of the word perfection *(perficere)* is closer to the nonjudgmental quality of being accomplished, completed, in this sense perfected. . . . But reality and perfection are the same thing."[26] Here a plurality of sexual behaviors and practices is recognized and emphasized regardless of any reference to an external standard or abstract ought of narrowly defined sexuality. Such a subtle, comprehensive, and nonjudgmental thinking of tolerance has profound implications for replacing and unsettling marginalization.

Just as Spinoza does not seek perfection in the abstract ideal but instead in that which actually exists, he defines power as the capacity to be affected; in other words, it is the most radical opening up of oneself to the world and that which exists. We could characterize this view of power as an ethical form of passivity. Yet in several places earlier in this chapter—such as the Greek sexual practices discussed by Foucault, the conscious hostility and the murder of Xaviere by Francoise from de Beauvoir, and the for-itself continually trying to ground out and fulfill its nothing in some other in Sartre, which leads to the eventual decline of each amorous relationship—we saw a very strong assumption always placed on activity and often on penetration.

Foucault's description of the implications of being penetrated on one's social role in ancient Athens still resonates with us today.[27] These ideas circulate not only regarding straight sex but are also alive and well in gay and lesbian practices in certain discourses of the "top" and the "bottom." Could it be that all these pieces of evidence point to a metaphysics of activity, which is also part of the sexual code of our culture? What are the implications for a self that is nondominative and is radically open to emptiness and the nothing? What dynamics of sexual marginalization are propagated by this emphasis on activity? The intentionality and holding of the active disposition here are likened to the grasping of the hand in a fist by John Welwood and Ken Wilber:

It is like the grasping action of the hand that makes a fist. If the fist remains clenched all the time, it would cease to be a hand, and would become a different kind of bodily organ. A fist by definition is the action of clenching the open hand. Just as a fist can only form out of the neutral basis of an open hand, the grasping of ego can only assert itself out of non-ego, out of a nongrasping awareness. Without this neutral nongrasping ground to arise from and return to, ego's activity could not occur.[28]

So, the desperate attempt to ground oneself in another, which Sartre describes, and the emphasis on penetration are not in a complementary dialectical relation to passivity. According to our ethics, they are passivity itself, only clenched into a fist as in the example above. Passivity is traditionally devalued in our culture and defined as weak, lacking will, dishonorable, and the like. But just what social and experiential costs are we drawing from ourselves as we continue to act out these frantically active roles? It is for us here in this performative ethics to revalue the places and reverberations of activity and passivity. The radical release and opening to passivity that we discuss here places us in the flow of an ontological dynamic. Drawing again on Hisamatsu and our way of existing in the world, Stambaugh asks: "What, then, is this Fundamental Subject? We are uncertain whether what is being discussed is what is being expressed or what is expressing itself. But, as we stated earlier, what is painting and what is being painted are the same."[29]

In the continually ongoing and changing register of the ontology of ethics, it is impossible and artificial to try to pull apart an actor and an acted upon, an active and a passive. Every "thing" is simultaneously acting and acted upon. This idea is also highly resonant with Spinoza's conception of *natura naturans* and *natura naturata*, or nature naturing and nature natured. These are not two separate natures for Spinoza, but one nature, which is in a continual process of writing on itself and being written on by itself.[30] Had Sartre followed his own thinking further, and had he not been hamstrung by a Cartesian subjectivity and a notion of binary heterosexual lack, he might well have seen the kind of implications that masturbation is starting to have for us here.

We see masturbation as a possible way to fulfill a radical ontological self-grounding: it does not view desire as a lack of another; it allows for the direct experience of one's materiality and thinking being; it permits a view of the subject as a discrete structural unity; and it provides some movement away from sexual marginalization. Alan Soble highlights some of the reasons why the discussion of masturbation addresses more than just a relatively common, pleasurable, harmless sexual practice. In his perhaps slightly tongue-in-cheek comments, he illustrates the cause for inhibitions resulting from discussion of masturbation:

> Masturbation is . . . unpaired, nonprocreative sex that relishes pleasure for its own sake and on demand, thereby violating the spirit and the letter of the ideal pattern. But, further, mockingly challenges the very categories of our sexual discourse itself. Masturbation is faithful sex with someone I care about, to whose welfare and satisfaction I am committed. Masturbation is both incestuous and homosexual at the same time. And, as Rousseau suggests, it is the promiscuous rape of every man or woman or creature to whom I take fancy. Little wonder, then, that we advertise our marriages, feel confident enough to admit our adulteries, but keep our masturbatory practices to ourselves.[31]

If, for Sartre, there is a problem that in desiring to attain gratification we are always threatened by inevitable objectification, then it seems that masturbation avoids it. Perhaps the main problem with his theory and its inability to attain success is the fact that he cannot envision this unity as occurring within the individual but requires a binary relation to fuse the two modes of being. If it were granted that this integration could be enacted on the unitary level, perhaps the vacillation and subsequent failure that occurs on the binary level would cease; there would no longer be the logically impossible need to appropriate some other's for-itself to ground oneself as a for-itself in-itself. Since his solution of using others to fill that deeply dissatisfying void in being has failed, perhaps it is possible that masturbation (as a more direct way of realizing this goal of uniting and grounding being) is a more plausible response to this fundamental problem.

It seems mistaken to accept any theory that banishes success from the arena of sexual behavior, because it is evident that certain unambiguous victories do exist. For example, people often pursue and subsequently fulfill sexual desires in a physical sense. Perhaps the implication is that there can be success in some facets of the sexual arena but, as Sartre is alleging, not in the metaphysical one. Even if that is what he is alleging, it seems manifest that Sartre has made a critical error.

It seems clear that sexual desires form prior to one's attempt to respond to "the look," which is what Sartre believes generates one's adult sexual response. It is possible that he would want to say that even a baby's sexual excitement originates when he or she experiences the look of the other as possessing his or her existence; however, we could not agree with this premise. Thus, we must first try to explain the nature of infant or childhood sexual desire. For the sake of clarity, we call this desire original desire.

We would like to propose that original sexual desire stems not from interpersonal relationships but rather from a for-itself sexual relation with itself. We do not agree that this desire originates in the for-itself's need to appropriate the other's in-itself and likewise form a unified whole as Sartre claims is the case with adult sexual behavior. Rather, the manifestation of this original desire is with itself, namely self–sexual arousal. It allows us to go forth into the world as a field of relationality, as the primordial unity of subject and object. This is not to say that the original sexual desire maintains the split between subject and object; rather, it precedes and subsequently elides it.

Since it is likely that one will experience this type of sexual behavior prior to any of the Sartrean models (that is to say, it is likely that one will masturbate before one ever engages in sexual activity of any sort with a partner), we think that it may be more indicative of the type of relation sexual behavior is. In other words, we might avoid many of the problems of marginalization by adopting this sort of early childhood masturbation paradigm, which advocates plenitude, versus the binary Sartrean paradigm, which is constituted by lack.

It seems that, if de Beauvoir and Sartre are correct and we are responsible for our own destiny, there must be an awareness both of our own facticity, or necessity, and our possibilities. This original desire is our first acceptance of that facticity. We desire ourselves, and we realize ourselves through both our embodiment of consciousness and our actualization of this incarnation through the successful attainment of these desires. Thus, we make ourselves flesh for ourselves in order to objectify ourselves and unify our facticity with our freedom. Since we have a more direct access to ourselves than we have to others, and we are permanently present in relation to ourselves (in other words, I cannot leave myself), it would be easier to prevent the division of the forces within our primordial being.

If we depend on another person to mediate our two modes of being together, however, we will be left with the contingency of their presence. That is to say, supposing that there was a way to adhere these facets of my being together by using the other, what would the outcome be if that other departed? Would the unity cease, and would I then be compelled to search for another in order to reinstate it? Because masturbation only involves one person, it eludes the fate of binary love and binary sexual desire. It will not degenerate into masochism and sadism (the dreaded Scylla and Charybdis for Sartre, in itself a moral judgment about sexuality in his work), for how could I ever lose my subjectivity to myself the way I do in the case of masochism if it would be to myself?

Although still within the Sartrean vocabulary of subject and object, this hypothetical extrapolation of Sartre's theory really speaks about a kind of ontological experience prior to the distinction between subject and object, which repudiates desire as lack. In the experience of masturbation the self experiences itself as touching and touched, desired and desiring, thinking and being. It is in such a situation that one can get an intuition of Spinoza's thoroughly immanent idea that "the mind is an idea of the body,"[32] and perhaps as well Parmenides' "for thinking and being are the same."[33]

And indeed, masturbation in this respect denies lack as the desire for an absent presence. Rather, the masturbator thinks to himself or herself, "I have (am) what I want." It seems that this supposition is very similar to the way that Diogenes the Cynic treated masturbation, as "he likewise found in masturbation the most direct means of appeasing his sexual appetite. He even regretted that it was not possible to satisfy hunger and thirst in so simple a manner: 'Would to heaven that it were enough to rub one's stomach in order to allay one's hunger.'"[34] Diogenes is very much the exemplar of an ethics of ontology rather than the metaphysics of a moral code. He is characterized by fulfillment rather than lack, and he recognizes no division between his thinking and his being. His ethics was along the lines of a personal exploration.

Diogenes was an early practitioner of what Foucault might call localized experimentation on the self. As one who fits squarely on the ethics side of Foucault's ethics-morality split, Diogenes did not care about the empty ought and the usual habits and rules. He did not look upon some behaviors as favorable and some taboo, but experienced them in terms of frequency and intensity of experience. He was truly one who practiced the ethics that Spinoza discussed—Diogenes was in touch with his relationships of speeds and slownesses, and he did what he enjoyed and what increased his power (in that Spinoza defines power as capacity to be affected).

Diogenes was so at ease with and committed to his own regimen that he defied conventions of privacy and public decency in sexual acts. Foucault describes this behavior in a way that is very attentive to the ontoethical grounding of Diogenes' practice and performative critique:

> The scandalous gesture of Diogenes is well known: when he needed to satisfy his sexual appetite, he would relieve himself in the marketplace. Like many of the Cynics' provocations, this one had a double meaning. It owed its impact to the public character of the act, of course, which went against every convention in Greece; it was customary to assert the need for privacy as a reason for making love only at night, and the care one took not to be seen engaging in this kind of activity was regarded as a sign that the practice of aphrodisia was not something that honored the most noble qualities of humankind. It was against this rule of privacy that Diogenes directed his "performance" criticism. Diogenes Laertius reports that in fact he was in the habit of "doing everything in public, the works of Aphrodite and Demeter alike," reasoning as follows: "If breakfast be not absurd, neither is it absurd to breakfast in the market-place."[35]

It is uncanny how much the prevailing habits and rules, which Diogenes was criticizing in action, are similar to the same problematic norms, habits, and rules we live with today. The strong pressure toward keeping sex private and the attendant debates over public sex seem to have been circulating in classical Athens as much as in the contemporary United States. Diogenes pointed out the deep hypocrisy of the society that tried to hide away and regulate natural functions. He not only hearkened to his own body and followed his own rhythm, but he also was aware that doing so was an enacted performative critique and it could have a transformative influence on his society. Indeed, even if somewhat tamed, his ideas did inspire the foundation of a philosophical school—the Stoics.

Diogenes was a marginal character who was enacting his own performative critique of marginalization. He scorned empty virtue and the static, abstract ideals of the Platonic school, preferring to combine thinking with the ongoing bodily performance of existence—a regimen and an ethics. His legacy has implications for a whole range of marginalized sexual behaviors because an ethics rather than a morality of sex shifts attention to the world of actual practice and phenomenological relation. Some people can find complete being in the world and a happy tempo of speeds and slownesses through celibacy or masturbation. Some will have their joy and power increased by same sex relations. Some will perform different genders and myriad roles.

Expressions of sexuality can be more various and more robust through the careful decoupling of erotic relations and misconstrued ontological relations concerning the nothing. Instead of vainly expecting amorous relations to answer our call of being or fulfill some sorely absent part, it is important for us to realize through this ontology that we already can be fulfilled because of being a positive field of relations. Through this plenitude of relation, and moving away from the static empty ought that has dominated Western sexuality for far too long, we are finally becoming able to move toward new organizations of sex and sexuality.

Conclusion

Sartre suggested that in sex what we seek to accomplish is the impossible ontological task of establishing the for-itself as an in-itself. What we have discovered here is that this project is in fact futile. However, with the turn toward masturbation, we have discovered a way in which this primordial plenitude can be successfully attained. We may still wonder why, given this picture, one would ever be inspired to look further than one's own hand and seek the binary relation. We must first admit that binary sex has ceased to serve the purpose of the Sartrean unification; interpersonal sexual relations are incapable of connecting the in-itself with the for-itself. As we have discussed, through originary masturbation, we have effectively elided the need for such an outward search. Thus, lack is no longer the only drive for sexual contact with another; rather, according to the experimental ethical ontology put forth here, desire has a healthier sexual and social grounding. We do not proceed with the view that we desire others simply to fulfill some need, but rather for the way in which we can mutually augment our joy and power through combinations of our ontological rhythms of speeds and slownesses.

Beginning with this more originary foundation, our ontological ethics allows a whole range of formerly marginalized behaviors and practices; it is evident that masturbation would account not only for those activities traditionally conceived of as sexual but also for many activities previously considered "deviant" or "incomplete." Hence, if what Soble says about masturbation is correct, the acts of homosexuality, consensual incest, nonprocreative sex, and sex for the sake of pleasure would have to be viewed and accepted as normal. This situation, then, would be preferable to what we face now when theorists advocating a metaphysics of morals feel compelled to judge certain sexual acts as morally wrong based on their deviation from the completed binary sexual act. In the words of Georges Canguilhem, "Without being absurd, the pathological state can be called normal to the extent that it expresses a relationship to life's normativity . . . the abnormal is not such because of the absence of normality."[36] Thus, the theories defining masturbation and the other activities Soble claims are suggested by it as abnormal can no longer be regarded as valid since we have recreated the paradigm of sexual analysis and likewise redefined the state of normality. As indicated by Canguilhem, we cannot look at normality in contrast to abnormality. We must simply define the states of normality as the different modes of living they are.

Notes

1. Roland Barthes, *A Lover's Discourse: Fragments*, trans. Richard Howard (New York: Hill and Wang, 1978), 54. The term *comblement* is a French word

meaning fulfillment in English. It is being employed as a metaphor to fore-shadow our notion of ontological ethics, or our solution to the metaphysical problem that will be discussed in this chapter. To preview, if the Sartrean meta-physical split can be resolved or fulfilled internally by an individual with her-self, sexual relations with another person can be successful and would not be doomed to failure as Sartre himself contends. Furthermore, solving this meta-physical dilemma and opting for an ontological ethics will enable us to recon-ceptualize and possibly overcome marginalization of sexualities.

2. Michel Foucault, *The Use of Pleasure*, vol. 2 of *The History of Sexuality*, trans. Robert Hurley (New York: Penguin Books, 1985).

3. Ellen Degeneres is a comedian and actor probably best known for publicly announcing that she is a lesbian. At the time of this announcement, she was starring in her own self-titled sitcom *Ellen* (1994–1998), in which the main character also made a parallel public affirmation of her sexual orienta-tion. This famous "Puppy Episode" (30 April 1997) spawned a great deal of controversy, which in turn motivated major sponsors to cancel their advertis-ing spots. Though the public coming out (static declaration) was received as controversial, it was not until she actually started living her lesbianism (lived practice) in the next season that the disciplining of her sexual regimen began, which was accomplished by the parental advisory messages and TV PG-14 rat-ings that preceded every show. Slightly shy of a year after the infamous episode, the show was canceled.

4. Paul Reubens was well known for both the Saturday morning televi-sion series *Pee Wee's Playhouse* (1986–1991) and the films *Pee Wee's Big Adven-ture* (1985) and *Big Top Pee Wee* (1988), in which he portrayed the character Pee Wee Herman. In 1991, he fell victim to a police sting operation when he was allegedly caught masturbating in a porn theater in Florida. After paying his fines and court fees (all under $100) and completing his "public service duty," which involved doing an antidrug commercial, his criminal record was erased. However, it is clear from the running dates of the television series that his ca-reer as Pee Wee Herman ended the moment his arrest became public.

5. It is interesting to note here that this procreative economy is situated as one response to an intuition of individual human finitude. The procreative economy takes on an existential valence as each subject experiencing or con-templating its own mortality can grasp at immortality by conceptualizing the survival of the race of humans. It seems that the valence becomes so strong that those who stand outside of the set arrangements of human procreation take on the status of traitors or enemies. We will be discussing the human re-lation to nothingness and finitude as it relates to sexuality and marginalization later in the chapter.

6. Friedrich Nietzsche, *The Birth of Tragedy Out of the Spirit of Music*, trans. Walter Kaufmann (New York: Vintage, 1967).

7. Betty Friedan, *The Feminine Mystique* (New York, Norton, 1963).

8. Gilles Deleuze and Félix Guattari, *Anti-Oedipus*, vol. 1 of *Capitalism and Schizophrenia*, trans. Robert Hurley, Mark Seem, and Helen R. Lane (Min-neapolis: University of Minnesota Press, 1993), and *A Thousand Plateaus*, vol. 2 of *Capitalism and Schizophrenia*, trans. Brian Massumi (Minneapolis: University of Minnesota Press, 1993).

9. Jean-Paul Sartre, *Being and Nothingness*, trans. Hazel E. Barnes (New York: Simon and Schuster, 1956).

10. This also has resonances with the phenomenology of the closet.

11. Sartre, *Being and Nothingness*, 472.

12. Hazel Barnes, "Key to Special Terminology," in Sartre's *Being and Nothingness*, 800.

13. Ibid.

14. Ibid., 802.

15. Sartre, *Being and Nothingness*, 471.

16. Barnes, "Key to Special Terminology," 800.

17. Robert Baker and Frederick Elliston, *Philosophy and Sex*, rev. ed. (New York: Prometheus Books, 1984), 252.

18. Sartre, *Being and Nothingness*, 59.

19. Ibid., 48.

20. Simone de Beauvoir, *She Came to Stay* (New York: Norton, 1954), 1.

21. Joan Stambaugh, *The Formless Self* (Albany: State University of New York Press, 1999), 85.

22. Ibid., 84.

23. Ibid., 85.

24. Ibid., 83.

25. Ibid., 81.

26. Ibid., 81–82.

27. As Foucault notes repeatedly in *The Use of Pleasure*, Greek sexuality was conceptualized in terms of act rather than identity. Thus, for instance, a different category of desire was not assumed to be at issue in determining male or female object choice. Desire was seen as a factor or trait that could be directed in a number of ways, but the latitude in sexual behavior was not total. Although identities such as "the homosexual" were not recognized in Greece, roles were emphasized. Thus, adult males were associated with an active role, and Foucault points out that it was perceived as a violation of role for an adult male to take a passive position, especially with a young man. Mirroring the active and passive sexual roles, there are sets of duties and practices accompanying each position. Foucault comments upon these regimens: "These practices—the reality of which has been amply documented by K. J. Dover—defined the mutual behavior and respective strategies that both partners should observe in order to give their relations a 'beautiful' form; that is, one that was aesthetically and morally valuable. They determined the role of the *erastes* and the *eromenos*. The first was in a position of initiative—he was the suitor—and this gave him rights and obligations; he was expected to show his ardor, and to restrain it; he had gifts to make; services to render; he had functions to exercise with regard to the *eromenos*; and all this entitled him to expect a just reward. The other partner, the one who was loved and courted, had to be careful not to yield too easily; he also had to keep from accepting too many tokens of love, and from granting his powers heedlessly and out of self-interest, without testing the worth of his partner; he must also show gratitude for what the lover had done for him" (196).

28. Quoted in Stambaugh, *Formless Self*, 93.

29. Ibid., 84.

30. Baruch Spinoza, *The Ethics*, trans. R. H. M. Elwes (New York: Dover, 1955).

31. Alan Soble, *The Philosophy of Sex: Contemporary Readings*, 2d ed. (Savage, MD: Rowman and Littlefield, 1991), 134.

32. Spinoza, *Ethics*.

33. "To gar auto noein estin te kai einai." See G. S. Kirk, J. E. Raven, and

N. Schofeld, *The Pre-Socratic Philosophers* (Cambridge: Cambridge University Press, 1983).

34. Foucault, *Use of Pleasure*, 55.

35. Ibid., 54.

36. Georges Canguilhem, *The Normal and the Pathological*, trans. Caroline R. Faucet (New York: Zone Books, 1989), 227–228.

Chapter Five

Persistent Problems, Illusions of Progress, and Mechanisms of Marginalization

Patricia Smith

Marginalization in some form is inevitable. If privilege exists, marginalization must also exist. If there are insiders, there must be outsiders; and there always will be insiders. That much is inevitable, but marginalization has many sources, and there is no reason to suppose that any particular form is necessary and ineliminable.

In this chapter, I will review some persistent problems and consider several mechanisms of marginalization that might help to explain the failure of reforms. In particular, I want to focus on what I call the "wind tunnel effect," a pervasive collection of devices by which any mainstream culture retards deviance and supports the status quo, thereby stunting reform.[1]

This phenomenon is found in many forms. Everyday rebellions, large and small, provide innumerable examples. Here is a little one, which illustrates the device of assimilation. In the 1960s, wearing Levi's was a symbol of rebellion, specifically to reject the commercial obsession of the mainstream establishment. Levi's are now manufactured, bought, and sold by the commercial establishment for somewhere between forty and eighty dollars a pair (and they symbolize, if anything, participation in the commercial establishment). Trying to change the course of mainstream culture is like trying to change the course of the Mississippi River with a shovel. Most of us find ourselves swept downstream without making so much as a dent in the bank.

Reform in the name of equality has been a particularly tricky proposition. Indeed, inequality is a fact of life: unavoidable, universal, and ineliminable.[2] In spite of this fact, certain egalitarian ideals have been widely recognized in this century as requirements of justice. Equal protection of the law is thought to be fundamental to any free and democratic society. Equal respect and consideration for all persons is widely regarded as a basic norm to be met by any adequate moral theory. Equal opportunity for all citizens is widely accepted as a baseline requirement for any fair social system.[3] The founding value of these ideals is not equality but justice, yet they stand for the proposition that all human beings are "created equal." We are moral equals entitled to fair treatment without preconceptions about our many nonmoral differences. Such presumptions at this point in time are, if not widely held in fact, at least widely declared as doctrine. They might be considered part of our official postmodern morality if that is not a contradiction in terms. That is, those who make authoritative public declarations of what "we" believe say that we believe this.

These ideals may be viewed as the motivating force of several significant social movements to alleviate prejudice based on race, sex, and class that took place during the second half of the twentieth century. All three provide excellent examples of reform movements, which have met with rather limited success, aimed at equalizing marginalized groups. I cannot address all three, given limitations of space, so I will focus on racism and the civil rights movement.

The Persistence of Racism and Marginalization of Blacks

Perhaps it should have tipped us off that reform would not be easy when, following a bloody civil war to eliminate slavery (since nothing else could do it), three constitutional amendments (plus the Civil Rights Act of 1964) explicitly requiring equal protection of the law for all persons failed utterly to protect black people anywhere from segregation, discrimination, or even blatant Jim Crow laws that basically eliminated every right they should have had as citizens, including the right to vote. After all, "equal protection of the law" has to be interpreted. It does not require equal privileges such as the privilege to be licensed for employment or the privilege to own property for the purpose of agriculture. These are privileges extended and determined by individual states. And of course, equal protection of law must be compatible with segregation of the races. Just because facilities are separate does not mean they cannot be equal. And of course, the right to vote does not mean a right without qualification, so that must be open to interpretation as well. Poll taxes, literacy tests, and legislative apportionment should surely be within the purview of individual states to control. So said the Supreme Court.

Such reasoning seems outrageous and hypocritical, but only because of its disregard for the history and circumstances.[4] It now seems obviously wrong, but apparently it did not seem so obvious at the time. That is the wind tunnel effect: efforts at radical reform tend to be reinterpreted to maintain the status quo or something very close to it. People do not tend to think in terms that stray far from what they are used to. The members of the Supreme Court, for example, simply could not imagine that equal protection of law would actually prohibit segregation, thereby allowing the races to "mingle." That was just too big a step for most of them to take. Today, the Jim Crow laws are gone—that much progress has been made in the space of almost a hundred years—but it is still the case that proportionally more blacks live in poverty, in ghettos, in prisons, and in cancer wards than any other definable group in this country.

One wonders what mechanisms of marginalization maintain the status quo at the expense of the vulnerable today. Invisible to us now, will those devices look as outrageous, hypocritical, and self-serving as the reasoning of the Supreme Court that supported states' rights to decimate black citizenship from 1883 to 1954? It appears that the most tenacious threat to revolutionary reform is not to be fought against and rejected, but to be accepted, absorbed, and reconstituted in a form analogous to (or compatible with) traditional categories that maintain the power of the powerful, the status quo intact, and the marginalization of those always marginalized in a new form that co-opts and incorporates the vocabulary of the reformer. Thus, discrimination against blacks remained profound for almost one hundred years after slavery was abolished.

The civil rights movement started slowly, but with the implementation of *Brown v. Board of Education* in Little Rock and the catalyst of Rosa Parks's courage in Montgomery, it exploded on the American scene in 1955.[5] Leaders emerged and protests began. For the first time since the Civil War, the issue of racial injustice became a focus of public attention. The movement was aimed at eliminating long-standing discrimination against blacks by challenging overtly prejudicial practices and replacing the social policy of segregation with integration. Once this view was recognized as implied in the equal protection clause, from the 1954 Supreme Court decision in *Brown* to the Civil Rights Act of 1964, removing legal barriers and enacting federal legislation that required equal treatment turned out to be the easiest part of the battle. As long as the focus was on legal reform, the nation seemed to move forward (grudgingly, to be sure, yet forward), and so there was initial reason for high hopes that racial justice might be achieved in general, even if not in all particulars.

The problem, however, was deeply entrenched. A culture built on a history of prejudice cannot be reversed merely by changing the law. Discrimination can be reinforced by law, but it cannot be eliminated by it. A society organized around a policy of segregation cannot be easily integrated even if the formal policy is reversed, which is particularly true if those who are expected to effect the reform disagree with the reversal or find themselves disadvantaged by it.

It is worth noting that some advances have been made. There are, today, fewer people who actually believe in racial inequality in fact or segregation in principle than there were in 1955, so in principle progress has occurred. But principle does not put bread on the table. The continued marginalization of blacks keeps a disproportionate number in poverty and seems to involve a complex of factors that combine to dissipate reforms. The most widespread of these factors is an attitude that I call functional racism. I will discuss this attitude in more depth in the next section, but I will relate it here in order to illustrate its effects in concrete examples.

Functional racism has two elements. First, no one wants to give up a position of privilege. Second, no one wants to acknowledge that his or her own position is, in fact, privileged or that it was obtained from a privileged position. Everyone wants to assume that their own situation constitutes the neutral baseline, and that any advantage they have was earned or obtained by merit. Consequently, so long as the proposition for racial justice is put in abstract terms or enforced against someone else, most people are in favor of it. But if the cost falls on our own doorstep, well, that is surely going too far. The trouble is, of course, so long as there is a cost (and there always is), it will inevitably fall on *someone's* doorstep and that someone will oppose it. More often than not, the someone who opposes it will be more powerful or more personally motivated than the representative of the marginalized group who seeks to compel inclusion.

It is reasonable to assume, for example, that Allan Bakke did not care if minority students got into the University of California (Davis) Medical School, so long as none of them got "his slot." Their getting in should not preclude his getting in—better to get rid of the program. Why should he bear the cost?[6] It is reasonable to presume that many people who fought against minority participation (or governmental interference, as they put it) in fire departments, police departments, trade unions, governmental agencies, private industry with government contracts, and so on thought that minorities were entitled to a job opportunity somewhere—but just not "my job" or, in other words, not the job opportunity that "I want."[7]

Parents in the North indignantly supported the forced integration of southern schools, but they were not nearly so cooperative when their own de facto segregation came to be scrutinized. Schools should be integrated, but not "my child's school."[8] Neighborhoods should be open to integration, but not "my neighborhood."[9] Equal protection of the law is a fine principle of justice—in principle, but not at "my expense." Expense requires a different interpretation, one that does not change anything or cost "me" anything important.

So laws have changed, but neighborhoods have not. Television programs have changed, but the distribution of income has not. Every single step toward equal treatment has been fought tooth and nail in the courts, despite general agreement that equal treatment is right in principle. The idea of equal protection of the law generated so little voluntary cooperation in the moral community, in the natural form of equal respect for all persons regardless of race, that it was necessary to enforce the law by mechanical measures (measures of last resort) such as school busing and affirmative action quotas. These are clumsy, heavy-handed measures for handling delicate moral relations—cracking nuts with a jackhammer—so of course they were resisted as governmental interference or artificial quotas, interpreted as reverse discrimination, and challenged again in the courts.

Thus, the most powerful form of marginalization possible (after slavery), namely, physical exclusion by legal barrier (or formal segregation), was replaced with the second most powerful form, personal rejection by informal discrimination: the smallest step possible, thus, the wind tunnel effect. By and large, the status quo has been maintained, and blame has been shifted to the victim. It can now be argued that if blacks succeed it is because they have been specially favored by reverse discrimination, and if they fail, of course, it is because they are inferior. The ironic double bind is that affirmative action makes the accusation impossible to disprove, but without affirmative action there is no counter to discrimination, which is, at this point, also impossible to prove.[10] After thirty years of integration initiatives and twenty years of affirmative action, the United States is almost as segregated and unequal as ever. After enormous reform efforts, only small progress has been made.

Mechanisms of Marginalization and the Wind Tunnel Effect

Consider the mechanisms of marginalization implicated in this history. First, the early history: you have a class of slaves considered barbarian inferiors across the board. They are freed by war and constitutional amendment, that is to say, by force against their oppressors. The southern reaction was immediate hostility and resolve to reverse, insofar as possible, any change mandated by the new legal regime. Every possible means of maintaining the status quo by segregation and restriction was implemented to reduce any freed slave to an impoverished, disenfranchised sharecropper. If blacks would not be slaves anymore, they would be the next thing to it. Thus, the wind tunnel effect is, in this case, manifested overtly.

Of course, the former slaves could leave—legally, that is. They had no resources by which to leave and nowhere in particular to go.[11] If they left, they left with nothing: no property, no education, and no skills of note. When they arrived at a new place, they would be greeted as a group with nothing to offer. Worse than that, they wore their badge of inferiority, like the mark of Cain, in the color of their skin. They might not be slaves, but they were still the next thing to it: the slave race. Here we see another manifestation of the wind tunnel effect, this time not overt but unconscious.

So, in the North, blacks were segregated in fact, if not in law, and were treated as congenitally low class and perhaps mildly retarded, occasionally dangerous, and more or less uncivilized. They were okay for low-level jobs if you kept an eye on them. Other than that, one kept one's distance: "They are different from white people, you know." I remember hearing such remarks at social gatherings. "I don't wish them any harm," someone would say, "but you wouldn't have dinner with one, would you?" I was a child at the time and found such remarks (I guess I never listened to the whole conversation) puzzling, but I do not now suppose that anyone else was puzzled. That was in the early 1950s, when racial stereotyping was still profound. Stereotyping is a well-known and powerful marginalizing device.

The effect of such treatment across the board was to produce an environment of poverty, deprivation, illiteracy, and a certain acceptance of inferior status, which was not universal among blacks but was certainly widespread, and, in turn, reinforced and internalized the stereotype of inferiority.[12] This is another example of the wind tunnel, the effect of which is cumulative. You may start with a revolutionary reform (in principle): the slaves will be freed and will be equal citizens with all others in the nation. But the wind tunnel of social organization and practice sucks this revolution back in line with the status quo, adhering as closely as possible to the original standard while also assimilating some interpretation of the revolutionary concept that was intended to generate the reform. Thus, it is an instance of reform efforts met by the retrenchment of privilege through the reinforcement of the status quo by the imposition of new forms of marginalization, which serve as a substitute and simulation of the source of marginalization just banned.

I do not suppose that any of this information is new. The marginalization of blacks has been widely discussed; and my presentation of it here is both superficial and overstated. A much more variegated and diverse account would be needed for accuracy. I have only tried to convey the profundity of the effect where the practice is pervasive. Since it has been extensively treated elsewhere, I will not pursue the idea here.

What I would like to consider in more depth, by focusing on the outline of events since 1955 that I sketched earlier, are some other mechanisms of marginalization at work today. It is not hard to understand the stagnation that occurred in race relations before the civil rights movement; the old ideas were hardly challenged in fact. Blacks were not considered equal; they just were not considered slaves. But after the challenge of Martin Luther King Jr., after the marches, debates, attention, analysis, scholarship, and scrutiny of the public eye, why has so little progress been made? Why have so many initiatives failed? Why does the marginalization of blacks continue despite the formal rejection of racism? How does the wind tunnel work?

Let me try out a few ideas as they apply to this case history. Part of the wind tunnel is structural; in fact, much of it is. Custom, tradition, and institutions of all sorts (the family, academy, legal system, market, and so on) are arranged to promote stability, or, in other words, to retard change. Whatever retards change tends to keep people in their places, whether top or bottom, inside or out. Even concepts, categories, language, and the structure of authority tend to create a drag on change and to restrict the possibilities of reform. The process of law is an easy example.

The general doctrine of stare decisis, or following precedent, explicitly attaches any current decision to a standard established in a prior case. Furthermore, to be considered by a court at all, any new case or appeal must fit within a cause of action already recognized. In addition, the structure of legal rights protects those already recognized as having legitimate claims, not those outside the established framework. These and other structural devices intended to maintain stability have the side effect of disadvantaging any marginalized group unless it can get itself recognized in some form or another.[13] Consequently, before 1955, despite the formal language of the Constitution, there was no protection from racism. After 1955, the Court interpreted the equal protection clause to provide special status for suspect classifications, especially race. With the Civil Rights Act of 1964 declaring special protections against discrimination based on race, one might have thought that blacks had finally made it to insider status, but these reforms were less effective than hoped for several reasons. These reasons may shed some light on the wind tunnel effect.

First, minority status in itself often marginalizes minority members, which might be called the problem of critical mass. If the society is otherwise uniform, then one or a few individuals who deviate from that norm (for it becomes a norm merely out of regularity) are exceptions, tokens, or outsiders just by virtue of being different. Of course, what counts as different is a matter of judgment and value. Given U.S. history, being black counts as different. One or two exceptions do not change that status; they just become exceptions. Considering that minorities are relatively few in number, having greater participation is more or less precluded by minority numbers. Thus, minorities are structurally condemned, in a sense, to be outside the norm, to be exceptional, and the law cannot fix that.[14]

Second, a unique problem of blacks in this country is that the issue of race is mixed with class. Given their historical background as slaves, they are identified with being low class—the lowest class. Changing their legal status did not change that. Furthermore, blacks are historically poor, without property or family connection to property. Traditionally and currently, law—the full, interconnected web of it—is set up to protect those who have property, not those who do not. The Civil Rights Act and the equal protection clause will be interpreted to be consistent with that general structure (even if there is an occasional temporary deviation, such as affirmative action).

Typical legal rights are negative: they are rights against interference, rights to be left alone, or rights to keep property one already possesses. Anita Allen has argued that the negative concept of rights leaves poor blacks at the mercy of majoritarian politics that protects the "haves" at the expense of the "have-nots." There is no right to a safe neighborhood or to shelter of any kind. There is no right to be provided with clothing, food, or medicine, let alone contraceptive protection or abortion. There is no right to a job of any sort, let alone one that provides a living wage. And there is no right to a basic education that meets any particular minimum standard of adequacy.[15]

These are actually issues of class that happen to affect blacks disproportionately. There is no necessary connection here, but this fact happens to create special problems. First, class bias is the one form of marginalization that is impossible to eradicate. Some utopian writers have always argued that it can be addressed, but look how well Marx did it. No, class cannot be eliminated unless privilege can be eliminated, and privilege cannot be eliminated.

What could be eliminated is poverty (at least, as a phenomenon of class); the lowest class need not live in poverty.

That there will be a lowest class is inevitable. What makes the existence of class more acceptable (besides the frightening alternative of uniformity) is that class is not an immutable characteristic. One can move in or out of it, although not easily. Whites move in and out of it. There are rich whites and poor ones; and the norm is somewhere in the middle. The problem for blacks is that their norm is poor.

If class is identified with race (which is immutable), it creates an additional disadvantage (a presumption or stereotype of poverty as normal) for blacks. Second, given the problems of majoritarian politics, if blacks are identified with being poor, then they have two strikes against them. They are twice as likely to go underrepresented, since both the poor and blacks are traditionally underrepresented. The marginalization of both class and race is less likely to be addressed politically if they are attached to each other.

A final structural reason for the relative failure of legal reforms since 1955 is that laws against discrimination turn out to be exceedingly difficult to enforce. Once people know better than to say anything racist aloud, it is relatively easy to give acceptable reasons for what would be discrimination, if it were done for discriminatory reasons. "Sorry, the job is filled. There were a lot of splendid applicants and you were edged out. . . . Sorry, 'so and so' got the promotion for 'such and such' reasons—we can't all be promoted. It's a judgement call. . . . Sorry, the apartment is rented—or it's not for rent right now because we are renovating it." And so it goes. Does anyone today actually say that you will not be hired, promoted, or anything else because you are black? Only if the intercom is accidentally left on will you get to hear such a reason, and proving it otherwise is no easy task. This discussion illustrates that beyond the problem of structure, which retards change and protects privilege in general, the challenge of alleviating marginalization is a matter of reforming attitudes.

Indeed, a large part of the wind tunnel effect is attitudinal. As the points just discussed show, structural elements interact with attitudinal ones, but they are distinguishable. I will discuss three sorts of racist attitudes that perpetuate the marginalization of blacks: classical racism, unconscious racism, and functional racism.

The first I will only mention: Classical racism is the irrational attitude of the hatemonger, who maintains fear of or disdain for others (perceived as significantly different and inferior) based on a stereotype of them. This sort of racism has been much discussed, so I will not analyze it here except to note a couple of points about it.

It must be acknowledged that racist hatred is remarkably resilient. This resilience supports the unfortunate conclusion that there is a nasty side to human nature, which will never be eliminated altogether and thus will always be a problem at some level. The interesting scholarship on this issue is psychological and sociological. What causes racism? Why does it persist? Can it be treated?

Another interesting point about the classical racist attitude is that although it is irrational, it is at the same time efficient and convenient for the beneficiaries in (at least) three ways. It is a convenient simplification device. It supports the status quo, and thus secures the social position of the beneficiaries. On the one hand, it maintains self-esteem for those who have status, because it equates the status quo with merit and explains inequality by presuming inferiority. On the other hand, it maintains self-esteem for those who do not have status, because it equates merit with innate characteristics and provides a scapegoat. This distinction is worth noting, because it is not exactly clear how to maintain those benefits without racism. Indeed, it may help to explain the resilience of racism.

Another point to notice about classical racism is that if it is isolated and idiosyncratic, it cannot marginalize another group of people. In order to do this, classical racism must be systematically manifested in centers of power and authority or supplemented and bolstered by some other racist behavior or support system.[16] I want to consider this latter possibility now. In fact, I want to argue that this problem needs to be identified and exposed in order to understand the failure of reforms.

One manifestation of racist behaviors that supplement and bolster classical racism can be seen in a second form of racist attitude that has also been widely acknowledged and discussed: unconscious racism. This sort of racism can be rather blatant, although it is not recognized as racist by its perpetrator, or it can be very subtle. The subtle kind is difficult to pinpoint and is not yet well understood. It may be behavior that reflects a certain picture of the look, feel, style, or focus of authority, appropriateness, or excellence in an area. That picture tends to reflect the current and traditional situation and to exclude deviation from it—the wind tunnel again. The new "deviant" person just does not "fit the picture." A great many evaluations and selections are made on just such amorphous, intuitive grounds—whether it "feels right." People tend to like, trust, respect, and even agree with (not to mention hire and promote) those who are more or less like themselves. People like the familiar, and many people in mainstream culture are unfamiliar with blacks, so blacks do not "fit the picture." Thus, they remain marginalized. Here the problem of critical mass is indeed critical.

It was precisely the purpose of affirmative action to address that problem. The idea was to make blacks less marginal, to get them included in a broader picture of normal life, and to affect the attitudes of enough people to put them in the picture. It worked to some extent. It fell far short of hopes and expectations, however, and the higher up the ladder of competitive success one attempts to climb, the less the traditional picture has been affected. That picture creates the glass ceiling for blacks and women. The glass ceiling, of course, is a metaphor for a particular form of marginalization, which is perpetuated by unconscious prejudice that favors the familiar.

The third set of racist attitudes is what I laid out earlier as functional racism. This attitude is not ordinarily defined as racism, nor am I committed to doing so, although I think there is some value in characterizing it that way here. What I do want to argue is that this phenomenon combines with all the other factors to perpetuate the marginalization of blacks in just the same way that racism does and thus becomes part (indeed, a major part) of racism. The primary elements of this attitude have already been laid out and illustrated earlier in this chapter. First, no one wants to give up a position of privilege; and second, no one wants to admit that such a position is privileged.

This attitude is clearly illustrated by the Bakke case, the fights over (discriminatory) testing for jobs in police and fire departments, and many situations ultimately involving quotas or "set asides" for positions or government contracts. All these involve "zero-sum games." If blacks get in, some whites get excluded. If some contracts are "reserved" for minorities, that means fewer contracts are available for whites. So the argument goes this way:

let all the contracts be open, and we will all compete in the open market. That would be fine if we could assume that the market were really open and minorities would not be subject to prejudice, but our entire history speaks against that assumption. Still the response is that the necessity for set asides is evidence that minorities "can't compete." This response raises the charge of reverse discrimination, because the discrimination that favors blacks in such a case can be identified, but the discrimination against them cannot be. Thus, it presumes the absence of overt or unconscious racism and ignores disadvantages that result from it. It denies the problem of critical mass or the value of diversity (at least, as a value that overrides any other). In other words, it denies the problem of continuing racial prejudice that reverse discrimination is supposed to counterbalance. In this way, it supports racism by denying its existence.

The integration of neighborhoods, public schools, and (possibly) trade unions involves a different, but analogous, set of attitudes. These are not "zero-sum games," but they are perceived as posing a serious threat or disadvantage to those who hold status quo positions. As exemplified by statements made at the time, some groups fighting to exclude blacks in all three cases were overtly racist: "No niggers in *my* neighborhood (kid's school, trade union)!" (These attitudes also generally presume a right of first occupancy or possession.)

Often the racism is more subtle and unconscious: "I have nothing against them, but we might be lowering the quality of our neighborhood (schools, trade unions) if they start moving in; and it is going to change the feel of the place, for sure. First thing you know this may become a black neighborhood (school, trade union). A white person won't feel comfortable here anymore." (This siege mentality is very common and may be provoked by as little as the appearance of two or three blacks, or women, in a place where there were none before. It is a worry over the possible loss of majority status or becoming an outsider oneself.)

Finally, the racism may be purely functional: "If the blacks come in, the property value (educational standard, wage, job availability) is going to fall. Statistically, that has been true, and I don't want that to happen to me or my family." Here it is noticeable that the difference between functional and unconscious racism lies only in the accuracy of the fear it represents. Each specific context has its own analogous set of claims and arguments and its own mechanisms of marginalization.

Conclusion

There are millions of such social phenomena in every walk of life that may involve classical racism and certainly involve unconscious racism that repels the unfamiliar, a vicious circle given the problem of critical mass. All of it is supported by the generalized protection of self-interest that I am calling functional racism.

The important things to recognize about functional racism are that it is more or less coincidental and we all participate in it. It just happens to be the case that the backs we are standing on to maintain our status quo position are black. It is nothing personal. Unlike the classical racist, we do not wish anyone harm; that is just the effect. Without this support, the classical racist would be isolated and weak. Thus, it is the common commitment to the status quo that keeps blacks marginalized and racism viable, which requires no hatred—only timidity, selfishness, and enough bad faith to maintain the illusion that our personal accomplishments are unconnected to the marginalization of others. Although this attitude is irrational in the sense that it rests on an inaccurate representation of social reality, it is immanently "rational" in the sense that it supports one's self-interest to hold it.

These I suggest are central features of the wind tunnel effect. Their presentation has been unavoidably superficial, since the wind tunnel is a cumulative effect of individual interactions and attitudes occurring within the channeling force of most of our social arrangements and practices. To switch metaphors, it is a river made up of a million raindrops. Each example given here represents only one drop, which is only a superficial and inadequate description of the river, and so one is left representing one metaphor with another. Still, a certain picture does emerge, and a conclusion as well. Reform on behalf of marginalized groups will necessarily be slow even when the marginalization is recognized as illegitimate in principle, because all the social mechanisms that maintain stability and privilege maintain marginalization as well.

Notes

1. A wind tunnel is a chamber through which air is forced at controlled velocities in order to observe its effect on objects within the tunnel. Obviously, it is difficult to walk against the wind in a wind tunnel.

2. Given that human beings are less than perfect and primarily concerned with their own welfare, security, or power, it seems that some degree of inequality is inevitable.

3. None of these ideals is accepted universally, of course, and what they require is subject to interpretation.

4. That is, the general legal principle that the federal government or the courts should not second-guess local governments in legislative matters is perfectly reasonable in the abstract.

5. The initiating events of the civil rights movement have been much discussed. The original decision in *Brown I* was made in 1954 (see 347 U.S. 843, 1954) and implemented in *Brown II* (see 349 U.S. 294, 1955).

6. See *Bakke v. Regents of the University of Calif.*, 97 Sup. Ct. 1098 (1977).

7. See, for example, *Griggs v. Duke Power Co.*, 401 U.S. 424 (1971); *McDonnell Douglas Corp. v. Green*, 411 U.S. 792 (1973); *Washington v. Davis* (police department test), 426 U.S. 229 (1975); and *Teamsters v. U.S.*, 97 Sup. Ct. 1843 (1977).

8. See, for example, *Keyes v. School District No. 1, Denver*, 413 U.S. (1973); *Miliken v. Bradley (Detroit)*, 418 U.S. 717 (1974); or *Miliken v. Bradley II*, 97 Sup. Ct. 2749 (1977).

9. See, for example, *Reitman v. Mulkey*, 387 U.S. 369 (1967), and *Hills v. Gautreaux*, 425 US 284 (1976).

10. On such "dilemmas of difference," see Martha Minow, *Making All the Difference: Inclusion, Exclusion, and American Law* (Ithaca, NY: Cornell University Press, 1990).

11. To say they could leave trades on the distinction between positive and negative freedom. See Isaiah Berlin, "Two Concepts of Freedom," in *Collected Essays* (London: Oxford University Press, 1978). On this sense of freedom, they were free to leave in the same way that you and I are free to cruise around the world or to live at the Ritz Carlton: No law prohibits it.

12. See Patricia Williams, *The Alchemy of Race and Rights* (Cambridge: Harvard University Press, 1991).

13. This point also has been widely observed. See Minow, *Making All the Difference*, chap. 1, n. 10, or Deborah L. Rhode, *Justice and Gender* (Cambridge: Harvard University Press, 1989).

14. This is a structural problem not shared by women, who could have enough participation to reach a critical mass that would make them numerous enough to be ordinary or typical, that is, part of the norm.

15. See Anita Allen, "Legal Rights for Poor Blacks," in *The Underclass Question*, ed. Bill Lawson (Philadelphia: Temple University Press, 1992).

16. Suppose only 10 percent of the population was racist, but that 10 percent was the top 10 percent, who did the hiring, admitting, promoting, evaluating, appointing, and so on.

Chapter Six

The Smartest Black Man in Union, South Carolina: Complimentary Racism and the Dialectic of Marginalization

Arnold Lorenzo Farr

I recall having a conversation with a young, white woman when I was a college student. I will never forget the close of that conversation. After I completed my hand waving and pontificating, the young woman said to me, "You're the smartest black that I know." Naturally, my head began to swell. However, before my head had swollen to maximum proportions, it began to deflate when I questioned the real meaning of this apparent compliment: Should I feel proud or offended? I recall other occasions since then when I was referred to as the "smart black."

Just as the Freudian slip is the outward expression of an unconscious desire or feeling, which is positioned against a social backdrop, the speech act wherein one refers to another as the "smart black" reveals a hidden history, a set of attitudes, and a social backdrop that make this speech act possible.[1] It is not possible to discuss this broader social context in detail here. In this chapter, I will simply examine the ambivalent nature of such speech acts. This type of speech act is an example of complimentary racism, which, due to its origin in racist myths, attempts to remarginalize people who shatter traditional racial stereotypes. Nonetheless, the oppressive narrative from which this speech act derives its possibility fails in its attempt to fully determine the marginalized subject. I will argue that, due to this failure to completely determine the subject, the margins are a site for transformative, emancipatory political activity.

Ambivalence and the Failure of Normalization

In her book *Excitable Speech: A Politics of the Performative,* Judith Butler writes:

> Speaking is not a single assimilation of an existing norm, for that norm is predicated on the exclusion of the one who speaks, and whose speech calls into question the foundation of the universal itself. Speaking and exposing the alterity within the norm (the alterity without which the norm would not "know itself") exposes the failure of the norm to effect the universal reach within which it stands, exposes what we might underscore *as the promising ambivalence of the norm.*[2]

The processes of normalization, subordination, and marginalization can never completely determine the subject. There remains an opening wherein resistance to subordinating social forces is possible. Butler shows that the very language on which we depend for communication and the construction of identity has its origin outside the individual's use of it. Therefore, it is external to the individual and cannot completely determine the individual. The "norm" (against which the margins are constructed) requires alterity for its very existence. This necessary alterity also limits the "norm" and its claim to universality. Butler's insight has some very interesting implications for a theory of marginalization, which I think are worth exploring within the context of my own experience of marginalization.

Butler describes ambivalence as the notion that the subject, which is the condition for and instrument of agency, is at the same time the effect of subordination.[3] Her thesis is that what we call the subject is the product of the opposing forces of agency and subordination. Without subordination, there is no subject. The subject is the product of internalized social norms, values, and restricted desire. What interests me most about Butler's position is her discussion of resistance: If the subject is the product of subordinating forces, how is resistance possible?

Butler explains that the subordinating, normalizing forces that subordinate and enact the subject into being can never fully constitute the subject. For various reasons, these forces often miss their

targets. The identity of the subject has no closure and therefore remains open to possibilities not intended by the subordinating
forces. Since all norms, values, systems of domination, and marginalized identities are the creations of finite human beings, they
are, by their very nature, temporal and transitory. Cornelius Castoriadis writes: "Each society also brings into being its own mode of
self-alteration, which can also be called its temporality—that is to
say, it also brings itself into being as a mode of being." He continues: "The alienation of heteronomy of society is self-alienation; the
concealment of the being of society as self-institution in its own
eyes, covering over its essential temporality."[4]

Society alienates itself in its attempt to conceal its temporal
and transitory nature. As the genealogies of Nietzsche and Foucault have shown us, society's values and norms have their origin
in human desire or will and are not established by some eternal,
absolute authority. In its attempt to conceal heteronomy, society in-
stitutes the margins. However, society's unwanted remainder is
necessary for mainstream society to construct its own identity. The
marginalized, then, have a function within society as that against
which mainstream society defines itself. Therefore, the "outside" is
never fully outside.

As society forms itself and its margins, it brings into being only
a particular mode of being; that is, society could have been otherwise. The process of identity formation in a society is always an incomplete process to the extent that the dialectic between inclusion
and exclusion perpetuates an ongoing process of reformulation,
readjusting, redefining boundaries, reexcluding, remaking, and so
on. That which destabilizes a society is at all times an essential part
of that society. The very process of identity construction harbors
within itself a deconstruction of the constructed identity and its
own mode of self-alteration. The margin is the space for deconstruction and self-alteration.

The Redemptive Potential of the Margins

As I discussed earlier, the margins can be a place for creative,
emancipatory, and critical activity. While much has been written
about the negative consequences of marginalization, very little has

been written about its redemptive potential. If the marginalized are to be emancipated, they must become conscious of the already active and critical nature of the margins. The margins have never been merely a place of passive silence; they have always posed a threat to the formation of hegemonic discourse. In her essay "Choosing the Margins As a Space of Radical Openness," bell hooks writes: "As a radical standpoint, perspective, position, 'the politics of location' necessarily calls those of us who would participate in the formation of counter-hegemonic cultural practice to identify the spaces where we begin the process of re-vision."[5]

For bell hooks, the margins may be chosen as a site for radical, emancipatory political struggle, which suggests that even nonmarginalized persons can choose the margins for political activities. She distinguishes between the margins as imposed by oppressive structures and the margins chosen as a site of resistance. However, I think that even marginality as imposed by oppressive structures has emancipatory or redemptive potential, which is largely due to the instability of the very process of marginalization.

Marginalization is very similar to subordination (in Butler's sense of the term). The difference is that while all subjects are the effects of subordination, not all subjects are marginalized. Although Butler's notion of subordination is very rich and complex, there is no time to fully engage it here. The point is that we all inherit a language and certain values from our society. We do not create language and values ex nihilo.

Marginalization is the effect of a double subordination, which produces internal contradictions that prohibit it from having a total or complete effect. Although all persons are subordinated in a general sense, the marginalized are subordinated more specifically. Subordination in a general sense subordinates one to language, norms, values, and so on. Subordination in a more specific or local sense is the subordination of one group by another. This form excludes the subordinated or marginalized group from certain rights and privileges allotted to the dominant group. However, the excluded group is still required to live up to the standards of the dominant group and is still evaluated in terms of the values of the dominant group. In this way, the marginalized can never be completely outside of the dominant group. The dominant group cannot fully exclude the marginalized without jeopardizing its own identity, which is thus maintained by only partially excluding them.

The marginalized are expected to cooperate with the dominant group and honor its morals and values even while not enjoying the respect that they deserve as human beings. For example, as an African American, I am expected to live according to traditional American and so-called Christian values, while my great-great-grandparents were not allowed to read or write and my parents and grandparents suffered from segregation. I, too, have experienced the attempt to maintain segregation: during my youth we had no movie theater or swimming pool in my hometown because the public pool and theater closed shortly after integration. This tension between trying to live up to the values of American society while being denied full citizenship creates confusion. This confusion has made me a "smart black."

The margins possess redemptive and emancipatory potential to the extent that they are conceivably critical spaces wherein society must face its own contradictions. Further, since the values or norms of society must be internalized by the subject in order to have an effect on the subject, these values cannot completely determine the subject. This problem is intensified to the extent that society often sends mixed messages to the subject, who is treated as a member and a nonmember of society at the same time. The marginalized subject is positioned at the margins of society, the outside, to the extent that he or she does not represent the "ideal" by which dominant members of a society define themselves. However, the marginalized are expected to conform to the values of the same society and to behave as good citizens. We are forced to conform to an "ideal" that is not of our own making and that is theoretically out of reach for the "lowly" creatures that we are.

The Christian mission to save the savage, to convert Africans to Christianity, is one example of what I mean by the contradictions and mixed messages of society. African Americans are expected to conform to a moral ideal while not being treated with the respect and dignity that such ideals promise. In America, the Christian idea of freedom somehow does not apply to persons enslaved and oppressed by white Christians. This reality creates a gap between Christian ideals to which African Americans are expected to conform and the social conditions in which they live. The subordinating function of the "ideal" fails to fully determine the marginalized subject and therefore creates a space for critical activity.

Conclusion: How I Became the Smartest Black Man in Union, South Carolina

Now I return to the issue posed at the beginning of this chapter. It has been a decade since my conversation with the young woman who proclaimed that I was the smartest black man she knew. Her comment created in me a sensitivity that I was not aware of before: as a black intellectual, I fit in everywhere and nowhere at the same time. I find myself serving a life sentence in the margins. Even as a university professor, I am the "black professor."

In recent years, I have learned how to approach this issue in a critical and constructive way. The task is to try to understand this situation and how it may be used for emancipatory purposes. *Am* I the smartest man in my hometown of Union, South Carolina? The answer to this question is as ambiguous as American identity politics. However, let us just assume that the answer is yes. What does this mean? What does it say about other blacks in Union, for instance, my family?

Let us say that as the smartest black man in Union, I am the symbol of African-American achievement. However, as a symbol, by my very nature I point to something beyond myself. I point to the social conditions for my own being and status as the "smart black guy." Once we begin to think about the condition for my being, matters become quite complex. What is disclosed is an entire history of struggle of which I am only a small part. My position is the product of generations of suffering by African Americans. The social/historical situation in which subjects are produced is often ignored when evaluating the specific subject, who is seen as an isolated individual who has become who he or she is by his or her own merits. It is not my intention to overlook personal responsibility. I simply want to look at the other side of the coin (which unfortunately gets very little attention).

The label "smartest black" is a form of complimentary racism to the extent that it still harbors the assumption that blacks in general are stupid. The so-called smart black is viewed as an exception to the rule. I recall once watching with a white roommate a movie starring James Earl Jones. At the end of the movie, I made a comment about the acting ability of James Earl Jones. My roommate responded, "Yeah, he's a good black actor." I immediately began to wonder if this meant that Jones could not compete with good white actors. How is one to take such a statement? I also began to wonder about my potential as the "smart black." Am I smarter than other blacks but unable to compete with smart whites? Not only do such compliments perpetuate negative stereotypes of African Americans in general, but they also remarginalize so-called accomplished blacks. These comments imply that the smartest black is still no match for the average white.

Although "complimentary" acts of racist speech serve to remarginalize, I am not as bothered by them as I once was. They indicate the unstable structure of racist ideology and the incompleteness of marginalization. The dominant group must always redefine itself as the marginalized define themselves. From the margins, the real story of identity formation can be told. I have worn the title "smartest black" in predominantly white institutions where many people are still under the spell of the traditional narrative of white superiority. This narrative fails to account for the real suffering that blacks experienced at the hands of whites. The idea that I am the "smartest black" is a part of the narrative constructed by the oppressors. As a citizen of the margins, my story differs.

The truth is that the smartest blacks in Union were never given the opportunity to acquire a formal education. However, they knew that such would one day be within reach—if not for themselves, then for someone else. It is from these people, these very smart, marginalized black folk, that I learned there was something for me beyond the boundaries of Union. If I am the smartest black man in Union, it is because I know I am not the smartest black man in Union. This disclaimer does not negate the intelligence of any individual; it merely opens what has hitherto been closed, that is, the living struggle of the invisible and the marginalized. It asserts that the smart black is no exception to the rule, because the so-called rule has been false all along, constructed in the process of marginalization and the formation of the identity of a group of oppressors. It is the result of systemic and systematic attempts to silence the necessary voice of the other, a voice that refuses to be silenced.

The failure of marginalization to completely determine the subject because of the contradictions embedded in the process of marginalization has created a tension in my own life. On the one hand, the feeling of not belonging can be quite disconcerting. On the other hand, it empowers me with the freedom to create or re-create myself from the ruins of history. As a marginalized person, I am in a position to create something new that destabilizes mainstream marginalizing forces. I find myself on the boundaries, not quite belonging to the margins or to mainstream society. Due to my intellectual concerns, I am displaced in my own community. Due to my blackness, I am displaced in the academy. One may argue that the choice to pursue an academic career is a choice to leave the black community. Such a claim is false. It does, however, signify a tension and uncertainty in the black community that is characteristic of the failure of marginalization to fully determine the subject (as I suggested earlier).

The idea of transcendence was inculcated in my consciousness early in childhood. I was made aware of my marginalized status as an African American in my youth. I was taught by those poor, uneducated, yet intelligent, black folk in my community that I must strive to rise above my present situation. The limits placed on me by society must be overcome. However, a person is never certain of what lies beyond his or her present predicament. To launch oneself beyond present constraints may force one to land in a mysterious place. My struggle beyond the constraints of color led me to the academy. But I entered the academy from the outside. Therefore, I am still in the margins.

The margins wherein I find myself are no longer a threat to me but rather a site for emancipatory struggle and self-creation. While the title of the "smart black" is a form of complimentary racism and serves to remarginalize one who has gotten out of place, it still liberates to the extent that it forces the dominant culture to recognize that I occupy a place that was once reserved for whites only. In this sense, I choose the margins as a space wherein I may present to the dominant culture (as others have done) something that it once thought impossible, a "smart black."

Notes

1. The term "speech act" is used in the same sense as what J. L. Austin, *How to Do Things with Words*, ed. J. O. Urmson and Marina Sbisa (Cambridge: Harvard University Press, 1962), calls a "perlocutionary act." Such speech is not merely an utterance that contains meaning (locutionary act) or an informative statement (illocutionary act), but is a linguistic utterance that produces an effect.

2. Judith Butler, *Excitable Speech: A Politics of the Performative* (New York: Routledge, 1997), 91.

3. Judith Butler, *The Psychic Life of Power: Theories in Subjection* (Stanford: Stanford University Press, 1997), 10. In this text, Butler draws on the work of Hegel, Freud, Foucault, and Althusser to explain how subordination enacts the subject into being, thereby producing agency as an effect of subordination. This type of thinking is also expressed in the work of the German idealist Johann Gottlieb Fichte, who claims that freedom is always a limited freedom that produces a striving.

4. Cornelius Castoriadis, *The Imaginary Institution of Society*, trans. Kathleen Blamey (Cambridge: MIT Press, 1987), 372.

5. bell hooks, *Yearning: Race, Gender, and Cultural Politics* (Boston: South End Press, 1990), 145.

Chapter Seven

Story of a Hyphenated-Consciousness

Sandra Bartky

Marginality and Identity

Are there patterns in the construction of personal identities? What part is played by dominant discourses that tell me who I ought to be and by my acceptance, rejection, or, most often, my personal reconfiguration of such discourses? This question is particularly acute when we ask it about marginalized groups, especially when the center, who regards itself as the rational, the normal, and, with some exceptions, the admirable, has in fact defined itself in opposition to the margins, wherein dwell the nonrational, the abnormal, the unusual, and, very often, the undesirable. I think that there are patterns in the construction, personal as well as social, of both mainstream and marginal identities, though it would take a major research project to ferret them all out. In what follows, I shall describe one such pattern—my own—which I characterize as "dialectical," and which I suspect is quite common to those of us who have had to salvage acceptable personal identities from an initial position of marginalization.

Sociologists are divided on the concept of marginality. There are at least two definitions of this term, which are conceptually distinct. The first defines marginality as "the state of being part insider and part outsider to a social group."[1] The other commonly used definition points to some of the harms that marginality can foster: "A process by which a group or individual is denied access to important positions and symbols of economic, religious, or political power within any society."[2] Using my own experience and that of my parents, I will show that personal identities can vary, depending on whether individuals feel themselves to be marginal in the first sense or in the second sense.

The postmodernists are right, I think, to regard identities as "multiple," even as "fragmented." They do not mean (although sometimes it sounds as if they do) that people suffer from multiple personality disorder but that I bear a large number of social inscriptions; I am able to function in a large number of capacities; some part of my behavior may well be unconsciously motivated and hence all but impervious to rational control. Thus, I am a woman, a teacher, a student, a lover, a daughter, a sister, a registered Democrat, a lover of antiques, a member of the Society for the Preservation of Old Theater Organs, a victim of several non-life-threatening illnesses, and so on. These "capacities" used to be (and in some circles still are) referred to as "roles," but this is a misleading metaphor.

The idea of a "role" suggests a unitary identity behind the role who "performs" it. Sometimes it may seem to me precisely that I am playing a role and that what I am doing is a performance. But most of the time there is no such distance between myself and what I am about. There is no way, for example, that I can choose not to be a daughter or a sister (though I can be these things differently than I have been in the past), that I can choose not to have been born in the United States, brought up in Chicago, and so on. Nor is there any way I can choose not to have been born a Jew in a society in which being Jewish has traditionally marked one as marginal. I can try to pass, as was done more commonly in my parents' generation, but in such a case, I am still a Jew, now a "Jew-passing." I will relate the story of my appropriation of a Jewish identity and then speculate as to the nature and pattern of this appropriation.

Jews: the ur-marginalized people of Christian Europe whose marginalized status did not disappear when they disembarked at Ellis Island. I grew up Jewish in the 1940s and 1950s in a prosperous, safe, attractive, and heavily (but not entirely) Jewish community on the northwest side of Chicago. Although my parents had a large circle of both Jewish and Gentile friends, and even though there had been considerable intermarriage on both sides of my family, Gentiles were still a curiosity to me. Two of my Gentile aunts, Rita and Peggy, were particular curiosities, especially Peggy, stunning in her little black hat with its half-veil, her doll-like beauty, her red-red lipstick, her mink and diamonds, bringing with her everywhere a heady aroma of expensive perfume and cigarette smoke. Peggy smoked the ladies' cigarette, red-tipped Marlboros (red to accommodate lipstick marks) before their regenderization as the favorite smokes of the Marlboro Man. Both Peggy and Rita drank Scotch in the afternoon. The Jewish matrons in the neighborhood found smoking (for a woman) a bit "fast" and drank nothing but a little sacramental wine at Passover. My uncles, the husbands of these aunts, had been successful bootleggers and, hence, had their choice of the choicest women of the demimonde.

There were anti-Semites in the neighborhood as well. The man across the street got drunk regularly, threw open his window, and shouted anti-Semitic slurs with such force that they could be heard up and down the street. There was a Catholic school at the end of our block, and several of the boys, on their way home, would sometimes taunt my brother and me with anti-Semitic slogans ("dirty Jews") and throw stones or snowballs at us. But as the neighborhood became increasingly Jewish, the enrollment at St. Timothy's shrank, our tormenters disappeared, and the drunken anti-Semite across the way must have moved as well. Perhaps he moved to Sauganash, a community west of us of beautiful homes (our neighborhood had mostly two- and three-flat apartments). Sauganash was "restricted," which meant that no Jew could buy property there; the deeds themselves specified that the property could only be transferred to Christians. Shortly after the end of the Second World War, the Supreme Court declared real estate "restrictive covenants" unconstitutional.

Near the end of the war, photographs of the death camps began appearing in the papers. All that was exposed had been rumored, but not in such ghastly detail. My father had been skeptical. As a boy during World War I, he and many other Americans had been taken in by trumped-up atrocity stories ("Huns cutting off the hands of Belgian children"), and he was not about to be taken in again. But the photographs and eyewitness accounts left no doubt about the horror of the Holocaust. The reaction in my household to pictures of the crematoria and to bodies stacked like cordwood was one of shock and horror. I do not remember that the shock at home was so much a response to the fact that most of the victims were Jews as to the idea that such barbarities could be inflicted on anyone.

Stage One: In Which I Appropriate the Jewish Identity of My Parents

My parents, like most of our neighbors, were children of immigrants, climbing rapidly into the middle and upper-middle class. Their lives were a balancing act between assimilation into mainstream American society and loyalty to Jewish tradition. My parents were atheists. They were also very strongly Jewish identified. Their identification was not with a religion but with an ethnicity and a history. The state of Israel was founded when I was thirteen; this—and the balancing act of most American Jews—gave momentum to a question that had agitated much of Jewry for decades: What is a Jew? Did all Jews have an obligation to immigrate to Israel and help build a national homeland? What were our obligations vis-à-vis the country of which we were citizens and Israel? Could you be a Jew but not a Zionist? Could you be a Jew and an atheist?

My father's answers to these questions became my own. My father, a very brilliant man, was the major intellectual influence on the first twenty years of my life. He was indeed a Jew as well as a nonbeliever. He was furiously anticlerical, seeing the local synagogue as little more than a fund-raiser for Israel. My brother was perhaps the only Jewish boy in West Rogers Park who did not have a Bar Mitzvah. We were given no Jewish education outside the home. I was always free to go to temple or to Sunday school with my friends. Of course, when I went, I saw "schul" through my parents' eyes.

My father was very much a Jew of the Diaspora, whose intellectual roots were in the Enlightenment and, like many Jewish intellectuals of his generation, in German culture of the nineteenth and early twentieth century. He had respect for the tradition of Jewish learning but little real interest in it. He gave generously to Jewish relief organizations but also to worthy non-Jewish causes. He supported the founding of the state of Israel as a homeland for other Jews, not for us. We were Jews but also Americans. As events unfolded in Israel, he came more and more to see that injustice had been done to the Palestinians and that if the Israelis refused to address this situation, there would never be peace. This position was (and perhaps still is) unpopular for an American Jew.

My only Jewish education was given to me at home, at the Passover service and ritual meal, the Seder. My father made a fine Seder, neither too long nor too short. He recited many prayers in Hebrew, so that we could hear the sound of our ancestral tongue, but the bulk of the service was in English. We circled the table; everyone read passages from the *Haggadah*, the ritual service. He hit the high spots and avoided the rabbinical commentary; nothing crucial was omitted from the embellished story of the Exodus: the ten plagues, the four questions, the wise, simple, and wicked sons, the "dyanus."[3]

All the ritual foods were displayed and some were eaten—of course the matzo, the unleavened bread (the Jews having left Egypt too quickly to let their bread rise); the bitter herb, usually horseradish, that symbolized the bitterness of the life of the slave; the *charoseth*, a finely chopped mixture of nuts, apples, and wine, symbolizing the mortar with which the Jews were said to have built the pyramids. The service is punctuated by the drinking of sweet sacramental wine, the first time, never to be forgotten, that a Jewish child is permitted to partake of alcohol. In the tradition of the rabbis, my father would discourse briefly on the meaning of the text. His interpretation varied from year to year, but mostly he saw in it, as I see in it, too, a universal message about the evils of slavery and a celebration of freedom.

Attention would then shift from Father to Mother, who served an enormous traditional meal (most of the time she cooked American)—from matzo ball soup and gefilte fish to the towering Passover sponge cake, a triumph made entirely without yeast. After her mother died, my mother, with joyous relief, stopped keeping a kosher kitchen. Keeping kosher is a difficult and complex business. Although she had what I would call a more "tribal" sense than my father, she damned traditional orthodox practices, even Jewish religious beliefs, as "superstitious" or "medieval." After dinner, my father sang traditional Passover songs, and we children searched for the "AfoKamen," the matzo hidden before the meal. The finder got a dollar, but so clever was my mother (who hid it) that we could never find it without very broad clues from the grown-ups.

The *Haggadah* instructs us to imagine that it was not those distant peoples, but we *ourselves* who were delivered out of slavery in Egypt; indeed, the point of the service is not only to praise God for deliverance but also to remember the event in its entirety, to actually try to relive it: "It is incumbent on every Israelite in every generation to imagine if he had actually gone out from Egypt."[4] This instruction raises the question of whether one has a moral obligation to remember the history and folklore of one's people, a theme neglected in the standard literature of moral philosophy. Perhaps the marginalized have a special duty to remember, as the center can more easily afford to be ignorant of its history and culture.

Some people are marginalized because of their culture, as opposed, say, to their race or religion (Southern Appalachians), while others have historically been under pressure to assimilate (Jews, Spanish Gypsies). It is against pressure to assimilate that memory must be mobilized: without shared memory, group cohesion is lost; without cohesion, the very existence of the group is threatened. Forgetting—for Jews in particular—does the work of our enemies; forgetting can lead to our disappearance, that fulfillment of the dream of the enemy—a world without Jews. Other passages from the *Haggadah* will resonate forever in my memory: "In every generation enemies rise against us, to annihilate us, but the Most Holy, blessed be he, hath delivered us out of their hands."[5]

In spite of his strong Jewish identity, my father had an ecumenical turn of mind. He had studied the New Testament and found the moral teaching there somewhat more elevated than that of the Old Testament. And we celebrated Christmas. I think that I have never had a Jewish friend who understood or approved of this practice, but without it, my childhood would have been deprived of some of its greatest joys. We celebrated Hanukkah as well. One, my father was fond of saying, is the celebration of victory in war, the other "the celebration of the birth of the Prince of Peace." The orthodox grandmothers had begun this tradition, thinking that Santa Claus was an American figure and Christmas an American holiday. So my mother and father and their brothers and sisters hung up their stockings near the coal stove on Christmas Eve. The bad children were threatened with lumps of coal, but all children got an orange, a rare and incredible delicacy in the poor, immigrant economy of their youth.

Christmas was celebrated at my school. We were taught mostly by female Irish-Catholic "losers" (old maids or widows) with two-year teaching degrees.[6] They never mentioned religion per se, but

the school was decorated with wreaths and pine branches and por-
traits of Santa. We were taught all the Christmas carols. Imagine
forty-five children, forty-three of them Jewish, singing lustily of
"Round John Virgin." Our parents, still having no sense of entitle-
ment to a critique of American institutions, never complained.

My brother and I wrote letters to Santa, were taken to see the
real Santa, i.e., the Santa at Marshall Field's, a huge figure bathed
in dazzling light (for the snapshots) before whom we were struck
dumb with awe. My father loved Dickens's *Christmas Carol*, which
he understood to contain the real values of Christmas—generosity,
compassion, and good fellowship. He talked a great deal about the
pagan origins of Christmas. On Christmas morning, my brother
and I ran into the magically transformed living room. The presents,
in two lines in front of the fireplace, his and mine, were arranged in
order of ascending psychological impact with the most spectacular
and unexpected at the end. Our stockings, hung up empty the
night before, were full of candy canes and little toys, and perhaps
there would be a half-eaten sandwich and a thank-you note from
Santa. One Christmas, my parents told me later, they were so broke
that they bought all the toys at Woolworth's. My brother and I did
not know the difference; this was long before the invention of intensive advertising to children of specific (and expensive) toys. But
my father would not have a Christmas tree; Christmas trees were
for Gentiles. That is where *he* drew the line.

Stage Two: In Which I Join the Unitarian Church

Stage two in the pattern of identity formation that I am describing
involves the rejection and negation of some of what had constituted identity in stage one. Characteristics of the moment of negation include resentment at having an "ascribed" identity instead of
a (freely chosen) "achieved" identity; internalization of negative
stereotypes of one's group; assumption (in bad faith) of a fantasized identity; hiding one's identity, i.e., "passing."

Though I was only sixteen, my overprotective parents were
persuaded by a family friend (my ally) to let me go away to college.
I went to a large public university downstate, the only university
my parents could afford. There I broke out of the largely homoge-

neous community in which I was raised and met an extraordinary diversity of students—from farms, small towns, foreign countries, and even the black south side of Chicago. It was there and then that I came to feel my Jewish identity as burdensome.

There were many complex issues that I dealt with in the painful, prolonged (and, I suspect, typical) identity crisis of late adolescence and early adulthood. My Jewish identity was only one such issue, and it was triggered by a long and agonized exchange of letters between myself and my parents having to do with the dating of Gentiles. My parents wanted me to promise that I would not date Gentile boys. I resisted this demand. In spite of my father's cultural and intellectual ecumenism and in spite of their wide and mixed circle of friends, both my parents believed that deep down, unknown perhaps even to themselves, all Gentiles were anti-Semitic. Dating eventually led to marriage, and one of their greatest fears was that I would marry out of the group. In the first really bitter argument, or even the last, they said, there would come that moment when he would look at me and say "dirty Jew."

Eventually I promised, tearfully, to do as they asked. Perhaps I meant it when I promised it, but in point of fact, I dated whom I pleased. In the course of my college career, it is true, I became seriously involved with two Jews, the first a musician, the second a published poet. Each expected me to marry him, but I knew I would marry neither. These men were so much like myself, in background and shared values, aesthetic and intellectual preferences, even neuroses, that sex with either of them would have felt incestuous. This being the fifties, one could be virtually engaged and not have to "go the limit."

I was secretly (and profoundly) attracted sexually to big blond jocks, utterly unlike my cerebral father and those doppelgänger Jewish intellectuals. The two men with whom I (serially) have spent most of my life are not Jewish; the first did have the sort of emotional self-control I then associated with Gentiles; the second is blond but scarcely a jock. (Nor did I ever find in either partner any trace of anti-Semitism.) An attraction to big, blond jocks: is this internalized anti-Semitism?[7]

I believed then that what I disliked most about being Jewish was the fact that I had not chosen it. I had been chosen by it. Furthermore, I would always be somewhat alien in my own country.

This label—"Jewish-American"—would follow me all the rest of my life. I would never be a real American, always a hybrid; I wanted to live in my country as someone truly *of* the country, not as a perpetual hyphen, straddling margin and center. I did not wish to be part insider and part outsider, but all insider. Mostly, I wanted to be free, free of all designations, free of all ascriptions, so that I could freely mold myself. Having not yet read Sartre, I did not know that the freedom I sought was impossible.

I discovered the Unitarian Church. A good number of faculty belonged, and the congregation took stands on political issues that challenged the McCarthyism of the day. I was apolitical then, but I approved of the stands they took. The church did not look like a church. It was built in the "mission" or "bungalow" style that was popular earlier in the twentieth century. There were no religious images anywhere. God and Christ were mentioned only in some of the traditional hymns we sang. The minister was an appealing young man who never mentioned God in his sermons; indeed, one Sunday's sermon consisted solely of a reading of Shelley's "Ode to the West Wind," that poem of hope that ends with "If winter comes, can spring be far behind?" And Unitarianism was *so* American! It was founded in America by high-minded New Englanders—representatives of the American spirit at its best—as an alternative to the narrowness and intolerance of Puritanism.

I especially liked the social hour after the service where one could meet faculty in a relaxed atmosphere, though I spoke mainly with other young people, a bit awestruck by the social distance between the faculty and myself. I especially liked to dress up on Sunday morning and to wobble down to church on my high heels; this was what real Americans did, they went to church on Sunday morning. One Sunday morning there was a ceremony of joining that involved inscribing one's name in a huge book on a stand in front of the altar. I signed, thus officially joining the church.

Several months later, I spent a weekend with a friend in Hyde Park, in the neighborhood of the University of Chicago. There is a large Unitarian congregation in Hyde Park, and so, on Sunday, I resolved to go to "my" church. This building looked just like a cathedral; indeed, it looked like the Episcopal church in Urbana, only bigger; and it looked nothing like the mission-style building where I had been hanging out. It was a huge gray stone affair, with high vaulted Gothic arches. The wooden church benches were carved with Gothic arches as well. There was an organ. The minister appeared, dressed in a floor-length black robe and white collar. He ascended a spiral staircase to a pulpit, carved with the inevitable Gothic arches, from which he proceeded to conduct the service. A paralyzing thought slowly took shape in my mind: "Oh, my God, I've joined a Protestant church!" I ran out of there, never to return, nor did I ever return to any Unitarian church, except for concerts. I have absolutely nothing against Unitarians and so I never thought to erase my name from the big book. So ends a tale of "being in denial" that I would match against any told in Alcoholics Anonymous.

After graduation, I was awarded a Fulbright Scholarship to Germany to study philosophy, even though I had only minored in philosophy. I had no particular desire to go to Germany as opposed to, say, France or England, but one had to show competence in the language of the country to which one applied, and the Fulbright Commission pretended that two years of college credit in a foreign language was evidence of competence, which, of course, it certainly is not. There was a contingency at work here. Thinking that every educated person should know, minimally, French and German, I went to register for French. But the lines at the French desk were extremely long, and there was no one at the German desk; so I registered for German. I was at the time in the college of music, so German seemed an appropriate choice. Later, when I transferred to liberal arts, I had so many liberal arts graduation requirements to make up that I could not fit French into my schedule. Hence the extraordinary year in Germany, in which I passed as *Evangelisch*, i.e., Protestant.

Given my flirtation with Unitarianism, this was not entirely a lie. Why did I do it? Was I still in flight from my Jewish identity? Or was the reason I gave myself the true one? I thought that if I signaled my Jewishness from the start, I would never know what the Germans really thought about Jews, the war, and the Holocaust. What I discovered there I think I would have discovered after a year of passing here in the United States: some Germans were guilt-ridden and conscience-stricken about what their parents had consented to (my German friends were mostly my age), while other Germans, apparently having learned nothing from the war, were anti-Semitic in fairly banal ways.

Seeing me carrying around a book about the Rosenbergs, my German landlord in Munich said, "Of course they did it for the money." "No," I answered, "I don't think they got any money; anyhow, I think they did it out of ideological commitment." "Impossible," he answered. "They were Jews, so they must have done it for the money." I spent a semester in Munich, and even though Dachau is now a war memorial and only a short train ride away, I never went there. I was unwilling to open myself completely to what Jewish identity had meant to *those* Jews. I have avoided reading Holocaust literature most of my adult life.

Stage Three: Two Shadow-Worlds

The first shadow-world was the world from which my grandparents had emerged: the world of the East European *shtetl,* the small Jewish village. My grandparents were all dead before I had a chance to know them, so I had no link to traditional Jewish life. Neither my father nor my mother ever related stories about that life that had been told to them by their parents. Perhaps these grandparents wanted to suppress their memories; but if this is true, then it is unusual, for my Jewish friends who had living grandparents were told such stories (generally about pogroms). Or perhaps the memory lapse, or the denial of memory, was my parents' doing—too much remembering might compromise their project of guarded assimilation.

But the shadow-world of Eastern Europe was not invisible. We used to go regularly to the Jewish cemetery to visit the family graves. This was an extraordinary place of marble and granite, photographs of the dead under oval bronze covers, statuary, and elaborate but ancient wrought-iron fences around the plots of immigrant burial societies, the societies and their members long dead. Very ancient men wandered about the cemetery, emaciated, with long, discolored gray beards, dirty wide-brimmed black hats, and long dusty black coats, which they never removed, even on the hottest of summer days. These men were religious beggars; they spoke to my parents in Yiddish, offering to say prayers for the dead for money. My parents always gave them money; a bit later we would hear them chanting and praying some distance from the graves.

Another very ancient Orthodox Jew, in the same disheveled costume and stained beard, would call upon my mother, carrying a can with Hebrew letters on it and a slot on top for coins. My mother always treated this man with great respect, giving his charity money and his clearly exhausted body a cup of tea while chatting a bit with him in Yiddish. My mother and father knew Yiddish but always spoke English at home with a fair smattering of wonderful, untranslatable Yiddish words, mostly insults. (Someone has said that Yiddish is rich in the vocabulary of human failure.) But it was eerie to hear my mother speaking this strange tongue to a figure who appeared to have come out of the past; in spite of this strangeness, I knew that this language and these sick old men in black were somehow connected to me.

The other shadow-world I took to be the real world, "the real America" I wanted to enter so desperately as a young woman. I knew it could not be found in Chicago or New York, where everyone was hyphenated or black. (Now that the term "Afro-American" has come into use, they are hyphenated Americans, too.) I imagined that the real America existed somewhere in the Midwest, in Iowa perhaps; it was a land of great civility and dignity, where people lived in large, white frame houses with ancient trees on capacious lawns, a land of largely virtuous WASPs. It was, in a word, the land of Andy Hardy movies; it was Radioland, from whence issued such serials as *Ma Perkins*, which I listened to every day at lunch.[8] Ma was wise, sagacious, and serene, as was Andy Hardy's gray-haired, dignified father, the judge. This "place," the Middle America of radio (I did much of my growing up before television) and the movies, was clearly the center; *we* were on the margins.

Urbana was full of somewhat more modest, white frame houses with porches and trees that met overhead. On those mornings that I clattered down to church I wanted desperately to have a grandmother in one of those old, white houses, a grandmother who, yes, baked cookies, a loving, serene, and wise soul with whom I could sit at dusk on the porch swing. I was eager to get into that world, to have parents who never raised their voices or lost their tempers, who would say to you, quietly and with dignity, if they were displeased, "Go to your room."

No such words were ever spoken in my family. Disagreements descended almost immediately into quarrels and then into shouting matches, often into screaming matches in which everyone's dignity was lost. I usually ended up out of control, crying hysterically. Looking back, I cannot remember what these frequent quarrels were all about; I remember only the overheated atmosphere and the rapid departure, on the part of my parents and myself, from rationality. Two ideas clung to me at that period: "Jews are too materialistic," which was believed by Jews themselves as well as Gentiles, and "Jews are loud." The latter claim, unlike the former, seemed, sadly, to be borne out by the decibel level of my home.

Stage Four: The Synthesis and Construction
of a New Jewish Identity

Clearly, there is a dialectical pattern at work here, for in this, the last chapter of my tale, I return, in a positive and deliberate fashion, to a Jewish identity, albeit an identity that in many ways still mirrors that of my father. As I continued to make my way in American society, I came to see that many of the things I had believed about Jews were either false or unobjectionable or just true of virtually everyone. Although I thoroughly disliked the overheated emotional climate of my family, the stereotypical WASP stiff upper lip, suppression of emotion, and silence about what is really important are perhaps even poorer ways to live.

I think now that the charge of "materialism" leveled against Jews is ludicrous. We thought that Jews were "too materialistic" only because most of the people we knew were Jews. The whole country, the culture of "late-stage" capitalism, encourages, indeed requires, high levels of consumption. In this, Jews are perhaps more like their neighbors than they are in any other way. As Jews tend to have a higher per capita income than most other Americans, perhaps we consume more, in which case the charge "materialistic" is just sour grapes.

For a time, I began to believe that Jews were better than other people. Weren't we, after all, overrepresented in progressive circles, given our numbers in the population? Weren't more of us at least liberals, surprising, given our relative affluence? Haven't Jews encouraged women's education when other groups did not? Weren't Reform and Conservative denominations quicker to ordain women than many other religious groups? Of the four men who are said to have influenced modern society the most—Darwin, Marx, Freud, and Einstein—weren't three of them Jews? Weren't Jews just smarter than other people? One could go on and on with this list, but one should not; Jewish chauvinism is no better than internalized anti-Semitism. If Jews have excelled in some areas, the reasons for this excellence are quite complex and are to be found in accidents of history and culture.[9] There is nothing intrinsically superior about Jews. I just wrote this statement, but do I believe it? I think I do, but only after many pendulum swings in the course of my adult life between pro- and anti-Semitism.

To speak at this time not just of Jewish chauvinism but of Jewish triumphalism, I confess to having felt joy and pride not now but in past Israeli military victories. Ever the romantic, I found irresistible the images of strong, bronzed Sabras sitting proudly atop their tanks as they rolled victorious through the desert. The sudden burst of pride that not just I but other Jews as well felt all those years ago is a measure of how deeply and consciously entrenched was the stereotype of the Jew as coward, the Jew as victim, as "he who is to be slapped." We needed new images of who we were, and we got them, in part, from Israel. But today I am no supporter of Israeli foreign policy; I am appalled, as are many Jews and non-Jews, by Israeli persecution of the Palestinians. Like my father, I hold the formerly unpopular but growing view among American Jews that the Palestinians should have their own state as was envisioned in the original UN partition plan. Israel is now just another nation-state pursuing what it (mistakenly) believes is its own self-interest. I owe no allegiance to Israel, nor do I recognize Israeli claims on me.

My turn away from Judaism was motivated by a sense of frustration at having been handed a marginal identity. Marginal or not, everyone is handed an identity that has somehow to be navigated. Furthermore, American Jews seem to have lost or to be losing their marginal status. Jews are represented in all professions, have gone straight to the top in many, have seats in the Senate and the House (albeit not many), had, for decades, a seat on the Supreme Court. There are Jewish scientists, professors, poets, bankers, brokers, artists, shopkeepers, criminals, musicians, university presidents, and, of course, doctors and lawyers. Jews have played and still play, through their influence in the entertainment business, a major role in the formation of American popular culture.

Jews have effective lobbies in Congress. Jews have been advisers to presidents (Henry Kissinger and Sidney Blumenthal). The appointment of a Jew to a cabinet post no longer elicits comment. Arguably, after the president, the most influential person in the country today is Alan Greenspan, head of the Federal Reserve System; I assume from his name that he is Jewish. True, there are still private clubs that refuse to admit us, but so what? We have our own clubs, and, anyhow, this sort of thing impinges very little, if at all, on the lives of ordinary Jews. The country is not ready to elect a Jewish president or, for that matter, a black, female, Hispanic, or Nisei president.

These days I feel entirely comfortable with my Jewish identity, having steered a course between the Scylla of Jewish self-hatred and the Charybdis of Jewish triumphalism. I sometimes find myself attracted to dark-haired, Jewish-looking men: the hegemony of the big, blond jock is over. I never fail to observe the Seder, either making it myself or managing to get invited somewhere. I mark the solemn Day of Atonement, Yom Kippur. I have just read my first Holocaust memoir, the superb *The Drowned and the Saved,* by Primo Levi. I celebrate Christmas as a pagan holiday marking the winter solstice. I have a Christmas tree.

How is my identity different from that of my father and mother? I lack their conviction that "deep down" all Gentiles are anti-Semites. I am not always aware, as when I was younger, of who is Jewish and who is not. My father had a strong professional identity and also an American identity. But if asked, "Who are your people?" he would most likely, and my mother would most certainly, have answered, "the Jews." The Jews are my people, too, of course, but I have other genealogies as well that are perhaps just as significant ingredients in my identity. I feel myself deeply connected to those feminists who struggled all their lives for women's equality despite deep flaws in the movement they built. I feel myself equally deeply connected to and part of the long line of homegrown American radicals (to name but a few): Albert and Lucy Parsons and the other Haymarket martyrs; Eugene Debs; Elizabeth Gurley Flyn; the "wobblies"; Norman Thomas; Dorothy Day; Martin Luther King Jr.; Fannie Lou Hamer; Rosa Parks; Noam Chomsky. My fantasy grandmother is no longer Ma Perkins but Emma Goldman.

Conclusion: A Short Reflection on the Pattern of My Identity

Earlier I described the unfolding of my identity as "dialectical." This unfolding resembles the tripartite unfolding of "thesis, antithesis, and synthesis" that is often associated with the idea of dialectic.[10] The thesis is the identity that is just given to me by the society in which I find myself at a certain moment in this society's historical development. This social identity is mediated by my parents and then uncritically adopted by myself. The situation is a bit more complex than this, as my father's own Jewish identity, much of which I just incorporate in the moment of "thesis," had already been filtered through his own personal and philosophical critique.

The "antithesis" in my tale is my rejection of Jewish identity. I have tried to describe its motives and forms. Finally, the return via a "synthesis" in which my negation of Jewishness is itself negated and a Jewish identity emerges that is similar to but more capacious (if less focused) than that of my parents. My father's identity and mine can also be regarded as syntheses of a commitment to Jewish identity, on the one hand, and on the other, to a European cultural tradition of art, literature, and philosophy (much of it influenced, often profoundly, by Christianity). It is the latter tradition that is formative in the education of Western secular individuals.

My narrative can also be positioned within the hermeneutic framework of Paul Ricoeur.[11] Ricoeur's concept of "narrative identity" fuses cosmological time and phenomenological time. What this means is that the space-time continuum does not map neatly onto the lived duration of the narrative of a life but that both are necessary to such a narrative. In the construction of identity, there are moments that are crucial: one can change in the blink of an eye. There are also periods of stasis whose chronological duration is not integral to the story. It is Ricoeur's view that, to have a personal identity at all, one must be capable of telling one's story, and that certain features are essential to any narrative.

What Ricoeur calls "narrative" is a process whereby the subject, in a constant interaction with others, makes and remakes itself.

Self-reflection, which is crucial to the construction of identity, is reflection upon the variations that a subject undergoes in time; the subject is in a continual process of dispersion and retrieval in which he or she attempts to combine persistence through time with dispersion and discontinuity.

The two construals of marginality that I mentioned earlier map onto not only the fate of assimilating Jews in America but also onto the differences between my Jewish identity and that of my parents. I was part outsider (but only part) growing up in a world in which Jews were becoming more and more insiders.[12] My parents, on the contrary, came of age at a time in which Jews were "denied access to important positions and symbols of economic, religious, or political power."[13] So similar in many ways, the differences between my parents' Jewish identity and my own stand out most clearly in their near-hysterical fear that I might marry outside the group.

My parents were Yiddish speakers of immigrant parents who must have told them of the pogroms. They grew up in an America in which discrimination was overt, blatant, and legally allowable. There were Jewish quotas in medical schools, indeed, in admission to many universities. When my father was twenty years old, one-third of the native-born white men in the bordering state of Indiana were members of the Ku Klux Klan.[14] In a state with few African Americans, the Klan leaders railed against the banks, the railroads, big business, Catholics, and Jews.

If the process of taking on an identity is, as Ricoeur has said, a constant juggling of discontinuity and retrieval, the discontinuity of discrimination in my parents' lives must have alternated far more dramatically with "retrieval" (here construed as the promise of social acceptance) than it ever did in mine. I came of age in an America made ashamed of overt anti-Semitism by Hitler and the Holocaust. Whatever anti-Semitism is out there has, as far as I know, never kept me from doing anything I wanted; nor, when the boys from St. Timothy's moved away, have I ever had to confront it directly.[15]

Notes

1. *The Harper Collins Dictionary of Sociology*, 2d ed., ed. David Jary and Julia Jary (New York: Harper Collins, 1995), 387.

2. *Concise Oxford Dictionary of Sociology*, ed. Gordon Marshall (New York: Oxford University Press, 1994), 304.

3. This is a long thank-you list of things that God did for the Israelites, assuring him that if he had done x, but not y, "it would have been sufficient"—"dyanu" in Hebrew.

4. *Passover Haggadah with Music* (New York: Hebrew Publishing, 1912), 29.

5. Ibid., 11–12.

6. "Losers" because it was considered a disgrace for a middle-class woman, unless she was single (and to be single was to have lost big—to be an "old maid" was a fate worse than death), to have to work for wages. This was a sign of the husband's failure to provide for his family—a misfortune and a disgrace.

7. Perhaps. Or perhaps it stems from an incompletely resolved Oedipus complex; anyone who looked like my dark-haired father would set off my unconscious oedipal anxiety. Or does it stem from the fact that my mother was blond as a child and bore a child, my brother, with a beautiful head of curly blond hair? A blond Jewish baby! Friends and relatives came to marvel at this miracle child, especially at his hair; five years older and a brunette, I was ignored.

8. The locus classicus of this kind of Jewish longing for the center is to be found in Philip Roth's unjustly maligned *Portnoy's Complaint*. I read part of this book with the sense that I was reading my own biography.

9. In Eastern Europe, from which most American Jews emigrated, it was illegal for a Jew to own land. As agriculture was the principal source of wealth, Jews were forced to learn crafts, to become petty traders or moneylenders. Moreover, it was a religious duty for male Jews to be literate and to study the Torah and, if possible, the voluminous commentary that had grown around the first five books of Moses. The community subsidized academically promising young men.

10. Of course, this conception has affinities with the dialectic of Hegel and Marx. But both thinkers describe historical transitions and transformations that are not always neatly packaged in the rather mechanical tripartite formula of "thesis, antithesis, and synthesis." See J. N. Findlay, *Hegel: A Re-Examination* (New York: Collier Macmillan, 1958).

11. See especially Paul Ricoeur, *Time and Narrative*, vol. 1, trans. Kathleen McLaughlin and David Pellauer (Chicago: University of Chicago Press, 1984).

12. See note 1.

13. See note 2.

14. William M. Lutholtz, *Grand Dragon: D. C. Stephenson and the Ku Klux Klan in Indiana* (West Lafayette, IN: Purdue University Press, 1991), 55.

15. I would like to thank Liz Goodenick and Yolanda Estes for their very substantial help in the preparation of this manuscript.

Chapter Eight

Marginalization and Political Identity: The Experience of Native Americans

Rebecca Tsosie

The Indian Wars officially ended in 1890 with the massacre at Wounded Knee. There were similar events, of course, throughout the history of the European conquest of the Americas, in which an estimated ninety-four million Native people lost their lives.[1] But Wounded Knee was different. The Ghost Dance movement swept across the Great Plains in the late 1800s, promising a vision of rebirth for Indian nations, regeneration of the buffalo, and a return to the freedom of the past.[2] It was all that the Indian people had to hold on to during the harsh winter in 1890, in the midst of the U.S. Army's campaign designed to starve the Indians into submission. Many Lakota and Dakota followers of the Ghost Dance were camped by Wounded Knee Creek, flying a white flag of truce, when the Seventh Cavalry fired into their midst, killing over three hundred Indian people, most of them women and children.

The massacre at Wounded Knee was different because it marked the symbolic death of a way of life as well as the physical death of hundreds of Indian people. Black Elk, a survivor of the massacre, reflected years later that "something else died there in the bloody mud, and was buried in the blizzard. A people's dream died there. It was a beautiful dream."[3] Today history books claim that the "Wounded Knee massacre . . . ended a quarter of a century of political, military, and moral struggle for the Sioux."[4] The Lakota and Dakota people of the Great Sioux Nation, they assert, have never "completely recovered, culturally or psychologically," from the military defeat, loss of buffalo herds, and forced dependency inculcated by federal policy.[5]

Contemporary ethnographers link the brutality of the past to the overwhelming poverty and despair that characterize many reservations today. Ironically, Indian people are now citizens of the same government that sought to exterminate them less than a century ago. As citizens, they are expected to share the same dreams and aspirations of other Americans. Yet, contemporary Indian people also cling to their separate political and cultural identities as a means to resist their assimilation as "citizens." Thus, while Native people clearly stand on the margins of contemporary American society, it is unclear whether this is a choice, one of the legacies of conquest, or both.

This chapter examines the political context of marginalization by evaluating the impact of Western imperialism on Native peoples. Marginalization is commonly understood to relate to the social oppression of groups such as women, the poor, and racial minorities.[6] However, Native Americans have experienced both political and social oppression. In that sense, for Native Americans, marginalization and imperialism are twin faces of the same phenomenon and represent the legacy of colonialism in a modern constitutional democracy. Today, there is still an ongoing tension between Native peoples' struggle to preserve their sense of group autonomy ("tribalism") and the assimilation of Native peoples into the United States as citizens.

Native American Marginalization in Historic Context

The colonial period of American history established the framework for European-Indian relations based on bilateral treaty negotiations, which secured political alliances and cessions of land for European settlers. After the War of Independence, the United States continued the treaty tradition with Indian nations first established by Great Britain and France. However, the balance of power shifted dramatically after the War of 1812, when the rapid westward expansion of the burgeoning nation set the stage for a series of brutal encounters between Indian nations, who were defending their territory, and American settlers intent upon claiming lands "from sea to shining sea."

A series of Supreme Court opinions in the early 1800s defined the separate political status of the Indian nations within the domestic territory of the United States. In a series of cases authored by Chief Justice John Marshall, the Supreme Court found that the incorporation of the Indian nations into the United States had divested tribes of their ability to enter into alliances with foreign nations yet upheld the tribes' sovereign authority over their own territories and their internal affairs.[7]

The tribes were designated as "domestic dependent nations" that were under the protection of the federal government but were immune from the reach of state law and from the general federal laws that applied to citizens. In *Ex Parte Crow Dog*, for example, the Supreme Court upheld the exclusive jurisdiction of the Sioux Nation over a murder involving two tribal members. The Court reasoned that the Sioux had by treaty pledged their "allegiance" to the United States and its laws as a "dependent community, as wards rather than citizens." Individual Indians were not "separately responsible and amenable in all their personal and domestic relations with each other, to the general laws of the United States."[8]

The flip side of this interpretation, however, was that the federal government had the authority to enact laws expressly for the Indian nations. Congressional legislation had the most direct and tangible impact on tribal sovereignty during the expansion era.[9] For example, the Removal Act of 1830 authorized the United States to "exchange" Indian lands east of the Mississippi for lands west of the Mississippi. Although the Removal Act contemplated "voluntary" exchanges, it was in fact responsible for the forcible relocation of over sixteen thousand Indian people from southeastern tribes such as Cherokee, Choctaw, Chickasaw, and Seminole, many of whom died on the infamous Trail of Tears. The Removal Act was predicated on federal policy that viewed the Indian nations as normatively deficient and called for their separation from encroaching white society.[10] Indian people were perceived as uncivilized, inferior, and subject to moral degradation. Policy makers claimed it was in the Indians' "best interest" to be removed to distant lands where they would not be subject to the tainting influence of the rough frontier settlers.

By the 1860s, however, the official policy of the United States had shifted to favor the assimilation of Indian nations. The Reservation Policy sought to confine Indian nations on gradually smaller land bases and inculcated a forced dependency upon government rations by restricting traditional subsistence practices, such as hunting and fishing. Christian missionaries were assigned to the reservations to serve as Indian agents. The Allotment Policy of the late 1800s sought to break up the reservation land base into discrete parcels of land, which would be allotted to individual Indians to farm and hold in "fee simple."

By enforcing the ideals of private property ownership, federal policy makers hoped to destroy the communal nature of tribal property systems and thereby destroy a central feature of tribalism. This policy was also promoted as being in the Indians' best interest because it furthered their civilization. Of course, the "surplus lands" left over after individual tribal members received their homestead allotments were sold off to non-Indian settlers, thus furthering another central government interest. The government asserted that the presence of non-Indian settlers on the reservation would have a beneficial "civilizing" effect on the Indians. However, under the Allotment Policy, Indian landholdings were reduced from 138 million acres in 1887 to 48 million acres in 1934, when the Allotment Policy was ended by the Indian Reorganization Act.

The Allotment Policy was part of an intensive federal policy of assimilation designed to break down tribal structures and institutions and supplant these with Anglo-American ideals. Under the Boarding School Policy, Indian children were forcibly removed from their homes and sent to distant boarding schools for periods of up to eight years, during which time they were prohibited from visiting their relatives, speaking their native languages, or practicing their religious and cultural traditions. On the reservations, the Indian agents banned the practice of native ceremonies and attempted to Christianize the Indians. This effort was one of the driving forces behind the Wounded Knee Massacre, which was intended in part to suppress the Ghost Dance. The Indian agents also established Indian police and courts of Indian offenses. These institutions were designed to supplant traditional tribal governments by appointing officials who answered directly to the Indian agent and received their authority from his office.

During the height of the Assimilation Policy, individual Indians who attained a measure of "civilization" were rewarded with citizenship. Thus, allotees who mastered agricultural practices and learned to manage their property in the same way as white citizens could achieve citizenship along with the fee-simple title to their lands. The more "backward" Indians, who insisted on retaining collective values and rejected assimilation, were deemed wards of the government and had their property held in trust by the government. Indians who became citizens were encouraged to leave the reservations and pursue opportunity on the same basis as white citizens.

This policy persisted throughout the 1950s and even into the 1960s in the guise of the Termination Policy, which sought to end the trust status of the more successful tribes, sell off the remaining tribal lands and resources, and distribute the proceeds per capita to individual members. Individual Indians were often convinced to move to urban areas, and the federal Relocation Policy offered vocational training to Indians who wished to move to big cities like Chicago and Los Angeles.

By the time the 1970s rolled around, President Nixon articulated a new policy of "self-determination," designed to "strengthen the Indian's sense of autonomy without threatening his sense of community." Finally, the federal government purported to understand the Indian nations' need to survive as distinct cultural and political entities. Yet, the last century of federal policy had left a lasting impact on Indian nations. Indian people were the poorest ethnic group per capita in the United States, and the conditions on many reservations rivaled those of Third World countries. Malnutrition, unemployment, alcoholism, suicide, high incarceration rates, and disease were endemic on many reservations. Racial tensions in border towns such as Gallup, New Mexico, and Rapid City, South Dakota, reached new heights in the 1960s and 1970s. For Indian people in the urban areas, conditions were often not much better. Indians tended to congregate in the lower-income neighborhoods, where they became yet another disadvantaged racial minority struggling to achieve economic parity with the white upper class.

This was the state of affairs in the 1970s, when Indian militants began to call for increased attention to tribal sovereignty and treaty guarantees of the last century. In 1973, the American Indian Movement (AIM) laid siege to the hamlet of Wounded Knee in a symbolic protest that sparked the nation's attention. It seemed that the dream of Native sovereignty and rebirth had not died at Wounded Knee after all. The dream was reborn during AIM's occupation, which was a cry for political recognition and cultural survival among Indian people across the nation.[11] This political activism spurred legal efforts by Indian nations to reassert the land, water, hunting, and fishing rights that had been guaranteed by federal treaties. The colonial underpinnings of U.S. policy were finally exposed for all the world to see, and in a global atmosphere of decolonization and nationalist fervor, Indian claims took on a new meaning.

American Indian Political Identity in Contemporary Society

Of course, the prior few centuries of conquest had lasting consequences for American Indian people. One of the most devastating consequences was the physical extinction of entire Indian nations such as the Karankawans, Akokisa, Bidui, and Tejas, who once inhabited what is now the state of Texas.[12] Other Indian nations were legally extinguished by court rulings that found they no longer existed as distinct political entities. In the United States, a distinction exists between "federally recognized" tribes and "non-recognized" tribes.[13]

Federally recognized tribes are eligible for federal benefits including health, education, and economic development services. Federally recognized tribes generally have a land base, reserved by treaty or statute, which is held in trust by the U.S. government. This means that the United States holds the "legal title" to the land, and the Indian nation holds the "beneficial title," including the rights to the mineral and timber resources of the land. Trust land may generally not be alienated from tribal ownership and is often exempt from state jurisdiction.

Nonrecognized tribes are not eligible for the same services, and most of these tribes lack a reservation land base.[14] During the 1970s, the courts established that the federal Nonintercourse Acts, first enacted in 1790, protected the land rights of all Indian nations.[15] The Nonintercourse Acts prohibited land transactions from Indians to non-Indians without the consent of the federal government. Not only were federally recognized tribes such as the Oneida protected by these statutes, but nonrecognized tribes such as the Passamaquoddy obtained recognition of their land rights, which had been wrongfully removed by the state of Massachusetts and later transferred to Maine. In the case of the Passamaquoddy, this legislation ultimately led to their recognition by the federal government and the establishment of a reservation land base.[16]

The Mashpee Tribe, however, never received the opportunity to litigate its land rights, because it was deemed to have ceased to exist as a separate political entity. When the Mashpee Tribe sued non-Indian landowners in the town of Mashpee on the basis that its lands had been removed from tribal ownership in violation of the Nonintercourse Acts, the landowners asserted that the Mashpee were not a tribe and therefore had no standing to bring such an action. A jury composed entirely of non-Indians found that the Mashpee were not an Indian tribe when the lawsuit was commenced in 1976, and that they did not "continuously exist" as a tribe during the relevant historical period.[17]

The jury was instructed to use a test formulated by an earlier court in *Montoya v. United States* to ascertain whether the Mashpee were still a tribe. The *Montoya* test asks whether the Indians are of the same or similar race; are "united in community"; are "under one leadership or government"; and inhabit a particular territory. The Mashpee had a long history of political interaction with the British and then the American colonists. They also had resided continuously in the town of Mashpee. However, the federal court of appeals agreed with the jury that the Mashpee had ceased to exist as a tribe because they were no longer "united in community" and were not under "one leadership or government."[18]

The court held that an Indian community must have some "boundary that separates it from the surrounding society" in a way that marks the community as "distinctively Indian." The court looked for evidence of discrimination by white people in a way that would establish a social boundary between whites and Indians. Ultimately, the Mashpee's "assimilation" into white society became the reason for their legal extinction. The Mashpee had intermarried with black and white citizens in the area; they appeared to have adopted the culture and manners of white people, spoke the English language, held their property as individuals, and practiced Christianity. According to the court, one could infer that by accepting private property rights and citizenship, the Indians "intended to give up their tribal organization and assume an English organization."

Unlike other tribes who had become dependent upon the federal government for their survival, the Mashpee had survived on their own, integrating into the larger economic and political structures that encompassed them. The Mashpee were in fact so successful at this integration that they had retained political control over the town of Mashpee until the 1970s. One of the primary reasons for the Mashpee's lawsuit was their desire to protect the coastal lands, which they still used for cultural and ceremonial purposes, from development. None of this influenced the court, however, which upheld the jury's conclusion that the Mashpee had ceased to exist as a tribe.

The federal government has now articulated regulations that define the mandatory criteria for acknowledgement as a "federally recognized Indian tribe."[19] Like the *Montoya* test, these regulations require that the petitioning group comprises a "distinct community and has existed as a community from historical times to the present." In order to prove this stipulation, the group must demonstrate significant rates of marriage within the group, show "evidence of strong patterns of discrimination or other social distinctions by non-members," and demonstrate shared cultural patterns among the group that are different from the local non-Indian population. Thus, marginalization is the key to the persistence of Native American political identity. To the extent that a tribe becomes assimilated into the non-Indian social, economic, or political structures, the tribe loses its rights to persist as a separate political entity.

Significantly, as both the *Mashpee* case and the federal acknowledgment criteria demonstrate, tribal identity is only provable according to the external factors of a system that has alternately excluded Indians and demanded their assimilation.[20] In the *Mashpee* case, the politics of historic domination forced the tribe to petition the federal government as "guardian" to allow it to exist as a separate political entity. The tribe was also forced to structure its petition according to criteria "recognized" by the United States: racial segregation, cultural *difference* (as measured against the Anglo-American "norm"), and economic and political subordination.

Furthermore, this evidence was required to be introduced through non-Indian "experts"—anthropologists and historians—in the language of those disciplines. The Mashpee themselves had oral histories rather than a written history, although they had, since the early 1600s, attempted to use European political and legal systems to advance their separate claims, resulting in some written documentary evidence of their existence. Moreover, the Mashpee had always welcomed outsiders to join the tribe, taking in other Indians, such as the Wampanoags, who had been virtually exterminated in wars with the Europeans, as well as escaped African slaves and Hessian soldiers. The obvious result was a tribe of mixed bloodlines, which still considered itself an "Indian Community." In the Anglo-American legal system, however, the Mashpee were penalized for maintaining a set of aboriginal traditions that did not conform to the dominant society's "racial" definition of community and society.[21]

As scholars have observed, the parties in the *Mashpee* case told two distinct stories. The defendant landowners told a story about "a small, mixed community fighting for equality and citizenship while abandoning, by choice or coercion, most of its aboriginal heritage." The plaintiff Mashpee Tribe told a story of cultural survival against incredible odds, pointing to the tribe's ability to keep the core of its Indian identity alive for over three centuries by "always attempting to control, not reflect, outside influences."[22] The line between these stories may seem faint, though the consequences are severe: it is the difference between "cultural adaptation," which promotes cultural survival, on the one hand, and "cultural assimilation," which results in cultural extinction, on the other. Both stories are implicated by the contemporary efforts of indigenous peoples to advance their claims for sovereignty and self-determination.

Native Self-Determination and the Global Context of Imperialism

The external characterization of Native American political identity under both domestic and international law has had a dramatic impact on Native communities. As Professor Gerald Torres notes, the regulation of groups within a polity "that has taken the individual as a foundation for its moral and political order assumes a special poignancy where cultures conflict irreconcilably."[23] American Indian tribes are defined by federal law as "domestic dependent nations," and thus their members may exercise rights different from those of other citizens. However, this characterization appears to conflict with the constitutional command for "equality" among citizens, leading to an increasing tendency to narrow the groups recognized as eligible for special status and the nature of the claims that may be asserted.

This tendency is perhaps best illustrated by the Native Hawaiian sovereignty movement. Native Hawaiians as a group do not qualify for most of the federal programs or statutory benefits accorded to American Indian tribes.[24] They may not seek federal recognition under the regulations that govern acknowledgement because those regulations are only applicable to "those American Indian groups indigenous to the continental United States."[25] Thus, Native Hawaiians remain largely without the special rights that pertain to federally recognized American Indian tribes, though they may share many similarities with these groups. This uncertain legal status, as well as the historical differences that underlie the status, have spurred Native Hawaiians to actively seek redefinition of their sovereignty.

The United States formally annexed Hawaii as a territory in 1898, after a group of Americans forcibly unseated Queen Liliuokalani in 1893 and replaced the Kingdom of Hawaii with a provisional government. The United States appointed a governor for the territory and set about suppressing Hawaiian traditional and customary institutions and cultural practices, including the Hawaiian language. After this annexation, the Native Hawaiian people were forced off their lands and precluded from using their traditional gathering areas. Many Native people were forced to move to urban areas to seek employment. In the crowded tenements of the cities, thousands of Native Hawaiians died of disease and other poverty-related social ills.

After Hawaii's admission to statehood in 1959, things did not improve for Native Hawaiians. Although the United States had set aside certain lands for long-term, low-rent leases by Native Hawaiians, the state of Hawaii, which had been entrusted with managing the lands, failed to allocate the majority of the lands. Today, Native Hawaiians number about 204,000 individuals, approximately one-fifth of the population of Hawaii.[26] Native Hawaiians are the most economically disadvantaged group on the Islands, suffering from high rates of incarceration, unemployment, poverty, and health problems. Native Hawaiians have lost their land base, for the most part, and have difficulty accessing their traditional lands for cultural and subsistence purposes.

While non-Native people often think of Hawaii as a playground for the rich and famous, Native Hawaiians have a much different perception. As outsiders flooded into Hawaii, driving up the real estate prices and marketing the Islands as a paradise for tourists, Native Hawaiians became increasingly alienated from their traditional lands. As Native Hawaiian activist Haunani-Kay Trask observes, "For Hawaiians, the inundation of foreigners decrees marginalization in their own land."[27]

Bereft of the protections that American Indians enjoy and marginalized in a society not of their making, Native Hawaiians have increasingly turned to international law for assistance. Self-determination is a foundational principle of international law that has particular relevance for the status and rights of Native Hawaiian people. Self-determination is a concept of international human rights law that speaks to the legitimacy of governmental regimes. The concept requires that the government should be created by the people it governs, and that the government should "be one under which people may live and develop freely on a continuous basis."[28] In the case of Native Hawaiian people, the government under which they now live was one that was forced upon them and has prevented their ability to survive as a distinct people.

However, there is a catch. The concept of self-determination under international law only applies to "peoples," defined according to Western European concepts of "statehood." In other words, while Native Hawaiians are certainly a distinct "people" in the common sense of the term—"a distinct community with its own social, cultural, and political attributes rooted in history"—they are not deemed to be a "people" in the technical, legal sense of the term.[29] The term under international law applies only to a set of "mutually exclusive communities entitled *a priori* to the full range of sovereign powers including independent statehood."[30] Because Native Hawaiians are considered to be an ethnic group residing in a state of the federal Union, international law does not consider them to be the type of group that is eligible for independent nationhood on the same basis as other "peoples."

Thus, the external characterization of Native Hawaiians defines them out of existence as a "domestic independent nation" under federal law and out of existence as a separate "people" under international law. They remain a distinct ethnic group with certain cultural attributes, which are protected to a very limited extent by federal and state law. But their political identity—as defined by external community—is predominantly that of "citizens." In fact, this ambiguous identity has now spurred contentions that special programs for Native Hawaiians may be constitutionally unsound because they do not share the same political status as Indian "tribes."[31]

Against this backdrop of domestic and international law, Native Hawaiians are fighting for recognition as a distinct people entitled to political and cultural survival. Their position appears to have been strengthened by a 1993 admission by Congress that the 1893 overthrow of the Hawaiian monarchy was unlawful.[32] In its joint resolution, Congress both apologized for the historical wrongdoing and pledged support for a "reconciliation" with the Native Hawaiian people. Although no concrete remedies are outlined in the joint resolution, it stands, nonetheless, as an admission of the wrongs perpetuated by Western imperialism. The legacy of Western imperialism has been the persistent victimization of Native people through colonialism and racism. Native people have been marginalized politically, economically, and socially by the dominant culture. As Haunani-Kay Trask notes, "imperialism" operates as a "total system of foreign power where another culture, people, and way of life penetrate, transform, and come to define the colonized society."[33] Thus, in asserting their distinct cultural and political identities, Native people are seeking to overcome this colonial history of domination and oppression.

Today, however, Native American people are part of a society that is seeking to atone for the sins of its past by adherence to constitutional ideals of equal protection and liberty. The common ideal of "citizenship" is trumpeted as a way to overcome the "differences" among constituent members of society, and separate treatment of different groups is viewed as inconsistent with the goals of post–Civil War America. In fact, even beneficial racial classifications (e.g., "affirmative action") are currently under attack as furthering the types of differences among citizens that are best forgotten. The approach of the majority society is to advocate "reconciliation" with Native peoples by stressing the moral logic of "unity" among citizens.

However, many Native people believe that the dominant society must recognize the separate identities of its victims and meet their claims to redress past and present injustice. Native activists argue that it is not enough to denounce the *practices* of the past (e.g., the massacre at Wounded Knee) that led to the present inequality of peoples while allowing the current inequality to remain in place. They argue that it is necessary to recognize the claims of Native people for cultural and political survival as separate groups in order to finally achieve justice. This movement to affirm "tribalism" is troubling to nations such as the United States because it raises the specter of ethnic Balkanization and political fragmentation.

Given the global tensions that have accompanied decolonization movements, commentators have expressed uncertainty about how the legal and moral claims of Native peoples should be adjudicated within modern pluralistic democracies such as the United States. It remains unclear whether indigenous peoples' claims to a separate cultural and political identity are inconsistent with the ideals of the "civic society" envisioned by American constitutionalism. The idea of the "domestic dependent nation" was intended to serve as an accommodation between the interests of Native people and those of the United States. However, many Native Hawaiian activists now argue against adopting the same status as American Indian tribes, asserting that this approach will limit their political and economic goals.

The next era will be one in which the nation-states must reach some accommodation with the Native peoples over the meaning of self-determination. If the Native peoples are to have a place in a civil society that is premised on equal respect, then it will be necessary to avoid imposing a choice between dual identities and citizenships. In other words, citizenship may be inconsistent with tribalism in a society founded upon racial, social, and economic stratification and difference, where "marginalization" is the only way to preserve the values of a different culture and political organization. However, citizenship should not be inconsistent with tribalism in a society that is founded upon mutual respect, trust, and recognition.

Notes

1. James P. Sterba, "Understanding Evil: American Slavery, the Holocaust, and the Conquest of the American Indians," *Ethics* 106 (1996): 430.

2. Elizabeth Grobsmith, *Lakota of the Rosebud: A Contemporary Ethnography* (New York: Holt, Rinehart, and Winston, 1981), 16.

3. John Geneisenau Neihardt, *Black Elk Speaks* (New York: Pocket Books, 1972).

4. Grobsmith, *Lakota of the Rosebud*, 16.

5. Ibid.

6. Iris Marion Young identifies the "five faces of oppression" as "exploitation, marginalization, powerlessness, violence, and cultural imperialism" (*Justice and the Politics of Difference* [Princeton: Princeton University Press, 1990]).

7. *Johnson v. McIntosh; Cherokee Nation v. Georgia; Worcester v. Georgia.*

8. *Ex Parte Crow Dog*, 109 U.S. 556 (1813).

9. For a concise description of the changing federal policies applied to Indian nations throughout the history of the United States, see Vine Deloria Jr. and Clifford Lytle, *American Indians, American Justice* (Austin: University of Texas Press, 1983).

10. See Robert A. Williams Jr., "Documents of Barbarism: The Contemporary Legacy of European Racism and Colonialism in the Narrative Traditions of Federal Indian Law," *Arizona Law Review* 31 (1999), 237–278.

11. For an excellent account of the events leading up to the 1973 occupation of Wounded Knee, see Robert Burnette and John Koster, *The Road to Wounded Knee* (New York: Bantam Books, 1974).

12. See Sterba, "Understanding Evil," 431.

13. See Felix S. Cohen, *Handbook of Federal Indian Law* (Charlottesville, VA: Michie, 1982), 3–27.

14. There is some exception to this rule for tribes that are recognized by state governments but not by the federal government, and which may enjoy some land rights protected by state law.

15. See *Joint Tribal Council of Passamaquoddy Tribe v. Morton*, 528 F. 2d 370 (1st Cir. 1975).

16. See Paul Brodeur, *Restitution: The Land Claims of the Mashpee, Passamaquoddy, and Penobscot Indians of New England* (Boston: Northeastern University Press, 1985).

17. 447 F. Supp. 940 (D. Mass. 1978).

18. *Mashpee Tribe v. New Seabury Corp.*, 592 F. 2d 575 (1st Cir. 1979), cert. denied, 444 U.S. 866 (1979).

19. 25 C.F.R. Part 83 (1997).

20. For an excellent discussion of this topic, see Gerald Torres and Kathryn Milun, "Translating Yonnondio by Precedent and Evidence: The Mashpee Indian Case," *Duke Law Journal* 4 (1990): 625–659.

21. Ibid., 639.

22. Ibid., 641–642.

23. Ibid., 657.

24. See James Anaya, "The Native Hawaiian People and International Human Rights Law: Toward a Remedy for the Past and Continuing Wrongs," *Georgia Law Review* 28 (1994): 311.

25. 25 C.R.F. 83.3(a); see also *Price v. State of Hawaii*, 764 F. 2d 623 (9th Cir. 1985).

26. Anaya, "Native Hawaiian People," 320.

27. Haunani-Kay Trask, *From a Native Daughter: Colonialism and Sovereignty in Hawai'i* (Honolulu: University of Hawaii Press, 1993), 2–4.

28. Anaya, "Native Hawaiian People," 323–324.

29. Ibid., 324.

30. Ibid.

31. See, for example, Stuart Minor Benjamin, "Equal Protection and the Special Relationship: The Case of Native Hawaiians," *Yale Law Journal* 106 (1996): 537–612.

32. Public Law 103-150, 103d Cong. (23 November 1993).

33. Haunani-Kay Trask, "Politics in the Pacific Islands: Imperialism and Native Self-Determination," in *Hawaii: Return to Nationhood,* ed. Ulla Hasager and Jonathan Friedman (Copenhagen: International Work Group for Indigenous People, 1994).

Chapter Nine

God, Us, and the World: Marginalization, the Role of Perception, and Conservative Christianity

Patrick D. Hopkins

Marginal Experience

To grow up an outsider. Seeing things from the periphery. Knowing not to assume that you will be respected or safe or treated well or given a say when you go "out there." Watching your culture and people mocked, caricatured, treated as villains or fools in films and books to entertain the majority. Perhaps not seeing yourself reflected in their representations of the world at all. Risking ridicule in standing up for your beliefs. Pushed to violate the values of your community and family. Pressured to assimilate. Endangered by the dominant culture, its law, and its government, which see you as a "special interest," an annoyance, a threat.

I know this feeling. I know this effect of marginalization. Growing up, especially in my later adolescent years, I lived my days in a community that dealt with this feeling constantly, a community that taught its children how to steel themselves against the way they would be treated by the world. My community fortified its children with love and self-esteem against rejection. It kept us safe while preparing us for being excluded, derided, ignored, or goaded to conform. It taught us what the world said our place would be and taught us not to accept it. We learned what it meant to be a cultural outsider, an experience both discouraging and empowering, painful and instructive. We learned how to resist.

But now, if you could be transported back to this community of my youth, this marginalized and disenfranchised culture, this minority that largely kept to itself and created its own literature, entertainment, and education to protest its erasure from mainstream society, what would you see? What skin, shape, houses, lifestyles would you find? Would you expect to see mostly white, able, middle-class, heterosexual, Christian Americans?[1]

For those writers, teachers, and activists who address issues of marginalization, particularly those associated with multicultural-ism, the notion that white, middle-class, heterosexual Christians would count as a marginalized group is absurd.[2] After all, they are the dominant culture; they are the ones who marginalize others based on race, class, religion, sexuality and who need to hear oth-ers' voices. But the story is not so simple. The concept of marginal-ization is widely used in political and cultural critiques, especially in feminist, multicultural, and postcolonial criticism. Although it is something of a nebulous concept and is used in different ways, generally it possesses at least two thematic functions. One, it is used to describe an actual sociopolitical state (broadly construed) in which a cultural group is marked for exclusion from mainstream society by both internal and external forces typically denigrating the group's differences as inferior and undesirable. Two, the con-cept is used to explain how social identities are formed in opposi-tion to dominant culture and how political resistance is often thereby motivated to overcome the marginalization and acquire a respected social "voice."

Although both of these uses are perfectly legitimate, they tend to assume a certain straightforwardness about the basic reality, structure, and motivational effects of marginalization. This is not to say that critiques that employ the concept of marginalization are simplistic; many are notorious for their complexity and exasperat-ing in their perpetual search for subtle and hidden prejudice. Nonetheless, such critiques often treat marginalization as a simple given, discoverable in the external facts of a group's existence. I, however, want to argue that (without ever ignoring the external facts) this approach is inadequate.

Taking as my example the case of conservative Christians—a community in which I grew up, was educated, and identified with—I want to address two things. First, I want to show how a group that many see as dominant, or at least as very powerful, can actually feel marginalized and be motivated by that fact.[3] Second, I want to show that we will understand marginalization and its ef-fects better by looking at the internal facts, that is, by looking at the belief systems of the individuals as they confront cultural externals, asking: What counts as being marginalized?

Marginal Culture

If the world hates you, keep in mind that it hated me first. If you belonged to the world, it would love you as its own. As it is, you do not belong to the world, but I have chosen you out of the world. That is why the world hates you. Remember the words I spoke to you: "No servant is greater than his master." If they persecuted me, they will persecute you also. (Jesus to his disciples)[4]

The particular church in which I grew up was not the main source of this sense of marginalization. That sense came from the nearby Christian high school I attended. My attendance there was primarily the result of proximity, not ideology—my parents and other relatives had gone to high school there, and so, automatically, did I. Whereas my church was doctrinally very conservative but culturally and politically more mainstream, the school was both doctrinally conservative (though in a different way) and culturally and socially self-contained.[5] In addition to its outreach work as a day school (which I attended), it was also a boarding school for children from broken homes, containing its own communal dining area, mail room, assigned faculty/staff housing, radio station, recreation, and work programs, and so ended up being a tightly knit community dependent both on outside donations and the dedicated work of its members.

Everything was very much dependent on the ideology of the community and its authorities.[6] With the few inevitable exceptions of contraband, more mainstream culture was supplanted by Christian entertainment, Christian education, and of course Christian worship.[7] Not everything was explicitly Christian, but nearly everything was filtered through a Christian cultural sieve (particularly material aimed at children and students), which excised anything considered against Christianity; and here is where the sense of a separate culture under attack comes into play.[8]

Television, movies, games, clothing, books, and so on that

were ruled out as against Christianity were not simply things that were *explicitly* anti-Christian, but rather things that expressed values or beliefs that were not consistent with conservative interpretations of Christianity.[9] As such, something did not have to be anti-Christian in the most literal sense to count as being *against* Christianity. Rather, something only had to present a point of view that did not agree with this particular conservative form of Christianity to be interpreted as dangerous and an affront to Christian beliefs and values.[10]

It is here, in beginning to see how a culture can *feel* marginalized, that it is crucial to understand the background belief system. The conservative Christians who ran this school were part of a religious culture and ideology that simply believes they have a direct line on the Truth. Taking the Bible as the literal, point-for-point, inspired Word of God and believing that the Holy Spirit would correctly guide their interpretations of that Word, they were certain that they knew the Truth, including God's plan for them and his plan for society.[11] They were also obligated to share this Truth with the rest of humanity, disabusing them of their false and ultimately damning beliefs. There is no relativism; and any pluralism that creeps in cannot impinge on any of the great Truth that they know.

Considering this background, then, it is eminently understandable how any belief, representation, or teaching that expressed some other view counted not merely as different, or even merely as wrong, but as *against* the Truth—and thus against them. These believers feel marginalized simply by the fact that others do not agree with their beliefs, the marginalization increasing as universal acceptance of their beliefs declines. It could not be otherwise. If a pluralist or multiculturalist were to argue that these Christians should "respect" other peoples' non-Christian beliefs, and respect here means something like not challenging those beliefs as wrong or allowing them to spread and influence society, then such respect is impossible.[12]

To refrain from accusing other belief systems of "false teaching" or to refrain from attempting to convert those other believers to Christianity *would itself constitute a violation of conservative Christian beliefs*, which is not simply a colonialist matter of conservatives wanting their own ideals to dominate but rather a serious altruistic and moral impulse. To be "respectful" of false beliefs in the pluralist sense is to ignore the eternal well-being of your fellow humans, to ignore their only hope of salvation.[13] The thoroughgoing multiculturalist, then, is in a real self-referential bind, unable to demand of conservative believers that they "respect" others' beliefs without in some way failing to respect the core (evangelical) beliefs of that culture itself.[14] The demand to accept the metaprinciple of pluralist respect is itself an attack on the core values of the conservative believer.[15]

In short, conservative Christians feel as though they increasingly live in an unjust world, a world that despises them, rejects the truth, and refuses to honor God by preaching religious and moral pluralism (along with other anti-Christian doctrines). They feel that they cannot even voice their core spiritual belief—that Christianity is the one true faith—without being attacked by pluralists. And keep in mind that for these people, God is not merely the abstract Creator, but a Person with whom they believe that they have a personal relationship. God is their Friend and Father, and they stand with their Friend and Father against a world of lies.

It is here that the term "the world" takes on a significant meaning. As it was used endlessly in the religious instruction I received, the world refers to the "out there," the human culture (and in particular American culture) dominated by humanist, secularist, relativist, hedonist, and materialist ideals. The world, and its popular insistence that people should find truth and love inside themselves rather than in God, was a constant danger to faith. It was an ever-present pressure that we had to resist so that we would not be corrupted by the world, which forever sought to undermine our faith. It is out of this notion that we regularly received the spiritual admonition "Be in the world, but not of the world."

The world crept up everywhere, in guises obvious and subtle. In its more obvious assault on and erasure of Christian values, the world presented no Christians of any consequence on television or in the movies (unless they were crazy fanatics). What was presented on television and in films and books, however, were humanist homilies on the virtue of "believing in yourself" (a favorite moral lesson of sitcoms) or endless violence and immoral sex praised as normal and liberating. During Christmas and Easter—two holidays where the Christian messages should have been strongest—the secular world erased the Christ from Christmas

(Xmas) and defiled the "true" meaning of the holidays with materialism, conspicuous consumerism, and suspiciously paganesque stories of reindeer, rabbits, and talking snowmen.[16]

Moving toward more subtle forms of anti-Christianism, Halloween was a greater threat than the Christ-less Xmas. And in this concern, there was some shift from the threat of the "world," which was mostly beset with humanism, to darker fears about diabolically motivated anti-Christianism, such as hidden forms of Satanism. Many of the faculty at my high school did not allow their children to celebrate Halloween in traditional ways because the holiday glorified the devil and his works and made Satanism attractive. Some families included among the list of censored television programs in their homes the old sitcom *Bewitched*, because it glorified witchcraft.

There were even more deviously concealed dangers. Rock music was feared to be filled with reverse-recorded Satanic messages that only backplaying could reveal. Secret Satanic communications were thought to be present in the logos and slogans of corporations (such as Proctor and Gamble's stars and moon and the supposed All-Day-Long-I-Dream-About-Satan message in the ADIDAS name). The United Nations was the first step toward a Satanic one-world government.

And while some of these anti-Christian messages and movements are more dubitable and salacious than others, the point to be gleaned immediately is that many of the conservative Christians I grew up with saw themselves in a struggle with "the world," whether predominantly a world of secular humanist values that constantly undercut Christian teachings or a world increasingly fallen under the sway of "powers of this dark world and . . . the spiritual forces of evil in the heavenly realms."[17]

All these reflections illustrate the background system of beliefs shared by many conservative evangelical Christians. This background, however, sets the stage for a full-blown sense of alienation and marginalization when confronted with two important cultural phenomena.

One, conservative Christians hold to the belief (more or less accurate) that the United States used to be a "Christian nation." Whether the dominant set of Christian beliefs had always been of the conservative evangelical variety is questionable, but in any case, Christian symbols used to be ubiquitous and basic Christian dogma so widely shared that it was reasonable to assume familiarity and often general agreement with Christian doctrine. Unlike many marginalized groups, therefore, the ideology of contemporary Christian conservatives is that the nation used to be moving in the right direction but has now fallen away from God, morality, and the Truth in the past forty or so years, deserting and mistreating Christians.[18]

There are several reasons why this sense of spiritual decline and the cultural sidelining of Christians arose, including the increased awareness of other creeds (through immigration, communication, transportation technology, and so on). But perhaps more important, we should point to the rise of a particular strain of so-called liberal and radical thinking that emphasizes the need to respect others' religious and cultural integrity while often laying the blame for years of oppression and injustice at the feet of the "dominant" culture—white, male, Christian. So, we have a general multiculturalism in the air that decenters (or tries to decenter) Christianity from its former position. And, as a matter of fact, the increased pluralism of U.S. society has reduced the prevalence of conservative Christianity and the assumption that this religion is a universal moral guide. Importantly, then, conservative Christians have experienced a decline of relative power and thus sense their situation as facing a loss.

Two, the very ideals and rhetorical strategies adopted by multiculturalists defending other cultures against the dominating forces of white, Christian, male society are themselves very much a part of American culture and intensely tempting. Thus, it is no surprise that a group who had formerly dominated the culture, who now feels displaced and marginalized by multiculturalism, would react against multiculturalism by adopting its methods.[19] In short, conservative Christians began to see themselves (in part) as a minority culture that was ignored, erased, and silenced by the new dominant humanist culture and that needs to fight for its right to be heard and respected. This is the direct political effect of perceived marginalization: the formation of a political unity, political response, and political identity centered around some special difference that the dominant culture neglects or disdains—in this case, faith and values.

Perhaps no rhetoric is so telling here as the now widely used phrase "people of faith." The phrase, which obviously parallels the political race-grouping phrase "people of color," began to be used by groups formed around a conservative Christian political identity who wanted to expand their concerns beyond that of Protestant evangelicals to other groups in the Judeo-Christian tradition, including Orthodox Jews and conservative Catholics. "People of faith" has become the latest name of a marginalized group that demands its rights.

Consider the informational statement at the web site of the Christian Coalition, probably the most powerful of the conservative Christian political organizations: "Christian Coalition was founded in 1989 by Pat Robertson to give Christians a voice in government. We represent a growing number of nearly 2 million members and supporters who believe it's time for people of faith to have a voice in the conversation we call democracy."[20] And later: "Today, Christians are playing an active role in the government again by uniting to stand up for families and people of faith. . . . Add your voice to the millions across America who have said it's time for people of faith to speak up and become involved."[21]

This emphasis on being heard is trumpeted elsewhere by former Christian Coalition leader Ralph Reed: "I've got news for our critics, the radical left, and yes, the liberal bureaucrats of the Federal Election Commission. We will not be harassed, we will not be intimidated, and we will not be silenced! We are Americans too!"[22] Such collectivizing speech serves to connect individuals and identify them politically with other groups who have been ignored or silenced by the dominant culture. However, while such rhetoric begins to mark conservative believers as wronged, the connection between the treatment of evangelicals and other groups unjustly discriminated against is often made in more explicit ways. According to Reed, "While some call for the inclusion of women, minorities, and Native Americans in a discussion of our history . . . they present a highly inaccurate portrait of our national past by ignoring the contributions made by people of faith."[23]

A Christian Coalition pamphlet carries the mistreatment idea further by showing a picture of a flag with a cross on it covered by muddy footprints, with the claim, "Christian Americans are tired of getting stepped on."[24] Even more explicitly, Coalition founder

Pat Robertson maintains that "in the 1930's . . . African-Americans in the South were classified by bigots as 'niggers,' not worthy of respect; today it is evangelical Christians who are considered by the liberal media as 'niggers' and not worthy of respect."[25]

Given that "people of faith" are now unified, grouped, and motivated by pluralist appeals to be given a voice, the political ground is set for organizations to begin providing that voice. The American Center for Law and Justice (ACLJ), which was founded by Pat Robertson, serves as a kind of legal defense collective for "people of faith." Its goal heralded as "defending the rights of believers" and trying to "undo the damage done by almost a century of liberal thinking and activism," the ACLJ is dedicated to "defending and advancing religious liberty" in such cases as "when students are told they cannot start bible clubs in their schools, or when their bible clubs don't receive equal treatment like other clubs, our legal teams spring into action to defend the student's rights." Given the moral work that the ACLJ performs, it is non-profit and relies "upon God and the resources He provides through the time, talent, and gifts of people who share our concerns over the erosion of our religious and civil liberties."[26]

Of course, the Christian Coalition and its offshoots are not the only organizations to represent people of faith, but the ideals, perceived enemies, and sense of marginalization of the general movement are by now well cemented in the cultural rhetoric. Focus on the Family, a multifaceted Christian and political organization headed by James Dobson, claims: "Secularism, moral relativism and self-centered individualism are prevailing ideologies that have put the family at risk. Rises in crime, substance abuse, out-of-wedlock births, abortion-on-demand, divorce, child abuse, etc. all point to the breakdown of the family and the unraveling of the social order." The organization wants to fight this deterioration by providing "a unique Christian educational community, that nurtures passionate and persuasive leaders who are committed to Jesus Christ" and by partnering with "colleges and universities in the development of the highest quality education program about the family and society from a Christian worldview perspective."[27]

The Family Research Council, connected to Focus on the Family, is more specific and actually maintains a public list of friends and enemies of the "family," specializing in listing the names of companies that promote immoral and anti-Christian values, such as domestic partnership health insurance programs for their gay employees.[28] Promise Keepers, a movement of mostly Christian men who want to restore the fabric of the family as intended by God and who are interested in "uniting men to become godly influences in their world," makes it clear that it "has no affiliation with the Christian Coalition" and "is not politically motivated in any way."[29] However, Bill McCartney, the leader of the organization, when speaking of the next major gathering the group plans on New Year's Day 2000, said: "Let's face it. Morality in this nation is spiraling downward, out of control. Christians are a minority, and we have to stand up and be counted."[30]

Although these sorts of statements help religious conservatives to unite around a political identity as a minority, to focus on the enemy of the world, and to draw on a long history of American antidiscrimination rhetoric, inevitably more extreme forms of rhetoric appear, which serve to magnify this sense of unity and identity through claims of group oppression. Robertson claims that "there's an incredible amount of religious bigotry . . . anti-Christian bigotry in the press," and "we must recognize also that the devil and his emissaries despise Christians. . . . Persecution is simply part of living as Christians in this world."[31]

Such claims, as with all claims of oppression, function best when the enemy is further specified. Robertson states that America "has become a largely anti-Christian pagan nation—and our government has become a weapon the anti-Christian forces now use against Christians and religious people."[32] A Christian Coalition press release maintains that "over the past three decades the Supreme Court has steadily suppressed religious speech, using the first amendment to defend censorship. The Court has usurped the constitution and converted it into a tool to drive religion from the public arena. But people of faith will have the last word. They want their religious liberties fully restored, and they will not be silenced."[33]

In response to criticism of his activity in Florida politics, Robertson draws the oppression idea out further: "Do you have a ghetto chosen to herd the pro-life Catholics and evangelicals into? Have you designed the appropriate yellow patch that Christians should wear on their garments to make certain that no Florida politicians become polluted by associating with them? . . . You are not going to get away with it. This is America, not Nazi Germany. Christians are Americans too."[34] This victimology makes its way down the political pipe. A campaign worker is quoted as saying: "Christians are the only people in this country who are persecuted. It's time we stand up and be heard."[35]

To summarize, then, many conservative, evangelical Christians have participated in a well-established political process. They have developed a new political identity based on their perceived marginalization and oppression, have organized political and cultural movements around that perceived outsider, second-class-citizen status, and fight in the social arena to be heard and treated equally.[36] They have, therefore, used a prevalent American political technique to establish their outsider-hood, in order to demand that they be taken seriously.

Conclusion: Marginal Theory

No doubt many multiculturalists (and others) who take recourse to notions of marginalization and oppression in their work and activism will simply say that this approach is wrong—wrong in the sense that white, male, heterosexual, middle-class Christians are not marginalized or oppressed as such; that such benefactors and purveyors of the dominant culture have no right to use such language; that this trivializes and further marginalizes those who have legitimate claims to being outsiders; that this is all a ruse to steal language and method in order to gain influence and reentrench white, male, Christian power.[37]

This sort of response, however, is problematic. On the one hand, it assumes that marginalization and oppression are objective political and experiential states that can justify political action, use of language, moral demands, and so on. Since these white, male Christians are simply not in such a state, their claims of victimhood are false; and they are unjustified and probably immoral in their demands. On the other hand, the concept of marginalization is also used in political and psychological analyses to explain political action, use of language, moral demands, and so on. Marginalization creates an experience, an identity, and often motivation.

The problem in the multiculturalist response is that it fails to see that marginalization is not meaningfully or usefully understood merely as an objective state. Since the harmful and politically motivating effects of marginalization are both to be found in the experience of being marginalized, it is important to understand the epistemic conditions under which this experience can occur. After all, if no one experienced marginalization, it would be explanatorily irrelevant as to whether they were or were not *actually* marginalized.[38] And it is not enough to say that the experience of being marginalized occurs when a group is actually marginalized (kept out of the political arena, silenced, discriminated against, and so on), because some sort of interpretive framework must react to those actual external conditions in order for them to be interpreted as marginalizing.

So, in order to understand the power of marginalization, we should recognize the importance of an antecedent belief system that interprets the objective features of social treatment and then move to inspect those beliefs.[39] Thus, we need to ask the following questions concerning a particular group of people and their belief systems: What actually counts as marginalization for them; what counts as "not having your voice heard, being silenced, ridiculed, persecuted, or attacked?" Only in asking these questions can we understand what objective features of the cultural and political environment will actually have marginalizing effects.[40]

In the particular case of conservative, evangelical Christians, what counts as being anti-Christian is often merely the expression of values that are opposed to or disagree with conservative Christian values or that fail to acknowledge or promote those values, especially in proportion as those expressions occur. In my own observation, for example, the mere existence of a positive gay character on television (such as Ellen) constitutes an "assault" on Christian values because it popularizes and "promotes" homosexuality. The fact that sectarian prayer was not led by teachers in the public schools counted as a government "attack" on faith by leading the country away from God. The existence of rock music whose lyrics talked in a normalizing way about extramarital sex was an "assault" on family and Christian values. Not putting a copy of the Ten Commandments in courtrooms, the existence of no-fault divorce laws, domestic partnership health insurance coverage in corporations—all of these things counted as anti-Christian. All of them also count as marginalizing.

At first, these claims may seem head-shakingly indigestible, but none of them is surprising if you actually examine the crucial components of the ideology itself. It is nearly built in. *If* you start with an ideology that claims to know the Truth and the Plan for society; that claims that anything which is not part of the Truth or Plan is against the Truth and Plan; that has a history of persecution for spreading the Truth; that has as an essential part of its mission the obligation to convert others to its beliefs and moral code; and whose adherents have experienced a decline in relative power, *then* it becomes clear how easily the sense of marginalization is produced in even a moderately pluralistic society. Unlike some identity groups, conservative Christians' ideological requirements cannot be satisfied without establishing a more pervasive dominance of conservative Christian ideas. In the presence of any resistance to this dominance, marginalization will continue to occur.

Although this chapter has dealt in part with the specifics of a particular religious identity, there are broader theoretical conclusions to be drawn that apply to any use of the term "marginalization." Namely, the social, political, and psychological effects of marginalization are best explained by the phenomenal experience of *feeling* marginalized rather than by some objective set of political features of marginalization. It is the experience of feeling marginalized that lends itself to identity formation and that motivates political activity. As a matter of explanatory method, we need to break the connection between the experience of marginalization and claims about who is and who is not really or genuinely marginalized.

While there may possibly be some more or less defensible definition of objective marginalization, this definition is largely beside the point if one wants to use the concept of marginalization to understand identity and politics. This supposition does not mean that empirical facts about such things as who is allowed to speak are not important. They are—but mainly because they tend to lead to the experience of feeling marginalized. I am not denying that empirical situation may *cause* a sense of marginalization; I think that it often does. However, empirical facts of political situation are less important in generating the *experience* of marginalization than empirical facts of ideological situation. The feeling of being marginalized depends on particular ideological commitments about what counts as having a say, as being free, or as being harmed.

If this position is correct, then at least two counterintuitive implications follow. One, it is possible for a powerful social group to feel marginalized or even oppressed and to be motivated by those feelings, especially in the face of a decline of relative power (the phenomenon I have examined here in the context of conservative Christian activists).[41] Two, it is also possible for a group who has no power or say not to feel marginalized and thus to have little or none of their identity or political activism shaped by the experience of being left out (such as fundamentalist Christian women, who may be compelled to remain silent in church and to submit to their husbands' authority, but who are still much more likely to feel marginalized and politically motivated as Christians than as women).[42]

To conclude, then, a phenomenally meaningful marginalization is felt, and therefore is largely in the perception of the experiencer and depends on what that experiencer believes about his or her objective situation. This realization simultaneously undercuts the moral power of marginalization as a kind of objective victim's badge of honor and yet expands the explanatory power of marginalization, demonstrating its amazing potency and centrality for political identity.

But what about the final nagging, unsettling questions? Are Christians really persecuted in the United States? Are they really victims who have their basic rights trampled upon? Isn't all this rhetoric just a classic manipulation of power by a still extremely influential group who cannot bear to lose total control?

It is very difficult to take seriously claims of victimization from a group who is wealthy, powerful, and massively overrepresented in political office. However, this reaction must be tempered by the theoretical conclusions drawn above. Given their particular religious and cultural commitments (which multiculturalists and pluralists are supposed to respect), conservative evangelicals do in fact feel genuinely marginalized and cannot be disabused of that notion merely by frustrated appeals to their perceived political power.

Perhaps the only appropriate response to these questionable claims of victimization is to engage in an analytical dialogue and critique that most multiculturalists do not seem to favor for any other group. Namely, since felt marginalization is relative to belief systems, we might demand that conservative evangelicals solidly argue for their belief systems and political goals and stop hiding behind the rhetoric of the oppressed. Feeling marginalized and claiming to be persecuted is not enough. Prove that you are oppressed. Prove that your rights have been violated. Prove that your beliefs have enough merit to be taken seriously. Prove that your demands do not unreasonably interfere with the lives, resources, and rights of others.[43]

Of course—and here is the deeply uncomfortable part for some multiculturalists—this kind of demand also involves that evangelicals actually defend their beliefs and justify the social treatment they think should be accorded to them. Their beliefs and practices are not simply unassailable givens. However, the demand to defend belief systems and justify any sort of special social treatment is one that applies to *all* groups. If it ends up that evangelicals are the only ones challenged to defend their beliefs, demands, and perceived marginalization while others are given a kind of pluralist immunity, then they really would have an objective mistreatment to point to.[44]

Notes

1. Of course, this is not all you would see. Not all were heterosexual, though all pretended to be. Not all were white, though in excess of 90 percent were. Not all were middle-class in the conventional sense of the term, though this characteristic was sharply mitigated by the fact that the community was essentially communal, with a central shared dining facility, assigned rent-free housing, paid utilities, and, in some cases, donated clothes and furniture from external supporters. This is all ironic, because while the members of this society were likely to rail against the immorality of communism, they participated in the closest thing to a small communist group I have seen directly.

2. Alternatively, if not multiculturalism, then some similar liberation-oriented movement.

3. The language here is difficult. To be dominant, to be in the majority, and to be powerful are all different things. Numerical minorities can be dominant; numerical majorities can be subordinate. As a purely objective matter, conservative Christianity is not the majority belief system of the United States. However, many of those who are suspicious and critical of conservative Christians definitely see them as dominant or, if not truly dominant, at least so powerful that no claim of being marginalized could be taken seriously. For my purposes here, the term "dominant group" will be somewhat imprecise but will certainly imply that the group is in no way without significant power and influence (regardless of its rhetoric).

4. John 15:18 (this and all following biblical references employ the *New International Version Study Bible,* henceforth abbreviated as *NIV*). In its footnote commentary, *NIV* succinctly defines "world" in this passage as "the human system that opposes God's purposes."

5. Though they shared similar racial, cultural, socioeconomic, and religious beliefs, my church and my school were significantly different. Theologically, my church disagreed strongly with the faith-only salvation and semicharismatic nature of my school's conservative evangelical beliefs — often to the point that they considered such beliefs to be false doctrines and the school's believers in danger of going to hell. Also, my church was much less political and much more likely to be active in the ordinary world. They were literalists and thought that no further revelation (through extrabiblical religious experience) was possible, so they did not believe in getting any personal messages from God or the Spirit. They also took seriously the idea that since Christians were ultimately going to heaven and this world would pass away, there simply was not much point in turning their faith into a political movement. Ironic, then, that my original spiritual conflict was being torn between two opposing conservative, literalist doctrines.

6. Many people supported the work that my school did with financial gifts, just like any organization. The school was considered a mission.

7. This is not to say that we did not learn about non-Christian things. However, all education got a conservative Christian emphasis. Even science classes were conservative Christian. Our biology class was dominated by a large section explaining why the theory of evolution was incorrect. We also had daily chapel meetings and required courses in Bible and Christian family living. For further information on this last class and its complicated content, see Patrick D. Hopkins, "How Feminism Made a Man of Me: The Proper Subject of Feminism and the Problem of Men," in *Men Doing Feminism*, ed. Tom Digby (New York: Routledge, 1998), 33–56. The notion of identity being addressed in this chapter is pervasive and certainly not limited to religion. Identity and culture formed around features of race, sex, ethnicity, or sexual orientation all lend themselves to subculture marketing, including bookstores, music, clothing, literature, television programs, movies, schools or departments, undergraduate majors, and so on. In the Christian context, there are Christian banks, Christian restaurants, Christian exercise videos, Christian video stores, Christian bowling leagues, Christian telephone companies, Christian lobbyists, Christian political groups, Christian therapists, Christian jewelry, Christian rock music, Christian rap music, Christian dances, Christian social clubs, Christian bumper stickers, Christian summer camps, Christian weight-loss programs, and so on. In short, like other groups, Christians want to be with "their own" in order to feel safe and to feel that their worldview is shared.

8. As one example, horror and romance novels were regularly rounded up and confiscated because of the Satanism and immoral sex they showcased. I remember a friend burning a Piers Anthony fantasy novel once he became convinced that it glorified Satan. This is not to say, however, that horror and romance themselves were verboten. In fact, there is a thriving publishing industry in both Christian romance novels and, surprisingly, Christian horror novels (mainly cast in narratives of the End Times and of good Christians fighting off demons).

9. I emphasize the conservative interpretation here, because even explicitly Christian materials would be ruled out if they disagreed with conservative doctrine. For example, openly gay people who considered themselves Christians would never have been permitted to speak at our daily chapel meetings, no matter how much they expressed their love for the Lord. In addition, even

explicitly Christian hard rock and Christian heavy metal were usually banned because such music relied on African percussion modes that were originally used in "devil worship" (one odd reason we were given).

10. It is impossible to get across the full sense of how my school worked in a single chapter, but I do want to guard against the misperception that some readers might have that this school was some sort of cultish compound. For the most part, students and faculty were ordinary people. There were no weird restrictions on hairstyles or cosmetics or clothes, though these were always watched to make sure they did not go "too far," exhibit rebelliousness, or express anti-Christian messages (so no shaved heads, miniskirts, or obscene tee shirts). The members of the community were very mainstream in some ways and would be indistinguishable from anyone else in the mall or at the movies (G- and PG-rated) unless you knew their particular beliefs.

11. These beliefs, of course, are held by many conservatives who nevertheless disagree with each other on doctrine and belong to a multitude of different denominations. In my own church, the particular belief that the Holy Spirit would intervene to help you correctly interpret the Bible through direct contact was considered a false doctrine that implied extrabiblical revelation, and thus I was admonished *not* to listen to what the preachers and teachers at my school taught but rather just "believe what the Bible taught."

12. This view is evident in what Christians call the Great Commission, which was the last direct message Christ gave to his disciples before ascending into Heaven: "Go into all the world and preach the good news to all creation. Whoever believes and is baptized will be saved, but whoever does not believe will be condemned" (Mark 16:15–16 [*NIV*]). I would like to point out that the admonition to baptize in this verse is one of the differences between my school and my church. My church took this passage literally and interpreted it to mean that physical baptism was necessary as an act of faith for salvation. My school interpreted this passage differently and believed that the act of believing itself was sufficient for salvation.

13. My thanks to Yolanda Estes for making this point clearer.

14. Although I am focusing on conservative Christians in this chapter, my analysis applies to all believers of whatever stripe whose ideological commitments share a similar structure.

15. Though I do not have time here to expand on this point, this is the reason that a truly complete cultural pluralism is logically impossible. Some belief systems cannot accept the pluralist metaprinciple because they are in fact obligated to do what they can to eradicate other belief systems. To give up that conviction is to change into a different belief system. Consequently, pluralism can never be a neutral position, because it must always be *against* some particular evangelical systems (religious or otherwise).

16. At my current institution, we are admonished to call the winter vacation the "holiday break" rather than the "Christmas break" so as not to offend non-Christians. This is the kind of thing that conservative Christians see as part of the erasure of Jesus from American history and culture.

17. Eph. 6:12 (*NIV*).

18. Justin Watson, *The Christian Coalition: Dreams of Restoration, Demands for Recognition* (New York: St. Martin's Press, 1997), 3–4, calls the dream of returning to the superior religious past "the restorationist thesis."

19. In many ways, this formerly dominant group has been itself muticulturalized by multiculturalism.

20. http://www.cc.org/about.html (27 November 1998).

21. Ibid.

22. Watson, *Christian Coalition*, 125.

23. Ibid., 141.

24. Ibid., 124.

25. Ibid., 135–136.

26. http://www.aclj.org/AboutA.html (27 November 1998).

27. http://www.family.org/welcome/aboutof/A0000080.html (27 November 1998).

28. http://www.frc.org/steward/ (27 November 1998).

29. http://www.promisekeepers.org/2a86.htm (27 November 1998).

30. Richard N. Ostling, "Man Trouble: Broken Promises?" *Time*, 13 July 1998, 63.

31. Watson, *Christian Coalition*, 40–41.

32. Ibid., 124.

33. http:www.cc.org/publications/ccnews/ccnews98.html#liberty (27 November 1998).

34. Watson, *Christian Coalition*, 137.

35. Ibid., 41. Watson describes several instances of this persecution, which were noted by Ralph Reed in a 1995 speech: "In Missouri, for example, a child caught praying silently over lunch was sent to a week-long detention. In Southern Illinois, a fifteen-year-old girl was handcuffed, threatened with mace, and shoved into the back of a police car. Her crime? Praying around the flagpole before school hours" (135).

36. I should point out that there are many conservative Christians who are not political in this way. They consider the constant concern about policy and Washington, D.C. to be a perversion of what Christian teaching is about. My own church was more of this opinion—Christianity is supposed to be about saving souls and knowing God, not fighting for school vouchers or against China trade policies or impeaching adulterous presidents.

37. Note that this last sort of criticism seems to assume that claims of marginalization and oppression are, in some sense, paths to power. This approach to gaining power, therefore, can be examined in the case of any marginalized group.

38. Obviously, this problem is familiar in the old question of whether someone can be oppressed without realizing it. Those who argue "no" to this question tend to see oppression as a phenomenal, psychological, perceived experience. Those who argue "yes" tend to see oppression as an objective political distribution of power and see those who do not realize that they are oppressed as victims of "false consciousness." The intuitive problem with the "no" side is that it implies that oppression is ultimately in the mind (so that, for example, happy slaves are not oppressed). The intuitive problem with the "yes" side is that it implies that oppression can be psychologically harmless (so that for example, blissfully contented housewives are victims in need of liberation).

39. This is not, of course, to say that belief systems are fixed and are not themselves alterable by objective external conditions. There very well may be a dialectical relationship. However, objective features of social treatment will always come up first against a belief system that is already in place, however malleable it may turn out to be.

40. This is not to say that a sense of marginalization cannot be produced

by the realities of political and cultural treatment. It certainly can. The point I am making here is less that marginalization needs a particular ideology to be produced or experienced and more that a particular kind of ideology can produce a sense of marginalization even without political mistreatment.

41. It is still a question as to whether a group can be objectively dominant and feel marginalized, but I suspect they can as long as they feel a decline of relative power or any threat to their power.

42. This implication is also relevant to the current debates over whether Muslim women are oppressed by having to wear the veil or whether African women are oppressed by being expected to submit to clitoridectomy. Those who hold to the notion of false consciousness for these women will obviously use the notion to describe fundamentalist Christian women as well. However, those who want to argue against the notion of false consciousness for Muslim and African women in the name of multicultural respect need to extend similar respect to fundamentalist Christian women or, if not, need to explain the difference.

43. This is not a demand that only comes from outside the evangelical community. I have heard conservative Christian activists, who fight against genuine religious persecution in such places as China and Sudan, rebuke American evangelicals for calling themselves "persecuted." These Christian activists have made the explicit argument that the U.S. evangelical experience of not being able to put up a nativity scene outside city hall does not compare with being imprisoned or shot to death for holding secret, peaceful Bible studies in one's basement.

44. I would like to thank those who were kind enough to read earlier drafts of this chapter and provide suggestions for how to improve it. I especially want to thank Perry Stevens, David Powell, Yolanda Estes, Jolene Jesse, and Bryan Smith.

Chapter Ten

On Evangelizing Children: Breaking the Cycle of Dogmatic Belief Systems

Wallace A. Murphree

The conventional way of grouping dogmatists is according to the content of their beliefs, such as those who are pro-this and those who are anti-that. This is a useful classification for many purposes since, for example, dogmatists holding one set of beliefs may reinforce unfair social barriers, while those holding another set of beliefs may not. However, another way that dogmatists may be classified is according to their motives for holding the dogmas they accept, irrespective of what the content of the beliefs may be. Specifically, I suggest that while many hold their dogmatic beliefs on the basis of self-interest, there are others who hold them from a sense of duty.

The overall purpose of this chapter is to illustrate the importance of this latter distinction in dealing with the ill effects of dogmatic belief systems. Since the concept of dogmatism based on self-interest seems clear on the face of it, I will attempt to elucidate the contrast between the two types by paying special attention to dogmatism based on duty. The approach will be, first, to look at one obvious and straightforward example of duty-based dogmatism in order to discern what its basic dynamics are and what the appropriate response to it is; and second, to show how these same dynamics are also at work in more common, complex, and subtle forms of such dogmatism (in, perhaps, a less conspicuous way). Since, no doubt, the most overt and straightforward form of dogmatism occurs in religion, it affords an instructive, introductory example.

Religious Dogmatism

The members of many conservative religious groups maintain that they have the duty to indoctrinate their children into the religion. Although the details of the indoctrination process vary, one common practice, reflecting one side of the distinction drawn above, involves convincing the child that the acceptance of the religion is in his or her own long-range best interest; another strategy, reflecting the side of the distinction that will be developed, works by exploiting the *good* child's desire to do the moral thing.[1] As will be explicated, I feel that this latter approach is especially appalling in that it tends to develop into a self-perpetuating form of "good-child abuse."

The type of religion in question might properly be called "evangelistic dogmatic exclusivism." In practice, all three labels may be unnecessary, since perhaps all religions that are dogmatic are evangelistic and exclusive as well; accordingly, I shall sometimes simply refer to them as dogmatic religions. However, the conceptual distinctions are necessary for the development of the points that follow.

First, a religion is *exclusive* if it teaches that any belief contrary to those of its own creed is literally false. Accordingly, any religion that embraces relativism or pluralism is "inclusive" rather than "exclusive."

Next, a religion is *dogmatic* if it teaches that it is a moral duty to accept the articles of its creed unconditionally. Thus dogmatists are exclusivists necessarily, but exclusivists are not necessarily dogmatists. The difference is that whereas the mere exclusivists believe the creed to be actually and absolutely true, dogmatic exclusivists believe the creed to be actually and absolutely true and also believe that it is a moral duty to accept the creed unconditionally. So, dogmatism brings an extracreedal, ethical belief to the religion.

For example, supposing the defining beliefs of Christianity to be those contained in the Apostles' Creed, then the articles of the creed would constitute the basic beliefs of the religion, and those who maintain that they are literally and absolutely true are exclusivists. But the Apostles' Creed does not contain an article to the effect that it (the creed) ought to be believed, and it is this extracreedal, ethical belief that is constitutive of the dogmatism.

Finally, a religion is *evangelistic* if it teaches that believers ought to try to win over nonbelievers to the religion. Perhaps all existing dogmatic exclusivist religions are in fact evangelistic to some degree or other, but in principle it is possible for such a religion not to be evangelistic at all. For the purposes of identifying evangelistic dogmatic exclusivism for this chapter, it is only necessary for the religion to be evangelistic in the minimum sense in which the parents believe it their duty to evangelize their own children. But to whatever the degree, the evangelistic feature of the religion, like the dogmatic feature, is also constituted by an extracreedal, ethical belief. In fact, it is the belief that "dogmatic exclusivism" ought be passed on to future generations.

Accordingly, being a Christian exclusivist consists in believing the Apostles' Creed (for example) to be absolutely true; being dogmatic is then produced by the addition of the ethical belief that it is a duty to believe the creed unconditionally; and being evangelistic is finally constituted by the addition of the further ethical belief that it is a duty to try to win others to the religion.

The particulars as to how such ethical beliefs enter the picture may vary, but the general structure that supports any such normative claims is that they are entailed by an ethical theory in conjunction with some factual belief or beliefs. A common source in conservative religions is a divine command theory ethics[2] in conjunction with certain factual claims about what God wills, such as: 1) It is our duty to do whatever God wills us to do [ethical theory]; 2) God wills that we accept the Apostles' Creed (for example) unconditionally [factual premise]; 3) God wills that we do all in our power to get others to do what He wills [factual premise]. Therefore, it is our duty to accept the Apostles' Creed unconditionally [dogmatic exclusivism] and to do all in our power to get others to do the same [evangelism].

Regardless of the details as to how the ethical claims are derived, it is to such religions that I call special attention, because I suspect that most who have not been reared in such settings fail to appreciate the strength of the moral grasp with which these religions bind their adherents.

Dynamics of Indoctrination

To those accustomed to freethinking, the view that one owes allegiance to any specific belief, or set of beliefs, may simply seem silly. In fact, this reaction is understandable, because one ordinarily comes to appreciate alternative positions by tentatively "entering into" them, and dogmatic religions cannot be visited this way. For example, a philosophy student may first provisionally and tentatively "be" a Platonist until the world becomes familiar from that stance, and then he or she may assume a Hegelian vantage point, and so on from perspective to perspective. Indeed, students are encouraged to do just this, for unless they are familiar with what it is like to be an "insider" of a position, their criticisms against it typically beg the question.

But, again, it is simply not possible to employ this method when it comes to understanding a dogmatic religion. Rather, to get "inside" a dogmatic religion at all requires absolute and permanent commitment, and, necessarily, one cannot do this provisionally or tentatively. One cannot decide to get "born again" for spring semester only. Of course, it is possible to make such a commitment and then later fall away, but to have made it at all is to have intended it for life at the time it was made.

Accordingly, a dogmatic religion is ordinarily considered only from the perspective of a fully committed member (from which its rejection is unthinkable), a question-begging outsider (from which its acceptance is unthinkable), or a backslidden sinner—an apostate. It is from the vantage point of a backslidden sinner in this respect that I attempt to convey something of what the insider's situation is like.

In this attempt, I think it will be helpful to trace in our imagination an indoctrinate's noetic history from childhood. So, suppose a good child, "Johnny," who is reared in a religiously dogmatic home. His parents have taught him its dogmas (e.g., the Apostles' Creed) and, in addition, have instructed him that it is a duty to accept them and to remain true to them no matter what. Of course, Johnny has no reason to doubt his parents, and, since he is a good child, he will make the commitment to embrace the beliefs for life because he truly feels that this is what he ought to do.

Furthermore, his parents and other adults of the religious community will nurture the commitment; they will forewarn him that there will be times when he will be tempted to doubt; and they will instruct him on how to keep the faith in the face of such temptations. They will warn him that from the sin of unbelief hardly any are able to return and caution him that this often occurs from the misguided attempt to be objective and fair. Accordingly, he is in-structed never to give the temptation to doubt a "fair chance" but to heed the scripture instead: "Trust in the Lord with all thine heart, and lean not to thine own understanding."[3]

So, given this general setting, Johnny is forced into a dilemma in which he can either make the commitment to accept the Apos-tles' Creed forever, or he can reject it by sinning; that is, the setting does not allow him to reject the creed without guilt, because essen-tial to the setting is the duty to accept the creed. As Johnny sees it, his only escape from the creed is to "sin" his way free; but since he is good, he will remain a believer instead.

Now, perhaps it will be countered that it would be no sin to abandon the youthful commitment if, for example, as an adult Johnny came to see it as unreasonable or as having been coerced; and this assessment certainly has appeal when looking at the situ-ation "from the outside." For example, if a freethinking adult hon-estly accepted a dogmatic religion one day and then came to see (or seemed to see) it was a hoax the next, it would certainly not be im-moral to reject it. Accordingly, the outsider would reason that if it would not be immoral for an adult to reject an adult commitment under these circumstances, then surely it would not be immoral for an adult to reject a childhood commitment if it should ever appear to be a hoax. However, although this point is compelling generally, it is not relevant to Johnny's case because he can never reach that state of seeing (or seeming to see) that the religion is a hoax with-out having already taken the path he believed to be wrong.

This conclusion should become clear by the imaginative con-struction of Johnny's situation when he first encounters the possi-bility of doubt. Suppose the thought "Jesus did not really rise from the dead and so the religion is a great hoax" has seriously occurred to Johnny for the very first time. What does he do with this dis-turbing idea? He has been forewarned that the time would come when he would be tempted to doubt and has been instructed to pray for sustaining faith on such occasions. So, if he is good—if he does what he believes he should—he will pray until the temptation to doubt is safely gone. Likewise, as he remains good, he will do the same with each successive temptation to doubt until they fi-nally come no more.

Thus, there is a great difference between Johnny's case and the scenario of the freethinking adult, because the freethinking adult can see (or seem to see) the hoax at once, but Johnny is programmed to go through an intermediate step of "being tempted to doubt." While the freethinker may doubt guiltlessly, Johnny can still only doubt by yielding to the temptation that he believes to be wrong. Of course, should he ever yield to the temptation, he then might honestly look back on the religion as a hoax and his earlier status as that of a victim. But, again, the only possible way for him to reach that state is through a path he believes to be wrong as he takes it.

Another avenue that might be recommended to Johnny "from the outside" is that of open and honest inquiry. Certainly this approach would be the proper recommendation when one feels unsure in other matters, and so it might seem appropriate here as well. But this route is also forbidden for Johnny, since his commitment is to accept the creed *unconditionally*. Accordingly, to submit it to the external test of evidence or reason would not only be to renege on the commitment of unconditional acceptance, but it also would amount to deposing the creed from its seat as the ultimate standard of truth and installing human standards in its place. Therefore, as long as Johnny does what he believes to be right, he can never allow anything to count as evidence against the truth of the creed.

It is possible, of course, that one should inquire openly and honestly in the matter and conclude on the basis of the research that the creed is literally true; indeed, many claim to believe precisely because they see it as the rational position, given all the evidence. In the terms developed above, such Christians are exclusivists but are not dogmatists; however, Johnny's situation is different, because he is committed to the creed as a dogma. This is a deep difference because, on the one hand, the ultimate appeal is to different touchstones, and, on the other, it is a difference with potentially far-reaching consequences: the one set of beliefs survives ever at the mercy of what new discoveries and changing circumstances may uncover, while the other is steadfast and secure.

For example, suppose a computer analysis of early New Testament texts reveals unexpected numerological codes that cryptologists decipher as pinpointing the location of records at some unlikely spot. Suppose further that archeologists explore the site and find a library detailing records of a Passover plot that fully describes how the crucifixion-resurrection-ascension hoax was carried out. Also, suppose it contains maps and burial records for Jesus, his mother, Mary, and a Roman soldier, and that skeletal remains are found at these exact places. Suppose, finally, that the community of professional archeologists agrees that one is indeed the remains of the historical Jesus (who had died at an old age), and that DNA tests on the three skeletons show Jesus to be the biological offspring of the other two.

Now here would be empirical evidence that conflicts with the basic articles of the Apostles' Creed: "Jesus Christ . . . was conceived of the Holy Spirit, born of the Virgin Mary . . . was crucified, dead, and buried; on the third day he arose from the dead, and ascended into heaven." Under these conditions, the nondogmatic Christian and Johnny would part company. The nondogmatist would either become an exclusivistic non-Christian, holding that the creed is literally false, or a nonexclusivistic Christian, holding that the essential truths of the creed are embedded in varying levels of metaphorical and allegorical meanings.

Johnny's beliefs, however, would remain unshaken since, as dogmas, they would be impervious to any such scientific claims. In fact, Johnny might feel a duty to organize think tanks, like the centers for creation science, to try to combat the rising heresy. After all, he has a perfectly good explanation—even one that should be anticipated—available to him, viz., that the powerful forces of evil fabricated the evidence to make the truth look like a lie in order to deceive those who would "lean to their own understanding."

Furthermore, what has been said of empirical evidence also holds for conceptual reasonability. For example, if the evil in the world became significantly greater so that every human being suffered the unrequited evils of Job and every animal lived its days in excruciating torment, Johnny's faith would never falter because he is good, and he has made a commitment to accept the creed unconditionally.

Poor Johnny; his whole intellectual life has been kidnapped because he refused to do what he believed to be wrong, which is the nature of the child abuse that was charged earlier.

The Dynamics of Self-Perpetuation

But the kidnapping of Johnny is not the end of the matter. Rather, the evangelistic character of the religion requires that Johnny impose the same conditions on his children that were imposed on him. So, conforming to the religion's expectations, he marries someone of the same commitment, and they have children of their own. Furthermore, since they are good parents, they are conscientious about their child-rearing responsibilities and, accordingly, instruct their children in the beliefs and duties of the religion. Moreover, "Brother John," his wife, and other adults of the religious community now nurture the children's commitments, warn them of false doctrines, instruct them on how to overcome temptations, and so on. As the children mature in the faith, the religion is secured for another generation. (In general, one survival technique such religions employ is that of using the indoctrinates of one generation to indoctrinate the good children of the next.)

It has been merely for convenience that I have used Christianity in the examples above, for the charge is not against exclusivistic Christianity but against evangelistic dogmatism wherever it occurs. Moreover, this mechanism need not be limited to existing religions, since any new cult or belief system can employ it once it gets the one-generation start.

For example, should a couple take a group of infants and inaugurate a new civilization on another planet, these nurturing and caregiving adults will naturally receive the trust of the children. When the adults give basic creedal articles ("a, b, and c") along with ethical precepts ("it is a moral duty to believe 'a, b, and c' unconditionally, and to teach others to accept them so") the good children, believing it to be their duty, will then accept the beliefs and faithfully deliver them, in turn, to the next generation. If as children the citizens are all good, and if as adults they are competent indoctrinators, then everyone on that planet will be forever bound to these beliefs. Again, the charge is not against the content of "a, b, and c"—whatever they are—but against evangelistic dogmatism as a technique for subjugating the population to them.

Best Response

It seems that outsiders typically try to defeat what they see as the evils of dogmatism by challenging (or ridiculing) the creedal beliefs of the indoctrinates. However, if the above analysis holds, the most that can possibly be accomplished by this approach is to persuade the indoctrinates to do what they believe to be immoral. Thus, given Johnny's indoctrinated perspective, when we try to convince him his creedal beliefs are false, we are, in his eyes, trying to persuade him to do wrong. So, even if we thought we could persuade him, it would seem improper to try for at least three reasons.

First, it would require extraordinary circumstances to justify any attempt to persuade someone to do what he or she honestly believes to be wrong. Second, as has been pointed out, it is not the exclusivism—i.e., it is not the set of creedal beliefs—that is the problem at all; rather, it is the dogmatism and the evangelism. Accordingly, it is these policies that rightfully stand to be challenged. Third, although indoctrinates are not morally free to question the creedal beliefs, they are morally free to question the policies of dogmatism and evangelism because they never made a commitment to accept these as dogma.

Rather, in the common case outlined earlier, suppose they accepted dogmatism and evangelism on the basis of the ethical beliefs that prescribed them as duties; further, they accepted the ethical beliefs because they are entailed by an ethical theory together with some factual claims as to what God wills. Since the indoctrinate is morally free to question any noncreedal claim, the beliefs supporting dogmatism and evangelism can all be questioned in complete moral innocence. Furthermore, if the ethical theory or factual beliefs were successfully challenged, then the ethical precepts, as well as the dogmatism and evangelism they impart, would be left without credit.

Of these, the challenge to the divine command theory does not appear helpful in the issue since not all evangelistic dogmatic exclusivists subscribe to it in the first place. That is, there are many Christians who do not hold that it is God's will that *makes* certain actions our duty; these Christians believe instead that God wills these actions *because* they are our duty, and this seems to be the Christian alternative available to the divine command theory. But in either case, whatever God wills *is* our duty—one way or the other—and this is sufficient, when conjoined with the factual claims, to yield evangelistic dogmatic exclusivism. (Incidentally, God's existence cannot be challenged in this context since it is an article in the creed: "I believe in God, the Father Almighty . . .")

Accordingly, the options left to challenge are the factual claims as to what it is that God wills. That is, it may be seriously asked of both of these claims whether God *really* wills what is alleged, or whether human beings are ever in a position to know God's will on such matters. Instead of being forbidden, these kinds of questions should be taken with all seriousness by evangelistic dogmatic exclusivists, because their goal is to obey God's will (whatever it is) rather than dogmatically to retain this or that view as to what God's will really is.

In addition, questions specifically relevant to each of the factual claims may be appropriately raised. For example, the support for the ethical precept undergirding dogmatism is the factual claim that God wills us to accept the basic creedal articles unconditionally, but the compliance with God's alleged will in this matter seems to necessitate dishonesty. That is, it seems that honesty demands that the acceptance of contingent propositions be conditioned by any known facts of the case, while the above claim is that God wills that the contingent creedal propositions be accepted with complete disregard for any known facts, i.e., that they be accepted unconditionally. Therefore, the question as to whether God would *really* will an exception to our basic sentiments of honesty in the case of the creedal propositions should constitute an open and important concern for the serious dogmatist.

Furthermore, the support for the ethical precept enjoining the indoctrination of children is the factual claim that God wills that we do all within our power to get others to accept the creedal articles unconditionally. But if the above criticism has merit, this precept would enjoin us to train children to be dishonest, which surely would be an important concern for any conscientious parent. In addition, there are numerous independent challenges that might be raised about this second claim that are very serious. Three samples of such questions are offered below.

When rival evangelistic religions indoctrinate their children, it is condemned as brainwashing, although the effective dynamics are the same. So a question that seems worthy of consideration is whether God would will that the very technique used to brainwash good children into false religions should be the same as the technique used to perpetuate the true religion.

It is theoretically possible that science could develop a pill (or hypnotists perfect a technique) that would produce the very same mental-spiritual-behavioral pattern in the child that otherwise would have been produced by parental indoctrination. Then the question arises as to whether God really wills the parental indoctrination of children when there seems to be no morally significant difference between it and the determination of the same effect by chemotherapy or hypnosis.

It seems possible that God wills to lead children to see cogent and authentic reasons for accepting the basic religious truths in his own season, and, if this is the case, then the early parental indoctrination of these truths would preempt God's perfect timetable. Accordingly, to recognize this possibility is to call into question the belief that God wills that parents indoctrinate their children, a consideration that every conscientious indoctrinate surely should take seriously.

So, again, I propose that the evangelistic dogmatist can question these factual beliefs as to what God wills with all moral freedom. This inquiry, I propose, is not just a "logical space that looks acceptable on paper" but a real moral space in which indoctrinates are free to operate. Thus, although they cannot directly question whether Jesus was actually resurrected (because they unconditionally accept the creed that says so), they can seriously question whether God would will dishonest belief or will that children be indoctrinated, since these contentions are not included in the creed. Accordingly, this questioning marks the area mentioned earlier from which I propose that the challenge to evangelistic dogmatic exclusivism can be appropriately mounted.

It is easy to suppose the lines of communication with evangelistic dogmatic exclusivists to be closed on all serious matters; but, if the above analysis is correct, they are only closed concerning the creedal beliefs. Moreover, since the evils of evangelistic dogmatism are consequences of its noncreedal beliefs, the indoctrinates are free to question these with full philosophical and theological rigor. In fact, since the indoctrinates are the good people, they likely have agonized over such issues already, and they should be expected to be remarkably earnest in any continued exploration of them. So then, having no vested creedal interest in retaining any factual claims as to what God wills, they should be fully open to whatever force any challenging argument may present.

Furthermore, if they should become convinced by challenging arguments, it seems clear that the moral force of their commitment to dogmatism and evangelism would thereby be annulled. That is, again, the indoctrinates were never unconditionally committed to dogmatism and evangelism; rather, their absolute commitment was to do whatever they believed to be their duty. So if they no longer believe it their duty to accept the creed unconditionally or to indoctrinate others to accept it unconditionally, this realization should break the cycle of religious child abuse. Moreover, to the extent that any challenging arguments should shake even the indoctrinates' confidence in the factual claims—and, by extension, in dogmatism and evangelism—it seems the abusive character of child-rearing also might thereby be correspondingly ameliorated.

It is important to remember that the exclusivism of believers need not be affected at all by their abandonment of dogmatism and/or evangelism. Rather, they might well continue to hold the articles of the creed to be literally and absolutely true, just as before.

Real-Life Complexity

In considering the religious setting above, the aim was to explore a simple form of dogmatism in the hope of discerning a basic pattern that is common to, but perhaps less obvious in, the more common and complex forms of dogmatism. However, the analysis of even this simple form has been oversimplified in various ways.

First, as was announced from the beginning, the form of indoctrination that works by exploiting the child's self-interest motive has been systematically ignored in the analysis, which may suggest the distorted picture that there are good children who are motivated by duty, and the rest who are motivated by self-interest. But, in fact, children are usually taught both that they should accept the faith because it is a moral duty and also because it is in their own long-range interest; and so it would seem likely that both motives are operative in ordinary cases of indoctrination. Accordingly, the analysis above is intended to describe those cases in which the motive of duty is the dominant, or decisive, one.

Second, the matter was presented above as if the indoctrinate would either retain or reject the creedal beliefs in toto, when it is possible that some creedal beliefs should be rejected while others are retained. Likewise, it is possible that the indoctrinate should reject one belief after another through an extended period, so that he or she would retain progressively fewer—and perhaps finally none—of the dogmas.

Similarly, the self-perpetuating character of indoctrination was presented as if the children of any generation were chained to the beliefs of the parents, and that the perpetuation could only be interrupted by breaking one of the all-or-nothing links. However, as with the individual case above, it is possible for the bond to weaken little by little across the generations, as fibers in the dogmatic tie give way one by one, or few by few.

But the above analysis seems to hold for these progressive cases as well. That is, either the dogmas are abandoned by successive little sins of doubt (which eventually add up to the ultimate sin of unbelief if the process is not checked at some point), or the original factual claims are revised little by little so as to require a progressively dwindling number of dogmas. For example, the original factual claim might be emended to become: "God wills that I believe all the articles of the Apostles' Creed except this one, or these two." (Perhaps this is what happened when earlier Christians relinquished the flat-earth theory, for example.)

Third, the above analysis presented only the spiritual or supernatural beliefs of religious dogmatism, whereas in actuality many such religions include dogmatic commitments to such social movements as racism, sexism, clanism, and "lifestyle-ism" as well. For example, Christians who take the collective assertions of the Bible (rather than the articles of the Apostle's Creed) as their dogmas frequently claim that these imply that one race, gender, nationality, or lifestyle is intrinsically superior to the other(s). Accordingly, anyone indoctrinated into such a position would necessarily think it immoral *not* to be racist, sexist, and so on. For example, if a good child were reared in a Christian Ku Klux Klan community, he or she would sincerely believe that egalitarianism is contrary to the sacred ranking established by God.

It seems, however, that the above analysis covers such complex cases as well. That is, here the indoctrinate likewise can abandon the bigotry only by doing what he or she believes to be wrong or else by rejecting some presupposed factual claim or other. For example, the indoctrinate may come to question whether God really wills all the assertions of the Bible to be accepted unconditionally, or whether God wills the Ku Klux Klan's interpretation of them to be the accepted one.

Secular Dogmatism

When racism, sexism, and so on abound in secular settings, the situation is significantly different in many respects. Nevertheless, I propose that the deep, general dynamics of these settings are the same as those of religious dogmatism in many instances.

First, such views are exclusive, for they hold it to be literally and absolutely true that "our ways and our kind are superior to all other ways and kinds," and, perhaps, "one should not relate to inferiors on an equal status." This might be called the Bigot's Creed, for it, or something similar, constitutes the basic beliefs of such orientations.

Next, such views are dogmatic since they hold the ethical belief that the Bigot's Creed should be accepted without question and with disregard for any evidence that might appear to the contrary. However, unlike religious dogmatism—but like stereotyping generally—such bigotry does not acknowledge the nonempirical character of its position; rather, any negative data that cannot be explained away are automatically taken to be isolated exceptions to the rule that is valid generally.

Finally, it is evangelistic in that it subscribes to the ethical claim that adherents ought to try to get others to accept the view. Especially such dogmatists claim the duty (or at least the right) to pass the bigoted beliefs along to their children so as "to keep our kind pure, and preserve our ways for posterity."

As with religious dogmatism, there seem to be various ways that these ethical beliefs may enter the picture. I suggest that an implicit social contract theory might be a prevalent ethical premise for such settings. That is, at some point, children become aware that the care and nurture formerly taken for granted come instead with strings attached; in other words, the children realize they are expected to accept the parents' values in return for the many benefits they receive. Then, since they continued to accept parental benefits even as they are fully aware of the parental expectations, they feel they have made an implicit commitment to abide by their parents' will in the matter. Moreover, parents are notorious for reinforcing such feelings by making children who contemplate deviation feel guilty: "For all we've sacrificed for you, you owe us this much."

Accordingly, the secular structure parallel to the religious setting can be summarized as follows:

(1) It is our duty to live the way our parents brought us up [ethical theory].
(2) Our parents reared us to believe the Bigot's Creed unconditionally [factual premise].
(3) Our parents reared us to bring up our own children in the Bigot's Creed [factual premise].

Therefore, it is our duty to accept the Bigot's Creed unconditionally [dogmatic exclusivism] and to rear our own children in this creed [evangelism].

Now, as with the religious child, the secular one will likely be motivated to comply with these injunctions both from self-interest and duty. That is, children reared in such settings know it is in their own best interest to comply, because otherwise they risk rejection by the family (and ostracism from familiar social circles) as well as an often heavy material loss. In addition, the good children will feel a moral duty to accept the Bigot's Creed because of the commitment they have implicitly made.

So, suppose a good child, "Jenny," who is indoctrinated into such a view, and consider how it might be possible for her ever to leave it. I propose that her situation is quite similar to Johnny's in that she is also put into the dilemma in which she either can comply by accepting the creed forever or reject it by violating her own ethics; thus, the very setting does not allow her to abandon the creed without guilt. Also, both instances of the indoctrination work by exploiting the strong sense of duty of these good children and so, no doubt, either Johnny or Jenny would have been a successful indoctrinate reared in the other's setting.

Accordingly, Jenny can never (seem to) see in a flash that the creed is false and innocently abandon it as one who first came to embrace it as an adult might, for the acceptance of her creed—like

Johnny's acceptance of his—has been imbued with an obligatory character by the indoctrination setting. That is, she cannot merely reject the creed if it suddenly appears mistaken, for she can only reject it by yielding to the temptation to doubt it, and she believes this choice to be immoral. Furthermore, even if she could be unbiased in her own investigation, she—like Johnny—could never submit her dogmas to an impartial test because that would be to go back on her tacit commitment to hold them without question.

Further, not only must she select her significant life's partner from the approved race, caste, and gender, but she also must select one who accepts the same bigoted values. Otherwise, it would be an outright betrayal of those who loved and nurtured her and provided her the many opportunities she has, and that would be a violation of the principles to which she has sworn to be loyal. And Jenny will not do that, because she is good. She has a strong sense of duty to the family legacy, and she will never allow its image to be tarnished.

Poor Jenny; her life has been kidnapped, too, because she refused to do what she believed to be wrong. Moreover, as in Johnny's case, she will become a link in the self-perpetuating chain that binds posterity to the cause. She will rear her own children to be true to the family legacy as well because she is good and she sees this as her duty, thus securing the bigotry for another generation. So, like dogmatic religions, part of the survival technique of such bigotry is that it has its indoctrinates impose the same conditions on their good children that were effective in their own indoctrination.

As in Johnny's case, outsiders often try to defeat the evils of Jenny's form of dogmatism by challenging her creedal beliefs. Also, as in Johnny's case, this challenge seems improper, because it is the attempt to persuade her to do something that violates her sense of ethics; it is the supporting beliefs, rather than the creedal beliefs, that are the root cause of the problem; and Jenny is morally free to question the supporting beliefs.

Supposing the prevalent case outlined above, Jenny's dogmatic and evangelistic bigotry is based on ethical injunctions derived from an implicit social contract theory ethics together with the two factual beliefs that her parents will that she accepts the values of bigotry and that she indoctrinates her children to do so as well. So, paralleling Johnny's case, although she believes these tenets to be true, she is morally free to question them because she is not committed to them as dogma; rather, she is committed to the secular dogmatism and evangelism on the basis of them.

However, it seems that the details of her case would differ from those of Johnny's at this point. Specifically, it will be recalled that the challenge of Johnny's ethical theory would seem not to ameliorate his situation, whereas the challenge of the factual claims of his case (as to what God really wills) seemed quite promising. However, Jenny knows the factual claims of her case (as to what her parents really will) are true, and so her only option is to question the ethical theory. However, unlike a successful challenge to the divine command theory, it seems that a successful challenge to the social contract theory would clearly leave the ethical precepts enjoining Jenny's bigotry without support.

Therefore, in general, I propose that it is appropriate to conceive of Jenny's and other such cases of secular dogmatism as instances of the same dynamics that are operative in Johnny's religious dogmatism; however, as was mentioned earlier, these operations seem less distinct in secular settings.

For one thing, although there are religious hypocrites who act as if they believe the dogmas when in fact they do not, there probably are many more who act as if they are bigots when they do not actually believe that their race, gender, and so on are superior. Instead, they simply take advantage of their privileged status in a basically bigoted society. Since there is ordinarily much more to be gained by assuming a bigoted role in a basically bigoted society than there is by assuming a religious role in a basically nonreligious society, it is understandable that more should exploit such a possibility. As a result, it is likely to be more difficult to distinguish the genuine dogmatist from the hypocritical impostor in the secular setting than in the religious one.

In addition, it seems that the distinction between the motive of self-interest and the motive of duty is much less clear in the secular setting than in the religious. In the religious setting, one's duty is quite independent of any past or anticipated benefits, while the self-interest motive is tied exclusively to anticipated benefits. However, in the secular setting, the duty is derived from benefits received, while the self-interest is tied to anticipated benefits. Accordingly, it would seem easy for the secular agent to conflate past and future benefits into a homogeneous continuum and rarely become aware of the ethical distinction.

Furthermore, while the call to the faith is absolutely central in the religious setting, it may be that the call to bigotry is only one among many calls in the eclectic patchwork of secular family values; that is, secular parents may claim their children owe them certain vocational, educational, recreational, and political commitments as well. Accordingly, as such "duties" multiply and diversify, the obligatory force of any given one may be lessened.

Finally, while Johnny feels a duty only to one God, Jenny may well feel conflicting duties to different people. For example, her parents may have some divergent values, and, given her ethical theory, she might well feel at least some loyalty to those of any race, caste, or lifestyle whose support and kindness she has accepted; this loyalty may then have the effect of dulling what otherwise would be a very keen sense of duty to one value or another.

Still, I insist that the same general dynamics are at work in her case as in Johnny's, although they may be spread half-hidden through multiple layers of other considerations. But if the analysis of these dynamics seems too Procrustean, I will be content with a wider claim, viz., that some who embrace and propagate secular dogmatism, like many who embrace and propagate religious dogmatism, do so because they have been indoctrinated in such a way as to feel that it is their duty to do so, and they simply are doing what they believe to be right. Also I propose that not only the most effective but also the most appropriate challenge to both positions is one mounted against the claims presupposed in the indoctrination process rather than one directed against the content of the dogmatic beliefs.

Conclusion

Whether in religious or secular settings, it is exclusivism—rather than dogmatism or evangelism—that draws the boundary that marginalizes, and, as mentioned earlier, I have no quarrel with exclusivism as such. Of course, I think many exclusive beliefs to be incorrect, but, when this is so, I think the opposite exclusive beliefs to be correct; so, the fact that a belief may be incorrect is no fault of exclusivism. Indeed, I think that even holding an incorrect belief is not such a serious matter in itself and perhaps is not such a serious matter at all if it can be corrected before it results in harmful consequences.

For example, I suggest that enlightened parents would not be appalled if their child returned from day care believing literally that the earth is round, there is a Santa Claus, and it is better to be of "my" gender (race) than the other, even though these parents firmly believe the latter two claims to be false. Rather, they would assume that as the child matures the authority of day-care lore will weaken and the false childhood beliefs will tend to become eliminated under the light of observation and reason, while the true ones will remain. Perhaps they would fail to see how the early belief about gender or race is *inherently* worse than the belief about Santa Claus (although they would recognize its potential for harmful consequences to be much more immediate and severe). They also might fail to see how the untested true belief based on the same authority is that much superior, if superior at all, to the false ones; and I concur with this point of view.

I propose the real culprit, instead, to be the dogmatism that would secure the early belief about gender or race by making it immune to the light of observation. Of course, such dogmatism can begin quite early as children realize it is in their own best interest to preserve the marginalizing boundary. But, again, it is the dogmatism rather than the exclusivism that turns the mere mistaken belief into a controlling ideology; likewise, I propose that it is the evangelism rather than the exclusivism that helps turn individual cases of dogmatic bigotry into powerful social movements. So, although evangelistic dogmatism is not the origin of marginalizing boundaries, it seems clear that it is a vehicle for securing and perpetuating whatever boundaries the exclusive beliefs first draw.

When contemplating marginalization, we tend to assume that those who accept it are always members of the privileged side of the boundary, and, no doubt, this assumption is correct for those motivated by self-interest. For example, selfish religious dogmatists deliberately assume a temporary self-marginalized status on earth for the purpose of gaining a place of high citizenship in the kingdom hereafter, in which "the world" will suffer eternal marginalization. Likewise, selfish secular dogmatists, doubting any kingdom beyond, clearly attempt to preserve and strengthen their privileged status in this one life that they have.

However, the theme I have tried to develop is that not all dogmatism is motivated by self-interest, and, if this premise is correct, there is no reason to believe that only members of the privileged side of the boundary embrace the dogmatism that secures it. For example, dutiful religious dogmatists would still assume their self-marginalized status on earth even if they believed there were no kingdom beyond. Likewise, dutiful secular dogmatists would still embrace the boundary even if they knew it would not be in their own self-interest. In fact, I submit that there are many such dogmatists today; that is, I believe there are those who truly would like to be full-fledged members in a multicultural society or would like to experiment in alternative lifestyles, but who refrain because they feel an obligation to protect their family from the perceived shame it would bring. They feel it their duty not to break their bigoted parents' hearts.

Accordingly, I contend that grouping dogmatists together solely on the basis of the content of their dogmatic beliefs overlooks an all-important distinction. Furthermore, I maintain that the failure to recognize this distinction not only amounts to an inherent conceptual confusion, but that it also has dire consequences, especially when dogmatic bigotry is concerned. For one thing, a program or policy that might be effective promoting egalitarianism against bigotry based on self-interest would be completely irrelevant to bigotry based on duty; conversely, the kinds of challenges suggested above against bigotry based on duty would be completely irrelevant to any bigotry based on self-interest.

In addition, I submit that it is unfair to dutiful dogmatists to group them into the same moral category with selfish dogmatists on the mere basis of the content of their creedal beliefs, since they lead radically different types of ethical lives. Finally, I suggest that the failure to recognize the distinction between the two forms of dogmatism is a conceptual confusion, and that our failure to act on the distinction is both unwise and unjust.

Notes

1. The issue as to whether one may rightly accept or teach a view based on such prudential considerations has long received wide attention. Blaise

Pascal, William K. Clifford, and William James set forth its classical treatments; see Pascal, *Pensées and Other Writings*, trans. Honor Levi (Oxford: Oxford University Press, 1995); Clifford, "The Ethics of Belief," in *Lectures and Essays*, 2d ed., ed. Leslie Stephen and Frederick Pollock (New York: Macmillan, 1986); and James, "The Will to Believe," in *The Will to Believe and Other Essays in Popular Philosophy* (Reading, PA: Longmans, Green, 1987).

2. Theists hold that whatever God wills, and only that which God wills, is morally obligatory. Proponents of the divine command theory, however, hold further that it is God's will that makes an action, or type of action, obligatory; and there are no moral constraints on what God may will. For a contemporary defense of this view, see Philip Quinn, *Divine Commands and Moral Requirements* (Oxford: Clarendon Press, 1987).

3. Prov. 3:5 (King James Version).

Chapter Eleven

Confessions of a Refugee:
My Life As a Loner/Rebel/Renegade

Yolanda Estes

"To the Reader"

The very banality of the lonely childhood inhibits a serious discussion. The universal figure of rebellious youth seems trivial. Where does one draw the line between the renegade and the ruffian? Nonetheless, I ask your indulgence in considering the loners, rebels, and renegades. I hope that by "obtruding on your notice my moral ulcers or scars," I might illuminate some general effects of social exclusion on the young and thus might contribute to some future inquiry.[1] My object is neither "gratuitous" recrimination nor "self-humiliation" but rather comprehension; and thus

> I here present you, courteous reader, with the record of a remarkable period in my life: according to my application of it, I trust that it will prove . . . useful and instructive. In *that* hope it is, that I have drawn it up: and *that* must be my apology for breaking through that delicate and honourable reserve, which for the most part, restrains us from the public exposure of our own errors and infirmities.[2]

De Quincey

When I was a child, I found a worn green book called *English Prose and Poetry* or something similar. The book was a treasure, because it contained "Beowulf" (I felt everyone ought to read that) and Robert Burns (I was obsessed with the Scots, the Irish, and all

193

things Celtic). My favorite, however, was a brutally abridged version of Thomas De Quincey's *Confessions of an English Opium Eater*. I identified with De Quincey without anticipating the strange parallel developing between our lives.[3]

Neither of us was a very good poet, but not for lack of trying. Detesting school, we ran away. We squandered our youth and vitality on dirty streets and hateful company because our heads were crammed with romantic dreams that lost no sweetness for being absurd. We spent the greater part of our adult lives paying for our indiscretions: tormented by guilty consciences, painful memories, and physical distress. Not least of all, we could say, "[in] the year we are now arrived at, as well as for some years previous, I have been chiefly studying German metaphysics, in the writings of Kant, Fichte, Schelling & c."[4]

As a youth, I read the *Confessions* as a work of fantasy. Today, it seems an eloquent reflection of my ambiguous sentiments toward a misspent youth. Suffering is one of De Quincey's recurring themes. In "Levana and Our Ladies of Sorrow," he expounds on the spiritualizing effect of suffering on children. Such motifs appealed to me, for I was a melancholy child and it pleased me to think that everything worked toward improving my soul. Moreover, De Quincey's interpretation contains some truth, but that truth is not the subject of this chapter.

My Solitary Childhood As a Loner

I lack a satisfying account of why children excluded me. My slight build, brown hair, and brown eyes failed to distinguish me as unusually attractive or repugnant. Incompetent with a ball and bat, I could dance with some grace. Neither wealthy nor poor, brilliant nor stupid, gregarious nor shy, I enjoyed drawing, collected rocks, and liked animals. I was verbal and an avid reader.

Probably my more extroverted fellows found my overactive imagination a cause for trepidation. I was cogitative and inventive whereas other children were pragmatically unreflective. To be sure, a degree of eccentricity—of queerness—contributed to my isolation. The social manuscript appeared to me as a farrago of symbols resisting translation. Perhaps, for that reason, I saw myself as a changeling, bewildered by a world for which I was constitutionally ill-equipped.

Whatever the reasons, the facts remain as follows. I failed utterly to negotiate the complexities of social interaction. Of this, my failure, other children informed me daily, hourly, verbally, physically, and so forth. My loneliness dismayed me, because I was not antisocial. There were a few "best friend" relationships, but several times with manipulative, sadistic children. Desiring companionship, I sometimes compromised or changed myself to win approval, but to no avail, and thus solitude became friendly. Next to reading and daydreaming, my main escape was to abstract from bodily feelings and external events by retreating within a "cotton wool baffle." Eventually, this "baffle" became an autonomic response, which evaded my authority (as it still does) but never by any means rendered me insensible. I suffered (and suffer) an excess of passion.

Since the social world seemed indecipherable, I dreamed of contracting some disease (tuberculosis, rheumatic fever, and polio were favorites) that might excuse me from society. I spent my most contented moments in solitary pursuits, such as reading, drawing, or taking "nature walks," so when I was not expiring on my imaginary sickbed, I fantasized about a little house in the woods. It would be a tiny cottage—just big enough for me—where I would retire with my books and keepsakes never to encounter another living soul. I talked to animals, caressed plants, and cut bargains with inanimate objects.

Between books, pencils, and my imagination, I could amuse myself for days. When no one trespassed on my private domain, happiness prevailed, but people often invaded my world, which became progressively dissimilar to theirs. Other fantasies supplanted my pastoral daydreams, but these generally had the same, painfully romantic, solitary themes. Escapism, Byronism, hermeticism, asceticism, and fanaticism of every sort appealed to me. Fiercely religious, painfully weird, I was mostly harmless. I read Tolkien and "Beowulf," wrote poetry, went to church a lot, and dreamed of joining the Irish Republican Army.

As time passed, loneliness became resentment. No more wistful yearning for companionship, I embraced my role as a pariah. Others thought me freakish; I played my part. Disgruntled by my adult protectors' failure to protect, I perceived all authorities as ringleaders of a vast conspiracy against truth, beauty, and difference. In school, I took to railing about politics, religion, television, technology, and everything else. Of course, my vendetta with society exacerbated my isolation, but what had I to lose? Often, I felt sad or angry, but discursive communication was difficult, so I expressed myself in self-destructive or cathartic ways. I did not feel "real" in the solid way that others seemed "real." Besieged in myself, my thoughts became increasingly solipsistic and incommunicable and, sometimes, incomprehensible to me:

> If in this world there is one misery having no relief, it is the pressure on the heart from the *Incommunicable*. And if another Sphinx should arise to propose another enigma to man—saying, What burden is that which only is insupportable by human fortitude? I should answer at once—*It is the burden of the Incommunicable*.[5]

My Reckless Adolescence As a Rebel

On the one hand, my late childhood and early adolescence were fruitful. I read voraciously and thought deeply about many subjects. Thus came about my atheism—not suddenly, but after an intense and painful summer's reflection. Indeed, I shed many beliefs during those years, because once asked, everything fell before the juggernaut: *Why* do I believe X? The dizzying answer was that most of my beliefs were groundless.[6] Ease in thinking even disturbing thoughts represents one of the more beneficial products of my adolescence.

On the other hand, my extremism and impulsivity remained unscathed by the scalpel of rational inquiry. A fanatic to the end, I became extravagantly, inauthentically, and externally skeptical. I found myself adrift in strange waters with no moral compass but many moralistic sentiments. Moreover, my suspicions about "everyone and everything" scarcely mitigated deeply internalized, insidious, dogmatic beliefs about women and men, good and evil, crime and punishment, and so forth, which I absorbed from various sources. My "second nature" remained firmly committed to a body of twisted notions: women are inherently inferior to men; love requires self-abasement; suffering confirms iniquity; punishment appeases guilt; an unyielding hand metes out just deserts, requiting good and evil in kind.

Intellectually, I was perhaps more mature—or at least, well-read—than the average adolescent, but too confident, in a sense, and too insecure, in another, about my intellect. I was burdened by a distorted belief system of which I remained but dimly conscious. Emotionally, I was not "immature" but deformed, vacillating wildly between unbridled passion and depressed indifference. My increasing, generalized sense of nonexistence, nonreality, invisibility, and disembodiment complicated matters. I was proud, stubborn to the bone, and hell-bent on self-destruction; and I had a—not necessarily bad—compulsion to "practice" everything I "preached."

Shortly before my sixteenth birthday, I abandoned home, family, and school. I laced up my hiking boots, shouldered my knapsack stuffed with books of poetry, notebooks, and toiletries, stuck out my thumb, and hit the road. It signified a crucial turning point. Indeed, it set into motion a series of events, the impetus of which I dimly comprehended at the time. (Many people believed me naive: Did I not realize I could be raped, hurt, or killed? On the contrary, I was acutely aware of those possibilities, but I disregarded physical risk because I viewed my body as an expendable appendage of my real, mental self. Moreover, I failed to recognize a subtlety: The dead, unlike the living, need never reconcile themselves with their pasts. These forces that I willingly, yet unwittingly, unleashed later generated guilt, regret, and sorrow.)

> Oh, Heavens! That it should be possible for a child not seventeen years old, by a momentary blindness, by listening to a false, false whisper from his own bewildered heart, by one erring step, by a motion this way or that, to change the currents of his destiny, to poison the fountains of his peace, and in the twinkling of an eye to lay the foundations of a life-long repentance![7]

My first adventure turned successfully into a *mis*adventure, which ended with my detention (for being a runaway) in a county jail several hundred miles from home. Later "trips" were lengthy, spanning the length and breadth of the United States. The main benefit from these travels was a feeling of self-direction and of respite from harassing teenagers. It was a terribly boring and unproductive time: working minimum wage jobs, talking to truck drivers, visiting (but not joining) a cult, and meeting survivalists, prostitutes, bored salesmen, battered wives, wife beaters, and so forth. (Oh yes, and I have "a million stories" I could tell, but not one of them interests me so much as a minute of my present "boring" existence.)

I spent my adolescence escaping, being captured, and working to save money, so I could run away again (along with a few normal activities like baby-sitting and my first/only date). A dismal period—attending college early and living with my first boyfriend—terminated my adolescent cycle; then—no longer a "child"—I left for good.

My Sordid Youth As a Renegade

My adolescent decisions provided no basis for a fulfilling life. Working, running, and living tumultuously consume a lot of time, so intellectually it was not very productive. College had its benefits: I read some good books, heard some interesting lectures, and discovered philosophy. Spiritually bereft, feeling cynical and jaded, I wanted desperately to devote myself to something, but nothing passed muster with my external skepticism. My internal dogmatism remained a forcible influence on my actions. Moreover, I still felt "unreal." Tired of living in my mind, I imagined that "experience" would "realize" me as fire smelts metal so I decided to inflict as many sensible "experiences" on myself as possible.[8]

> So shall he be accomplished in the furnace, so shall he see things that ought not to be seen, sights that are abominable, and secrets that are unutterable. So shall he read elder truths, sad truths, grand truths, fearful truths. So shall he rise again *before* he dies, and so shall our commission be accomplished . . . to plague his heart until we had unfolded the capacities of his spirit.[9]

I believed myself to be psychically *and* physically impenetrable, which is not to say that I possessed the sense of invulnerable immortality that teenagers purportedly have. I simply felt myself beyond caring and thus being "really" affected by emotional or physical harm. I was still proud and stubborn, but deeply insecure about my intellect, appearance, and sexuality. I did not want love, some involved relationship, or anything that smacked of commitment. Moreover, my internal dogmatism exerted a profound, half-conscious influence on my decisions. Determined to graduate summa cum laude from the school of "experience," I made an abrupt shift from a primarily intellectual-emotional existence to a raw physical life.

The first year of my youth was spent in the subculture of a major city, where I endured the self-imposed regimen of "experience." There, I was sometimes homeless, sometimes hungry, and often bored witless. Older people—castoffs, villains, aesthetes, fools like myself—populated my social environment. Everyone (except me) was very "cool." Thus, I—the social incompetent—embroiled myself in a web of human interaction. It was a nihilistic, hedonistic, anarchistic mix that I resolved to drink to the dregs. I applied myself conscientiously to pursuing the decadent, dissolute, and dissipated. What lunacy for one so keenly sensitive (reflective, emotional, moralistic) to presume to move "in but not of" that world. Thus, "experience" rendered detachment impossible. Morally and psychologically, I made a lousy aesthete.

The last four years of my youth, I was an outsider living among the lowest class in a marginal country. A giver of quarters to junkies, a receiver of leftovers from locals, I wore "dead peoples' clothes." I was an artisan: friend of the homeless, the student, the avant-garde. My daily activities, however, reflected the traditional roles of woman's drudgery: caregiver, maid, cook, worker, concubine, mother, scapegoat. I recall a tourist who, spying me at work, paused to edify his young lover. Since I could not "understand" because I did not "speak a word of English," I overheard the whole eloquent account of my "many" children (Catholics), who worked alongside "the rest" of my family in the *taller* (craft shop) where we had lived "for generations." I rather wanted the story to be true; that life sounded a lot better than mine.

Hunger, fatigue, and sickness dispelled any doubt about embodiment. Being directed by animal instincts disgusted me. The urgency of life precluded everything but a grueling struggle for psychic and physical survival. In a state of intellectual penury and emotional depletion, I trudged on for the sake of personal and moral obligations. So, time passed, youth passed, and I emerged: battered, conscience stricken, and too painfully "real."

My Age of Reason As a Refugee

When I was twenty-two, I reassembled my life. In the short term, this required some grief and humiliation. I severed the bonds of destructive personal relationships, which seemed like betrayal to me. Admitting misdeed wounded my pride; it meant that everything suffered and lost was meaningless. To be wrecked was one thing; to be wrecked and wrong, another. To be wrecked, wrong, and wracked was an entirely different story: that meant life had penetrated me, had *affected* me.

In the long term, there was work to be done and damage to be undone. I believed myself to be mentally retarded, physically repugnant, and morally depraved. Somehow, I had become pathologically shy and tongue-tied. Simple events, like going to the store, seeing a movie, or eating in a restaurant, terrified me. Overwhelmed by compunction and embittered by regret, I wondered how to restore a life that felt tired and sick. I feared people discovering that I was a refugee from the refuse.

I got an apartment, wore decent clothing, and returned to college. Reclaiming my intellectual life salvaged my passion and joy. A good many family members, friends, and teachers repaired my sense of self-worth. Today, I am almost certain that I am not retarded, repugnant, or depraved. Many would attest that I am neither pathologically shy nor tongue-tied. Simple events, like going to the store, seeing a movie, or eating in a restaurant, make me nervous. I gave up on trying to escape guilt; I just try not to enlarge my present burden. You, reader, know that I *am* a refugee from the refuse. You can decide whether I am a "demirep, adventurer, or swindler."[10] My self-inflicted "suffering" is trivial in the grand scheme of things, so I do not wish to aggrandize it when I second De Quincey: "I believe that minds which have contemplated such objects as deeply as I have done must for their own protection from utter despondency have early encouraged and cherished some tranquilizing belief as to the future balances and hieroglyphic meanings of human suffering."[11]

Responsibility

The structure of my narrative suggests a connection between my lonely childhood and my life as a rebel, a renegade, and now a refugee. Indeed, I see a relationship, which I shall discuss later, but not a causally determining one. Social exclusion occasioned many choices, so the responsibility for mine belongs squarely on me. Sometimes, guilt and painful memories goad me, but I would rather keep my guilt, regret, and memories, because my life is nothing if not for freedom. I was no victim in the affair. Although unwittingly directed by many foolish notions, half-conscious desires, and so forth, I chose my life freely as my own. Therefore, I assume the right to regret my folly.

Well-meaning folk say that "you would not be 'you' without your past" or, worse still, that "experience is the best teacher." Experience is a hard teacher. For that reason, few forget her lessons, but if people really believe in her methods, they should reintroduce the rod and the dunce cap to schoolrooms. Such methods are not best, because the gain in one area rarely exceeds the loss in another.

Sorting out my past is always a difficult business for me. Sometimes I leave it aside for years. Call that sanity. Sometimes—now, for instance—I force myself to analyze my history. Call that comprehension. Long ago I scrutinized and eradicated those internalized beliefs that so distorted my youthful thinking. I know that women *are not* inherently inferior to men; love *does not* require self-abasement; suffering *does not* confirm iniquity; punishment *does not* appease guilt; *no* unyielding hand metes out just deserts. To be sure, fresh wounds awaken a primitive emotional self who still believes, so I strive to not comport myself like a medieval monk on a guilt binge at those times.

Today, my life is good. It remains my life freely chosen, but I like to think my choices improved with age. Something was lost during my life as a rebel and renegade, but I retrieved most of what was good in that loner child. Still passionate, I channel my passions into my family, my teaching, and my work. Ever thoughtful, I surround myself with people who want to think even disturbing thoughts. To be sure, a degree of eccentricity—of queerness—marks me. I *am* weird, but my resilience to intolerance and pettiness prevents that from being painful. Perhaps I *am* a changeling, but if so, I am equipped for this—however bewildering—world. The social manuscript appears to me as a farrago of symbols resisting translation, so I am a sleuth.

> They utter their pleasure, not by sounds that perish, or by words that go astray, but by signs in heaven, by changes on earth, by pulses in secret rivers, heraldries painted on darkness, and hieroglyphics written on the tablets of the brain. *They* wheeled in mazes; *I* spelled the steps. *They* telegraphed from afar; *I* read the signals. *They* conspired together; and on the mirrors of darkness *my* eye traced the plots. *Theirs* were the symbols; *mine* are the words.[12]

Effects of Social Exclusion on Children

Social exclusion of the loner manifests itself primarily in four ways. First, children discourage or prevent the loner from participating in their activities. Second, they disregard the loner's presence, expressed feelings, and thoughts. Third, children verbally or physically abuse the loner. Fourth, children maintain these exclusive and abusive actions for a prolonged period. My narrative described the experience of social exclusion, noting distinctive attitudes, perceptions, and behaviors in order of chronological appearance. Here, I intend to reconsider those attitudes, perceptions, and behaviors in a more general, and somewhat more systematic, fashion.

I think social exclusion commonly affects the loner in five ways: perceptually, cognitively, emotionally, communicatively, and relationally. I shall discuss briefly each of these effects, which also appeared in my narrative. The effects may correspond to the severity and duration of the exclusion, but they also depend on the individual's psychic constitution, his or her freely determined choices, and the availability of adult support. Almost certainly, social exclusion affects loners in other ways, so my list is neither exhaustive nor exclusive. Many loners are probably not affected in exactly these ways, but I suspect the commonalty of these features is strong enough to warrant future inquiry.

Moreover, these effects are mutually determining, and thus my arbitrary divisions are intended for the sake of convenient organization. Each effect discussed might form the basis for an extensive inquiry, so my treatment is but a cursory introduction to several potential lines of inquiry. I shall present these effects as facts, since most of them were facts of my experience, but I intend them as possibilities.

Social exclusion affects the loner's perception of the world. Particularly, it affects the loner's self-perception. Degrading words and deeds impinge on the loner's sense of self-worth. Profound destruction of self-esteem results from attenuated exclusion. Severe exclusion produces insidious effects on the loner's self-perception, particularly if the loner withdraws or barricades to preserve a positive self-concept. These effects include feelings of unreality, invisibility, disembodiment, and emotional or physical impenetrability. A grossly distorted self-perception results.

The loner may see himself or herself as deformed, obese, stupid, insane, sinful, and so forth. (Alternatively, he or she may construct a magnified self-image.) These distorted perceptions extend to other people or to the world generally. The loner may perceive others as unduly powerful, significant, perfect, intelligent, beautiful, and so forth. (Alternatively, he or she may view others unfairly in a negative light.) The loner's perception of the external world may be more confused and frightened than warranted, thus resulting in feelings of paranoia or disconnection.

Social exclusion results in cognitive distortions because of lack of intellectual interaction, unfair criticism or disregard, and incommunicability of ideas. The loner's thinking becomes solipsistic due to isolation and fear. Extremist views and intellectual rigidity are common. The loner may adopt extravagantly dogmatic or skeptical attitudes. Indeed, both attitudes may be present at once. The outwardly skeptical loner may harbor internalized, barely conscious, dogmatic beliefs. Cognitive distortion is especially harmful when it results in conceptions and beliefs on the basis of which the loner acts.

The loner's emotional expressions rarely elicit empathy from other children, whose responses tend to be antipathetic or incongruent. This situation may lead to a permanent state of emotional incongruity between the loner and the world. Lacking the tempering influence of emotional interactions, the loner's emotions appear disproportionate. For instance, the loner exhibits passionate impulsivity or dispassionate indifference or, indeed, vacillates between these extremes. Depression and anger need hardly be mentioned.

Children rebuff the loner's attempts to communicate, thus reducing his or her opportunity to practice the art of communication. Incongruent responses to the loner's articulations increase these difficulties. As the loner becomes emotionally withdrawn and intellectually solipsistic, thoughts and feelings seem incommunicable. Discursive incommunicability may lead to nondiscursive or aggressive communication, such as "nervous habits," repelling others, fulfilling negative expectations, or vengeful, violent outbursts.

Subjective states that others ignore seem disproportionate, unjustified, and thus incomprehensible to the loner. Many loners articulate and justify their subjective states by equating them with well-defined, visible objective states. For instance, self-mutilating, risky, or sadistic and masochistic acts manifest subjective states objectively. Alternatively, loners may seek to deny the visible and objective as a way of negating the invisible and subjective. The struggle to produce a tangible realization of the invisible sorrow or to derealize visible pain leads to callous or self-destructive behavior: a compulsion to inflict pain or to deny its existence.

Initially, loners exhibit a willingness to compromise or to change in order to win friends or approval. When repulsed, the willingness to adapt may be surrendered for an avoidance of relationships. The loner may be obsessive about the occasional friend and may impose impossibly high expectations on those friendships. Many loners settle for manipulative, one-sided, or abusive friendships. Alternatively, the loner may wreck promising friendships in order to avoid rejection or to fulfill expectations. Eventually, these relational "strategies" extend to relationships with sexual partners, mentors, colleagues, and other adults.

Conclusion: Educing Children

Loners will always exist unless children or society or human "nature" changes. Many become rebels, some renegades, but not all refugees.[13] What if our contemporary loners and rebels are not hell-bent on *self*-destruction? Were they reared on "Beowulf" or bullets? Vengeance is romantic, too. Our contemporary renegades may not sink quietly into the underground. Who knows what refugees hide in the shadows of our society? Without caution and foresight, we may find ourselves contemplating "statistics" rather than "confessions."[14] Lest that prophecy be fulfilled (if it is not being fulfilled right now), we must consider the forces that educe the attitudes, perceptions, and behaviors of loners.

The forces in question constitute the process called education or socialization. Socialization, or education in the broad sense, is the process whereby children become social beings. Children enter the public arena partially socialized by their families, but the greater part of their education will occur in the children's world: nurseries and schools. Our society embraces "education" as a panacea, but education and schooling are not equivalent. Possibly the greater part of education occurs at the hands of children rather than of parents and teachers, who merely set the parameters of socialization.

We would do well to remember the fine line between education and indoctrination or socialization and brainwashing.[15] Indoctrination or brainwashing may occur on the small or the vast scale. Some governments are accused of systematically brainwashing their entire citizenry. Societies indoctrinate particular genders or racial groups.[16] Religious "cults" and churches indoctrinate their members.[17] "Deprogrammers" purportedly rebrainwash and reindoctrinate former members of religious "cults." Kidnappers, interrogators, and terrorists sometimes brainwash captives. Prisons try to indoctrinate prisoners. Wife beaters and pimps try to brainwash individual women.

Although I cannot explore the question in the context of this chapter, I think a worthy line of future inquiry might consist in investigating the similarities between social exclusion of children and certain well-known forms of indoctrination or brainwashing. Indeed, I would hardly find it surprising if we discovered parallels between the methods and effects of the social exclusion of children and the brainwashing of adults.[18] If that were the case, it might help us in revising our modes of educing children.

Whatever *educes*, or develops, *educates*. By the education . . . is meant,—not the poor machinery that moves by spelling books and grammars, but that mighty system of central forces hidden in the deep bosom of human life, which by passion, by strife, by temptation, by the energies of resistance, works forever upon children.[19]

Notes

1. Thomas De Quincey, *Confessions of an English Opium Eater* (London: Penguin Classics, 1986), 29 (my paraphrase).
2. Ibid.
3. It should be noted that, despite our similarities, De Quincey and I differ in one crucial respect (relevant to this chapter): De Quincey was almost universally adored by classmates, teachers, and virtually everyone he met. He became a loner and rebel because of deeply rooted fears of failure.
4. De Quincey, *Confessions*, 85.
5. Ibid., 182.
6. If I had read Nietzsche, I would have been able to call my attitude nihilism (for whatever good that would have done), but I had not read Nietzsche.
7. De Quincey, *Confessions*, 146. De Quincey admits that it was not the stomach pain resulting from his starvation in London but rather his memories of London that led to his opium addiction: "I repeat again and again, that not the application of opium, with its deep tranquilizing powers to the mitigation of evils, bequeethed by my London hardships, is what reasonably calls for sorrow, but that extravagance of childish folly which precipitated me into scenes naturally producing such hardships . . . . For in these incidents of my early life is found the entire substratum, together with the secret and underlying motive of those pompous dreams and dream-sceneries which were in reality the true objects—first and last—contemplated in these Confessions" (147).
8. If I had read Kierkegaard, I would have known that this particular brand of hedonism never works and thus could have skipped straightaway to the rotation method. If I had read all of Kierkegaard, I would have run like hell from the "aesthetic life," but I had not read Kierkegaard.
9. Thomas De Quincey, "Levana and Our Ladies of Sorrow," in *English Essays from Sir William Philip Sidney to Macaulay,* ed. Charles W. Eliot (New York: P. F. Collier and Son, 1937), 325.
10. De Quincey, *Confessions*, 29 (my paraphrase). A demirep is a woman of ill repute.
11. Ibid., 52.
12. De Quincey, "Levana," 321.
13. I do not mean to suggest that every loner rebels or that every rebel is a loner. It just so happens that the path for some takes the route: loner, rebel, renegade, refugee.
14. While writing this chapter, I thought often of these statistics. Of course, I thought of the multiplying numbers of children killed in the schools. More, however, I thought of individual young people I knew who did not get a second chance as refugees: Jimmy Slattery, Joseph Slattery, and Jared Hutson. I dedicate this chapter to them.

15. I, in fact, believe that such a line exists and that it depends on the methods of instilling values, attitudes, and beliefs. To be sure, many people would object that brainwashing is not socialization but rather resocialization, but I would argue that all socialization is resocialization. That is to say, incorporating a person as a member of society is not simply a cumulative process but rather a dynamic, dialectical process whereby attitudes, beliefs, and behaviors are continually transformed, revised, and replaced. In either case (brainwashing or socialization), the goal is not only to produce particular behaviors but also to provide a way of perceiving the world; hence, we can recall from George Orwell's *1984* that one must not simply say that $1 + 1 = 3$ but also see and believe it.

16. See Diana Tietjens Meyers, Chapter 1; see also Christine D. Overall, Chapter 2.

17. See Wallace A. Murphree, Chapter 10.

18. Another thought, which I cannot explore here: I believe rebels and renegades (though in many respects products of their indoctrination) are not the victims but the survivors of social exclusion. The confidence and self-esteem of the truly successful indoctrinate is so shattered that he or she eventually has the "grace" of slipping into obscurity. However self-destructive, immoral, or distorted the rebels and renegades may be, they demonstrate a resolve to fight for the preservation of their "self" against considerable opposition. In many respects, their responses show a healthy instinct for self-preservation and not a little courage. Here, exploring possible parallels between the social exclusion of children and other forms of brainwashing might be revealing as well.

19. De Quincey, "Levana," 320. In closing, I thank Clelia Smyth and Heather (Kate) Kennedy for encouraging me to tell this story. (To be sure, I do not know if I should thank or curse them.) I am much obliged to Sandra Elaine (Mommy), Katarzyna Paprzycka, Clelia Smyth, Timothy Hunter, Heather Kennedy, Wallace Murphree, and Patricia Smith for reading drafts of this chapter. Additionally, I thank Sandra Bartky for her inspiration.

Chapter Twelve

Toward a Poetics of the Disabled Body

Rosemarie Garland-Thomson

My eighty-two-year-old mother told me about an unnerving experience she recently had at the beauty shop. Slow and unsure on her feet now, wobbly and often confused about her surroundings, this woman who has spent a lifetime being brisk, efficient, and unobtrusive rather suddenly is experiencing a new relationship with her aging body. But more than that, to her surprise, she is having to cope as well with her own sense of being conspicuous. "Everyone was staring at the crippled up old lady," she said accusingly and disparagingly of herself, distancing herself from the "old lady" others saw in place of the person she imagined herself to be. Her point was that being looked at as "crippled" was for her more dismaying than actually being "crippled."

This was an interesting moment for me, the daughter who has spent a lifetime deflecting the stares of strangers by cultivating a demeanor of dignity and authority that ranges from haughty to congenial, from gregarious to aloof. What my mother is learning too late, and with too little self-consciousness to help her, is something I have known my entire life. For me, this knowledge is best expressed in the language of critical theory: that difference is constructed relationally. In other words, my body, my "congenital disability," becomes different, abnormal, disabled, only in comparison to the socially established and enforced bodily standards and expectations that interpret it so within a social context. Being stared at is one of the social practices that creates my disability, my sense of myself as different from what I should be.

As anyone with a visible disability knows, enduring stares is one of the universal social experiences of being disabled. Staring is one of the definitive, unifying social practices that establishes disability identity and gives the disabled body meaning in the collective cultural imagination. We are marked not by our bodies themselves, but by responses to our bodies: by the stares that record our otherness, by the narratives that establish our inadequacy, by the barriers that keep us out, by the norms that render us abnormal. Even disabilities that are considered "hidden," thought of as internal functional impairments such as seizure disorders, HIV status, or chronic fatigue syndrome, always threaten to erupt as physical signifiers, no matter how subtle, that will visually announce difference as surely as the wheelchair, the empty sleeve, the unfocused eye, or the unregulated tic.

My aim in this chapter is twofold: first, to outline how the stare creates disability identity; and, second, to analyze the performance art of two disabled women artists, Mary Duffy and Cheryl Marie Wade, in order to lay out what I call a poetics of the disabled body, one that is grounded in the staring dynamic. This poetics of the disabled body exemplified by Duffy and Wade directly engages staring both as an oppressive social mechanism and at the same time as a visual interaction that can be appropriated to protest and to redefine disabled female subjectivity.

Staring is a social relationship between the starer and the object of the stare that constitutes the starer as normal and the object of the stare as different. The exchange between starer and object registers both the anonymity that confers agency on the starer and the singularity that stigmatizes the one who is stared at. Staring is the ritual enactment of exclusion from an imagined community of the fully human. As such, it is one of the cultural practices that creates disability as a state of absolute difference rather than as simply one more variation in human form. Many other cultural practices, of course, create disability as well. For example, medical discourse pathologizes certain bodies and deems others "healthy" or "fit." Architectural features such as stairs disable those with mobility impairments, while ramps do not. A print-reliant workplace turns the impairment of blindness into a disability, while Braille and voice software mitigate it. My blind friend, for example, became much more disabled—more "blind"—when she left an urban area with good public transportation and moved to a suburban area that required driving for mobility.

In this sense, disability is not simply the natural state of bodily inferiority and inadequacy that my mother took it to be that day in the beauty shop. Rather, disability is a culturally fabricated narrative of the body, similar to what we understand as the fictions of race and gender. Disability is a comparison of bodies that legitimates the distribution of resources, status, and power within a biased cultural and architectural environment. As such, disability has three aspects: first, it is a system for interpreting bodily variations; second, it is a relationship between bodies and their environments; and third, it is a way of describing the inherent instability of the embodied self. The category of disability exists as a way to exclude the kinds of bodily forms, functions, impairments, changes, or ambiguities that call into question our cultural fantasy of the body as a neutral, compliant instrument of a transcendent will.

Moreover, disability is a broad term within which cluster ideological categories as varied as sick, deformed, ugly, old, maimed, afflicted, abnormal, or debilitated—all of which disadvantage people by devaluing bodies that do not conform to cultural standards. Thus, disability functions to preserve and validate such privileged designations as beautiful, healthy, normal, fit, competent, intelligent—all of which provide cultural capital to those who can claim such status, who can reside within these subject positions. It is, then, the various interactions between bodies and world that make disability from the raw material of human variation and precariousness.

Staring

Staring, as I have suggested, is one of those interactions between body and world that disables people. Yet, the dynamic of staring remains understudied in the burst of critical analyses from academics and activists as disability has emerged over the last twenty years as a social identity, a critical category, a political cause, and a civil rights issue.[1] Whereas feminist scholars have elaborated theories of the gaze that confront the sexualized display of women, disability studies has not yet fully conceptualized the implications of the stare.[2] Although it is not possible to undertake so complex a project here, I will nevertheless sketch out briefly the centrality and operation of staring in the social construction of disability and then turn to the performances of Mary Duffy and Cheryl Marie Wade.

The history of disabled people in the Western world is in part the history of being on display, of being visually conspicuous while being politically and socially erased. For example, the earliest record of disabled people is of their exhibition as prodigies, as "monsters" taken as omens from the gods that were read as indexes of the natural or divine worlds. In religious discourse from the New Testament to miracles at Lourdes, the lame, the halt, and the blind provide the spectacle for the narrative of bodily rehabilitation as spiritual redemption that is so essential to Christianity.

From antiquity through modernity, the bodies of disabled people considered to be freaks and monsters have been displayed by the likes of medieval kings and P. T. Barnum for entertainment and profit in courts, street fairs, dime museums, and sideshows. Moreover, medicine has from its beginnings exhibited the disabled body as what Michel Foucault calls the "case," in medical theaters and other clinical settings in order to pathologize the exceptional and to normalize the ordinary.[3] Disabled people have variously been objects of awe, scorn, terror, delight, inspiration, pity, laughter, or fascination—but we have always been stared at.

Staring simultaneously centralizes and marginalizes the disabled person. As it confers the stigmata of difference, staring literally foregrounds the person viewed at the same time that it objectifies and challenges his or her position as an accepted member of the human community. Staring interrupts—if not precludes—the comfortable, yet highly conventionalized, interactions that make up social intercourse between anonymous fellow humans. The established, predictable social rituals that characterize exchanges among seeming equals dissolve into tense and confusing relations when one person's disability is introduced into the social dynamic. Staring often disrupts the assumption of commonality and enforces a difference that usually makes both parties uncomfortable and unsure of how to respond to one another in any way other than the staring relation.

Moreover, staring frequently incites an embarrassment in both people that engulfs the relationship. For example, one of my own worst staring experiences occurred when a particularly bold child followed me around the grocery store taunting me while his horrified mother stared not only at me but at the scene her child created by demanding that I show him my arm. As this incident suggests, staring starkly registers a breach of commonality that occurs when one of the majority confronts one of the minority, when the ordinary encounters the extraordinary. In short, staring produces an asymmetrical relation that imparts what Erving Goffman calls "a spoiled identity" to the disabled person at the same time that it verifies the normative status of the starer.[4]

Disabled people, however, must eventually learn to manipulate the stare, to use it as a forum for asserting our dignity and humanity. It is a matter of survival, for one cannot endure such constant visual stoning and remain psychically intact. For example, in the grocery store incident I just described, I tactfully refused the role of the monster and instead asserted my humanity by authoritatively diverting the child's attention, aligning myself sympathetically with the disconcerted mother, and reassuring her that her child had not really bothered me. Thus, my strategy was to control the encounter with firmness and grace, the only tools I believed I had to defend myself from being, as cultural critics awkwardly say, "othered" by the stare.

Repeatedly, other disabled people testify as well that the hardest adjustment to moving into the disabled subject position is becoming visually conspicuous, of losing the privilege of anonymity. A psychiatrist friend tells me, for example, of a man who cannot go into a restaurant ever since the end of his little finger was amputated. For the prominent anthropologist Robert Murphy, his wheelchair became a flagrant sign that exposed his literally lowered status.[5] The writer Lucy Grealy, who lost her jaw to cancer, found that Halloween masks allowed her each year to "walk among the blessed for a few brief, sweet hours." Masks became her only deliverance from the intrusive stares constituting the "ugliness" that defined her.[6] Each of us has our own strategies for dealing with the daily stares that enact our status as different and threaten to cast us out of the human circle.

Staring Back

As performance artists, Mary Duffy and Cheryl Marie Wade make their manipulation of the stare into an art form. I will limit my analysis of this art form to these two women, although other fine disabled performance artists abound, both male and female, whose work engages on the staring dynamic. Bob Flanagan and Orlan are perhaps the best known. Duffy's and Wade's performances in particular fold together in suggestive ways critiques of both the gender system and what Lennard Davis suggests we call "the normalcy system"[7] that produces disabled identity.

In other words, these women's performances explore the intersections of femininity and disability, subject positions both constituted within patriarchal culture by visual appropriation. One might ask why these women, who have bodies that so disrupt the expectations of the complacently normal, would deliberately invite the stare in a public setting. Duffy, an Irishwoman, who presents herself nude in performance, is armless, with one delicate hand attached directly to her shoulder. Wade, an American, emphatically gesticulates from her wheelchair with hands that she describes as "gnarly." Both women would be characterized as "severely disabled" by the standards of what my colleague Paul Longmore calls with great irony the "severely able-bodied."[8]

The answer, of course, is that such performances are forums for profoundly liberating assertions and representations of the self in which the artist controls the terms of the encounter. In addition to allowing individual expression, their artistic engagement with self-display also provides a medium for positive identity politics, an opportunity to protest cultural images of disabled people, especially of disabled women. Simultaneously, these performances renarrate the scripts of disability and femininity.

The disabled performance artist faces a complex challenge by placing herself in the public view. In her performance, she must invite the staring that objectifies her body and then orchestrate that performance so as to create the image she wishes to project. It is the same task writ large that all disabled people encounter. Duffy's and Wade's performances make serious art from the quotidian stuff of my grocery store encounter with the curious and persistent youngster. Displaying the disabled body as a work of art involves, of course, more than just managing the stares we all face.

First, presenting the disabled body as art confounds aesthetic notions of beauty. Indeed, disability's departure from the ideal human form has been traditionally cast as an aesthetic violation.

Second, regardless of how prevalent staring at disabled people may be, it is fugitive looking, considered variously impolite, disgusting, tasteless, insensitive, sensational, or kinky. In short, the disabled body is imagined as an inappropriate art object. Social norms endorse looking at art as a proper visual practice, whereas staring at disabled bodies is illicit looking. This is the paradox that Duffy and Wade exploit in their performances.

Simply by using her body as an art form, the female artist invokes a perdurable tradition of displaying the female body as a beautiful ornament, decorative object, or work of art. As John Berger has described so succinctly and as countless feminist critiques have affirmed, women are the ones looked at in Western culture.[9] In the highly visual culture of modernity, female display, from classical art to contemporary media, has been a way to establish the literal contours of female appearance and sexual norms. How women are looked at is determined by the ideology of feminine beauty.

Lynn S. Chancer asserts that this ideology produces what she calls—not without irony—"looks-ism." Looks-ism, according to Chancer, is "a discriminatory phenomenon [that] sets up categorical divisions, placing far greater importance for one sex than the other on the cultivation and maintenance of particular bodily appearances to gain love, status, and recognition." Moreover, she continues, these "beauty expectations are systemic," that is, they are a "social fact," to use Emile Durkheim's term for an aspect of culture that "exist[s] above and beyond the ability of individuals to control."[10] Beauty, then—not unlike disability—is a system of practices and meanings, a historically shifting ideology of the female body that is at once culturally determined and yet by no means unalterable.

Disability, like feminine beauty, involves a politics of appearance based on culturally established body norms. The emergence in modernity of the ideological concept of the norm, in both the statistical and scientific discourses, controls our interpretation of physical impairment. The rationalization of the body in modernity uses scientific measurement and medical diagnosis to create the abstract, culturally validated figure of the "normal person" against which bodies are measured and evaluated. With the normal as a standard of value, both impairment and anomaly are seen not as part of the continuum of human variation or the inevitable transformation of bodies over a lifetime, but rather as the pathological exception, as the abnormal.[11] So while bodies that are impaired and anomalous have always been interpretive occasions in history—often as sources of wonder and awe—modernity has made them visible as medically deviant, a theme that informs both Duffy's and Wade's performances.

Mary Duffy

Duffy and Wade summon controversial questions as they braid together the several cultural traditions of looking at the body that I have discussed above. First, their performances raise the issue of what is appropriate looking; second, they query what constitutes beauty; and third, they ask what the truth of the body is. These women's performances unsettle cultural assumptions about humanity, femaleness, disability, and self by invoking and juxtaposing all of these categories. By simultaneously using the traditional format of female display to present bodies with disabilities, Duffy and Wade turn their performances into critiques of the politics of appearance and an inquiry into what it means to be an embodied person. To do this, Duffy primarily uses her body, whereas Wade mainly uses words.

The dominant aspect of Duffy's performance is the allusion to the classical female nude that her body announces. Her performances begin with a totally darkened room that wipes away all ocular options, clearing the audience's visual palate. For an almost uncomfortable period of time, the viewers see nothing. Amid the darkness, a series of enigmatic black and white images seem to float up; they are piles of smooth stones that increase in number as each image changes to the next. During this critical introduction, the clusters of stones grow, and the sound of a chugging train that transforms into a beating heart begins to accompany the images. The suggestion of embryonic development and fetal heartbeat becomes clear.

Then, out of the darkness, the form of Mary Duffy suddenly appears spotlit from the front and against a black background. The scene dramatically obliterates all visual alternatives except Duffy's ultrawhite form, forcing the audience to look at her completely naked body, posed in the posture of the Venus de Milo, the quintessential icon of female beauty. Young, full-breasted, voluptuous, beautiful, and armless, this living Venus demands with her silent presence that the audience stare at her. This arresting choreography hyperbolically, almost parodically, stages the dynamic of two opposing modes of looking: staring at the freakish body and gazing at the female body as a beautiful work of art.

The observer has been trained by the discourses of modernity to see Duffy's body as a pathological lack, a deviation from the norm that either has been hidden away in the asylum or displayed in medical photographs with a black bar over the eyes to obliterate personhood. For modern viewers, hers is the sensationally abnormal body that has been glimpsed furtively in the tabloids and yet proscribed as an object of proper bourgeois looking. Like gawking at a fatal traffic accident or the primal scene, looking at Duffy is at once compelling and illicit. But while Duffy's body calls up these visual discourses of the disabled body, it also invokes the familiar contours of beauty.

Duffy's simultaneously starkly disabled and classically beautiful body elicits a confusing combination of the rapt gaze and the intrusive stare. The literally in-your-face white figure against the black background is at once the degraded and the exalted body of Western tradition of looking. The templates that culture has supplied her audience are inadequate to make sense of her body. Framed as a work of art, her body is paradox incarnate, leaving her viewers' sense of the order of things in ruins. Hers is the art that transforms consciousness, granting a new way of seeing the known world.

While the visual aspect of Duffy's performance is central, words nonetheless are fundamental to her performance as well. Shifting the classical allusion from Venus de Milo to Pygmalion, Duffy begins to speak:

You have words to describe me that I find frightening. Every time I hear them they're whispered or screamed silently, wordlessly through front to middle page spreads of newspapers. Only you dare to speak them out loud. I look for them in my dictionary and I only find some. The words you use to describe me are: "congenital malformation." In my child's dictionary I learn that the first part means "born with." How many times have I answered that question, "Were you born like that or did your mother take them dreadful tablets?" How come I always felt ashamed when answering those big staring eyes and gaping mouths? "Did you have an accident or did your mother take them dreadful tablets?" Those big words those doctors used—they didn't have any that fitted me properly. I felt, even in the face of such opposition, that my body was the way it was supposed to be. It was right for me, as well as being whole, complete and functional.[12]

Unlike Pygmalion, however, in this performance Duffy does not affirm the perspective of her creator when she turns from silent object of the gaze/stare into a speaking subject. The words she cites are the verbal equivalents of the stare she sets up between herself and the audience. Yet here the words come from her own voice in performance rather than from the array of starers she has faced during her lifetime. By appropriating the words that have been used to describe her body, she upsets the dynamic of the stare, repeating in a kind of testimony the words of her starers while forcing the audience to look at a classic image of female beauty bearing witness to its own enfreakment by those words.[13]

Duffy flings the words, the questions, and the stares back at her lookers, rebuking the aggregate "you" who have tried to create her as a pathological specimen, freak of nature, or quintessential lack. She accuses them with their own accusing questions to her about being "born like that." She stares out at them, upbraiding them for their intrusive "staring eyes and gaping mouths" that made her feel "ashamed." Dismissing their perceptions of her body, she insists upon her own self-definition, asserting that "words" such as "congenital malformation" do not accurately describe her experience of herself. Her soliloquy moves from exorcizing the language her oppressors use to determine her to voicing her own version of herself as "being whole, complete and functional."

Another of Duffy's performances continues this critique of "the words you use to describe me" by redeploying them in the context of her own self-presentation. Highlighting her own agency, she affirms: "I'm winning battles every day against my own monster, my inner critic, who has internalized all my childhood oppressions: the oppression of constantly trying to be fixed, to be changed, to be made more whole, less visible, to hide and to be hidden."[14] Here Duffy appropriates the word "monster," which traditionally has been used to define her body. The words "congenital malformation" are a recent medical term for the older religious and early scientific designation "monster," which named the extraordinary body and gave rise to the nineteenth-century science of teratology, the study of monsters.

Duffy insists that the "monster" is not her body, as the dominant culture would have it, but rather the "monster" is the abstract, internalized version of herself that they have created and that she has absorbed from being stared at. "My monstrosity," she avows in another performance, "is in your imagination." Her perspective differentiates her body from the audience's interpretation of her body as monstrous, as a lack that needs to be "fixed." Her oppression, then, arises from the perceptual conflict between Duffy's sense of herself as "complete" and the dominant view of her as incomplete, as deficient rather than "whole."

The perception of the disabled body as lacking or excessive has consequences that go beyond staring, however. The power of the dominant culture to enforce this view by "fixing" our bodies is a constant threat for Duffy. In another variation of her performance, she succinctly protests the compulsory practice of medically normalizing the disabled body with procedures that are euphemistically known as "reconstructive surgery." Reaffirming that her perception of her body is "an essential part of [her] being," Duffy clarifies the "you" she addresses as the doctors who promote a medical model of disability. "You were always trying to change me in your image," she charges, "always trying to slice off my hand."[15]

This arresting image of mutilation, of having her hand sliced off, alludes to an experience common to people whose bodies are marked with what medicine terms "congenital malformations." For example, fashion model Aimee Mullins and performance artist Nomi Lamm both had their legs amputated when they were young in order that they could wear cosmetic prostheses. Intersexed children and conjoined twins are special targets of routine surgical normalization because they so challenge our cultural understanding of persons as unambiguously sexed and unambiguously separate. Such disciplinary practices maim disabled persons by standardizing their appearance and functioning, which is skin lightening and hair straightening with a vengeance.

It is part of the fantasy of the plastic body described by both Mike Featherstone and Susan Bordo as one of the hallmarks of consumer culture. The notion of what Bordo calls "postmodern plasticity" assumes that the body is infinitely sculptable into multiple variations of itself, into a range of simulacra that conform to the mandates of postmodernity.[16] Whereas cosmetic surgery has been critically analyzed by feminists as a violent and coercive practice that normalizes the female body so that it conforms to beauty standards, reconstructive surgery is excluded from these critiques, suggesting that such procedures are justified in the case of disability.

In the name of making these children more acceptable to other people, their bodies are surgically altered to assuage the anxieties of those who look at them. In the collective cultural consciousness, reconstructive surgery is imagined as an act of rescue, a medical miracle that redeems the disabled body from its suffering and delivers it from a state of deviance. To the child whose body is simply the given of her or his existence, however, the "reconstruction" we are often subjected to repeatedly at early ages is a violent trauma that brands into our flesh the message that our bodies are simply intolerable to the world we live in.

Cheryl Marie Wade

Complementing Mary Duffy's display of her body as an art form, Cheryl Marie Wade's performances provoke and manipulate the stare. Whereas Duffy is a soliloquist, Wade is a poet. Nevertheless, Wade's body is essential to her poetic project. Like Duffy, Wade also appropriates the dominant culture's words for her body and hurls them back at her starers in a new context of empowerment, agency, and sexuality—the three aspects of personhood that have been denied the disabled subject. In "My Hands," Wade parodically puts on the monster role she has been assigned, using its potency and taunting her starers with it:

Mine are the hands of your bad dreams.
Booga booga from behind the black curtain.

Claw hands.
The ivory girl's hands after a decade of roughing it.
Crinkled, puckered, sweaty, scarred,
a young woman's dwarf knobby hands
that ache for moonlight—that tremble, that struggle.
Hands that make your eyes tear.
My hands. My hands. My hands
that could grace your brow, your thigh.
My hands! Yeah![17]

With her invocation of "your bad dreams" and her truculent "booga booga," Wade mocks her position as monster by conjuring up popular culture's formidable anxiety-turned-fear response to bodies like hers that has thrilled and titillated normals. The hands that she invokes verbally are at the same time emphatically shoved in the audience's faces as she speaks, forcing her viewers to enact the stare they might try to suppress or furtively commit in some other social context. But here, Wade controls the terms of the encounter.

Like Duffy's shockingly naked body, Wade's shockingly naked hands breach the rules, both social and physiological. She acknowledges the normative ideal of "the ivory girl's hands," only to override that commercialized image of feminine beauty with a string of descriptors for her own hands that trounce its authority. Hers are "claw hands" that are defiantly "crinkled, puckered, sweaty, scarred . . . dwarf knobby hands." Wade's hands do not look beautiful, indeed they are a sight so evocative as to "make your eyes tear," perhaps with shock, repugnance, or sympathy.

Rather than displaying the soft static beauty of the "ivory girl's," these hands are the agents of Wade's subjectivity: they "ache," "tremble," and "struggle," exhibiting not loveliness but the evidence of a life of "roughing it." Moreover, these hands are sexual, not in the normatively feminine way of attracting and pleasing the male gaze, but rather as sexual agents. Wade's hands "could grace your brow, your thigh." "Could" here functions ambiguously as a proposition both threatening and tender, at once an offer of gentle love and a menacing "booga, booga" to the squeamish who imagine that the only legitimate caress might come from hands like the "ivory girl's."

Wade avows this version of her hands as active rather than

passive with her final line, "My hands! Yeah!" as she gazes admiringly and lovingly at her own hands with a sign of satisfaction reminiscent of sexual release. Here she reclaims the stare from her audience and transforms it into the look of love, a self-love here that is not narcissism but rather the affirmation of her own body as whole and right.

Wade's, like Duffy's, is a project of redefinition, of offering counternarratives to the prevailing cultural images of the disabled body. As I have suggested, theirs is a dual project both verbal and visual. Wade's best-known poem, "I am not one of the physically challenged," echoes her effort in "My Hands" to forge a self-description that captures the power and the pervasiveness of the disabled body:

I am not one of the physically challenged—

I'm a sock in the eye with a gnarled fist
I'm a French kiss with a cleft tongue
I'm orthopedic shoes sewn on a last of your fears

I am not one of the differently abled—

I'm an epitaph for a million imperfect babies left untreated
I'm an ikon carved from bones in a mass grave at Tiergarten, Germany
I'm withered legs hidden with a blanket

I am not one of the able disabled—

I'm a black panther with green eyes and scars like a picket fence
I'm pink lace panties teasing a stub of milk white thigh
I'm the Evil Eye

I'm the first cell divided
I'm mud that talks
I'm Eve   I'm Kali
I'm the Mountain That Never Moves
I've been forever   I'll be here forever
I'm the Gimp
I'm the Cripple
I'm the Crazy Lady

I'm The Woman With Juice[18]

Wade dismisses the awkward terms for the disabled that attempt to flatten the power of the disabled body. Instead, she invokes the archetype of the monstrous, awful, wondrous, primal body that is everywhere and always. She is "not one of the physically challenged," the "differently abled," or the "able disabled." Wade instead aligns herself with "Eve" and "Kali," becoming "the Gimp," "the Cripple," "the Crazy Lady," whose difference is the potent stuff of myth and legend. In this performed poem, Wade's body operates very much like Whitman's poetic body in "Song of Myself." Her body here is a communal body that absorbs and represents the aggregate individual members of her group, which extends beyond the disabled community to incorporate all humanity throughout history.

Whitman announces in "Song of Myself" that he begins his poetic project in "perfect health," suggesting that his national body empties out all the diversity of his catalogs into a normative image.[19] In contrast, Wade becomes the universal body that registers singularity rather than typicality. She is "the Mountain That Never Moves," "the first cell divided," and the primal "mud" that has "been forever" and will "be here forever." The body that represents the human experience is disabled, not in "perfect health." As "a million imperfect babies left untreated," the "ikon" of a "mass grave," and "withered legs hidden with a blanket," her incarnations range across human existence from birth to death to old age.

Such a portrayal suggests that embodied differences are the rule rather than the exception and that bodily stability is a fantasy. What we call "disability" is simply particularity intensified, the quality that makes us most fully human. Moreover, in our singularity is power: our bodies become marked with life experience, making us into "black panther[s] with green eyes and scars like a picket fence." This is the power of the body that bears witness to its own history, a figure that Toni Morrison portrays, for example, in *Beloved*'s Sethe, whose scarred back bears the oppressive history of her enslavement.[20]

The marked body functions here as the transgressive body, overturning at once the cultural scripts of femininity and disability. Countering the stereotype of the disabled person as asexual, Wade creates a poetic persona whose difference is sexual: she is "a French kiss with a cleft tongue." She claims erotic agency in the tradition of the poet-warrior, Audre Lorde,[21] by asserting herself as "pink lace panties teasing a stub of milk white thigh." Wade rejects standard disability imagery as well. She is no sweet poster child, no victim displayed to elicit sympathy and contributions. Instead, her position in a wheelchair is one of agency, even aggression.

Manipulating the dynamic of the stare, she reimagines her role as the object of the stare not as a passive acceptance, but as an active visual assault, as "a sock in the eye with a gnarled fist." Her final self-proclamation, "I'm The Woman With Juice," invokes exuberance and sexuality, affirming—as was evident in "My Hands"—Wade's embodied self as fully human and vital. Her performance, then, is a kind of outlaw lyric that reimagines disabled female subjectivity by rejecting the limp and dry "physically challenged" label and embracing her self-description as "the Woman with Juice."

Conclusion

This chapter augments my larger scholarly aim, which is to introduce disability as a category of analysis in literary and cultural studies. My goal is to advance what Eve Sedgwick has called a "universalizing view" of disability that will cast disability as "an issue of continuing, determinative importance in the lives of people across the spectrum."[22] This process involves helping to define and launch the new field of disability studies in the humanities. The fundamental goal of disability studies, in my view, is to reimagine disability. The most important contribution that a literary studies approach brings to the subject of disability is a focus on the issue of representation. I mean here representation in its broadest sense, of course: as the saturating of the material world with meaning. In this sense, disability is a story we tell about bodies. The important point, of course, is that these stories shape the material world, inform human relations, and mold our senses of who we are.

The cultural work of Duffy's and Wade's performances is to challenge our collective stories about disability: in other words, to renarrate disability, to reimagine it as an integral part of all human experience and history, rather than an isolated misfortune that ruins bodies, evokes a patronizing pity, or prompts rejection. Duffy's and Wade's performances inaugurate a poetic genre of the disabled body that is necessarily visual; it is a poetics of the stare. Body and word signify together in an act of self-making. Unique to disability, this genre manipulates the stare in order to renarrate disability. The body is integral to the poetry, operating as a material signifier that generates the stare. By appropriating the social practice that constitutes their oppression in order to reimagine their identities, Duffy and Wade enact a kind of communal exorcizing of the objectification that they so commandingly reject in these poetic performances. In creating such an art form, they boldly reimagine disability on behalf of their community: other disabled people for whom the daily business of life is managing, deflecting, resisting, or renouncing that stare.

Notes

1. The emerging critical field of disability studies, which is most fully developed within sociology and the humanities, lays out in various forms a theoretical model of disability as a social construction. In doing so, it reframes disability according to a social or a minority model rather than the traditional medical model.

2. See Rosemarie Garland-Thomson, "Narratives of Deviance and Delight: Staring at Julia Pastrana, the 'Extraordinary Lady,'" in *Beyond the Binary: American Identity and Multiculturalism*, ed. Timothy Powell (New Brunswick, NJ: Rutgers University Press, 1999).

3. Michel Foucault, *Birth of the Clinic: An Archaeology of Medical Perception* (New York: Vintage Books, 1994).

4. Erving Goffman, *Stigma: Notes on the Management of a Spoiled Identity* (New York: Simon and Schuster, 1986).

5. Robert Murphy, *The Body Silent* (New York: W. W. Norton, 1990).

6. Lucy Grealy, *Autobiography of a Face* (New York: Harperperennial Library, 1995).

7. Conversation with the author.

8. Conversation with the author.

9. John Berger, *Ways of Seeing* (New York: Viking Press, 1995).

10. Lynn S. Chancer, *Reconcilable Differences: Confronting Beauty, Pornography, and the Future of Feminism* (Berkeley: University of California Press, 1998), 83.

11. Georges Canguilhem, *The Normal and the Pathological*, trans. Caroline R. Faucet (New York: Zone Books, 1989).

12. Mary Duffy, *Vital Signs, Crip Culture Talks Back*, directed and produced by David T. Mitchell and Sharon Snyder (Marquette, MI: Brace Yourself Productions, 1996).

13. "Enfreakment" is a term coined by David Hevey.

14. Duffy, *Vital Signs*.

15. Ibid.

16. Mike Featherstone, "The Body in Consumer Culture," in *The Body: So-*

cial Process and Cultural Theory, ed. Mike Featherstone, Mike Hepworth, and Bryan S. Turner (London: Sage Publications, 1991), 170–196; Susan Bordo, *Unbearable Weight* (Berkeley: University of California Press, 1995).

17. Cheryl Marie Wade, *Vital Signs.*

18. Ibid.

19. Walt Whitman, *Leaves of Grass* (New York: Bantam Classics and Loveswept, 1983).

20. Toni Morrison, *Beloved* (New York: Plume, 1998).

21. Audre Lorde, "The Uses of the Erotic," in *Sister Outsider: Essays and Speeches* (Freedom, CA: Crossing Press, 1984).

22. Eve Kosofsky Sedgwick, *The Epistemology of the Closet* (Berkeley: University of California Press, 1992).

Chapter Thirteen

Cultural Change and Institutional Entrenchment: Single Mothers, Working Mothers, and the Crisis of Caregiving

Patricia Smith

Times change and so do institutions, but rarely is the transition smooth. Institutions, once established, tend to remain entrenched; and basic institutions, such as the family or motherhood, are of particular concern. The social revision of such fundamental institutions is invariably characterized as clear evidence of the disintegration of fundamental values and perhaps as the potential destruction of society itself.[1] Consequently, it is viewed as cause for the utmost resistance.

Given the changes in family structure and reproductive practice that have characterized the second half of the twentieth century (at least in the industrialized world), the attitude of institutional entrenchment just mentioned has had the odd effect of marginalizing the majority of family arrangements in the country. While some scholars have argued that the stereotype of the middle-class nuclear family with its stay-home mom, its breadwinning dad, and its two and a half children has never represented the majority of families, interwoven social and economic arrangements are nevertheless premised on this "Ozzie and Harriet" model.[2] The increasing discrepancy between this model and social reality in the late twentieth century has caused a "crisis of caregiving" in this country. It is generally associated with "working mothers," "broken homes," or "unwed mothers," all of which are said to be its cause.[3]

The crisis of caregiving is real enough. There certainly are not enough caregivers to go around for the children, elders, invalids, and others who badly need them. Moreover, this trend can be explained historically by the shift from domestic care to participation in the workplace on the part of huge numbers of women since about 1970.[4] While acknowledging this point of fact, I will argue that a variety of causes (or cures) can be postulated for the crisis of caregiving, including the entrenchment of formal institutions that no longer meet the needs of the people. This situation is partly due to, and certainly aggravated by, the marginalization of women in any role except the outdated traditional middle-class homemaker. The dynamics of this marginalization at this point in time are enormously complex and surprisingly subtle, so I do not expect to do them justice in a short space such as I have here. Still, the primary outlines can be sketched, so after noting some major features of the problem, I will offer a few preliminary suggestions toward addressing the crisis of caregiving.

"Abnormal" Mothers

Motherhood has many constraints, as illustrated by the modifiers appropriate to the term "mother." There are, for example, single mothers, unwed mothers, welfare mothers, and working mothers.[5] The implication is that normal mothers, or at least the general class of mothers, are none of these things but rather are married, supported by their husbands, and do not work outside the home. Of course, no one thinks that standard actually represents an accurate description of the typical American mother today, not even those who think it should or wish it did. We all know (or should know) that more than half of our children live in single-parent households for some part of their lives. People move in and out of marriage and other relationships these days. The divorce rates have hovered around the 50 percent mark since the 1970s, and out-of-wedlock babies retained by their birth mothers are at an all-time high.[6] Moreover, in 75 percent of dual-parent households and 83 percent of single-parent households, mothers work outside the home.[7]

Yet the modifiers to motherhood linger on, maintaining a background picture of normal or ideal motherhood and family life that seems to retard institutional reform, which could better address the needs of children and parents alike. That is, to put it crudely but briefly, social practice suggests that if single mothers lack income, the cure is adding a father with income. If single mothers lack authority, the cure is adding a father with authority. If working parents lack time for their children, the cure is restricting the work responsibilities of mothers by devices such as flextime, part-time work, mommy tracks, serializing, and so forth, to give mothers more time with their children by restricting and marginalizing them in the workplace.

Thus, the cure for problems associated with single mothers and working mothers is to eliminate single and working mothers, to maintain their marginalization, and to push them toward the old norm. This approach is especially clear in the case of single motherhood: social practice implies that it should not be accepted as normal even if it is the norm.

Consider the most common form of single motherhood, namely, that derived from divorce. Obviously, divorce cannot be considered a good thing. It is at best a failed experiment, even if it may be better than a bad marriage. On the other hand, it is so common that it can hardly be considered abnormal. More children today are the products of "broken homes" than of unbroken ones. Of course, it does not follow that this is a good thing, and, indeed, studies abound regarding the financial, emotional, and intellectual impact of divorce on children.[8] Unfortunately, there can be no comparative studies of what the impact would be if their (unhappy) parents stayed together for the children's sake. Thus, it is unclear what any investigations show except that divorced families are not ideal. They invariably purport to show that the traditional family paradigm is "indispensable for the good of children and society."[9] The implication is that divorced mothers, if they care about the good of their children and society, just should not be divorced.[10]

Consider the ideology of single motherhood as such. Here the marginalization is even clearer. Unwed motherhood is deviant behavior that creates a deficient family unit, widely condemned while it is at the same time widely and openly practiced. The shameful status of unwed motherhood is now unclear. Unwed mothers were literally hidden from public view before the 1960s, while now they are open, acknowledged, and common. But it would be going too far to say they are accepted.

Consider the furor created over the *Murphy Brown* television series that presented a professional woman undertaking single parenthood as a considered choice. The very thought that this choice could be seen as a positive role model generated paroxysms of outrage and indignation broadcast nationally at its apex during the 1992 Republican presidential convention. There can be little doubt that a significant segment of society is deeply troubled by what they see as an assault on the family. But the general apathetic response to a decade of ranting over "family values" reflects the ambivalence of the common public over the "normalization" of single motherhood.

The primary focus of concern has been on the problem of teenage pregnancy, but the condemnation of that condition can be more easily justified by reference to the youth, emotional immaturity, and financial dependence of the potential mother rather than to her marital status. Furthermore, none of these arguments applies to Murphy Brown, nor do they explain the furor caused by the episodes on single motherhood. Rather, it is the very idea of a fully independent, emotionally secure, and financially self-sufficient woman who decides calmly and rationally to produce and raise a child with absolutely no need for any contribution from a man except an impersonal sperm donation that sends shivers of inchoate fear through the historical memory of our patriarchal species. This is the ancient goddess reclaiming her heritage from the Titans who stole it away three thousand years ago.

It is the traditional patriarchal family that is threatened by single motherhood, not the family under any description, since Murphy and her child would otherwise *be* a family. Although it is far from uniform or universal, there is a deep distrust and anxiety about the idea of single motherhood as a permanent family structure. So long as the basic idea is not accepted, institutional reform to accommodate it or ease its problems will be restrained.

Similar claims can be made with regard to working mothers, about whom attitudes in this country are so ambivalent as to have reached a point of schizophrenia. Unlike single motherhood, which might at best be described as condoned by society, working in the marketplace is strongly encouraged for all, including middle-class women. Self-esteem for young women today is so strongly based on accomplishment in the workplace that some conservative commentators and feminists complain that traditional roles are being disparaged,[11] and indeed the practice of nurturing or caregiving traditionally associated with women by role or by nature is being undervalued.[12] This is the source of the contradiction embodied in our current social schizophrenia. While *women* are encouraged to participate in wage labor, no revision of our economic structure has been made to accommodate the valuable work *mothers* have always done or the needs they have always filled.

In 1963, Betty Friedan suggested that women "could have it all."[13] Unfortunately, this suggestion turned out to imply that women "could *do* it all." Women were to raise their children and compete in the market at the same time. The predictable result is that women are systematically disadvantaged and marginalized in the market, and modern institutions are singularly unresponsive to the needs of contemporary families. The feminization of poverty is clear evidence of the penalty exacted against mothers for wage work, while at the same time social structures that supply self-esteem give women no choice but participation in the public sphere. And the final straw that seals the schizophrenia is that this systematic disadvantage for women is explained as the result of our choices. We choose to disadvantage ourselves by choosing to be mothers!

Joan Williams has addressed this viewpoint perspicuously.[14] Beginning with the idea that gender is a system of power relations reflected in all aspects of human social life, she argues that the gendered structure of wage labor provides two bad choices for both men and women: career or family but not both. Wage labor, as currently designed, presumes an ideal of a perfect worker: dedicated, undistracted, and able to work when, where, and for as long as needed. The perfect worker is not interrupted by family emergencies or child-care needs. Thus, he is the gendered correlate of the domestic caregiver (the perfect mother), all of which reflects the bifurcation of the male public sphere and the female domestic sphere that became the middle-class ideal after the industrial revolution.[15] This gendered division of labor is today obsolete, and to suggest that the change is simply a result of personal individual preferences is to ignore the profound effects of social structure on personal life and individual opportunity.[16]

Choices, especially practical ones, are never made in the abstract or in isolation. They are always made within a social context that structures and constrains as well as informs them. Women are socialized to sacrifice for their families, to put their family responsibilities first. Men are socialized to be breadwinners, to put their career obligations first. The fabric of our social and economic structure is woven around these behavioral presumptions. Ignoring such facts is the only way our current economic situation can be attributed to the choices, or at least the free choices, of women. The economic system today offers women (and secondarily men) the same choice a robber offers a victim: your money or your life. Two bad choices add up to no good choice at all. We must rebut the claim that the crisis of caregiving is caused by the choices of individual women, for that suggests that the solution lies with them.

Conclusion

What should be done about the crisis of caregiving? It is a complex problem, so of course there is no single solution, and proposals always carry costs and drawbacks as well as benefits. Three different groups need care: children, the elderly, and the infirm. There is no reason to suppose that all their needs can or should be approached in the same way. I will not offer specific policy suggestions, but I would like to note three ideas that need to be accepted in order to free up the possibility of a broader range of practical suggestions and experimental programs to address the problem. All three ideas question dichotomies long rejected by feminists.

First, the crisis of caregiving exists not because of individual "choices" but because modern economic systems are not structured to allow for the personal needs of workers. We need to recognize that workers are human beings with personal needs that sometimes can and should be accommodated within work structures, during work hours, and even at the workplace. (On-site child care, for example, is an experiment that is functioning well in some businesses. Telecommuting enables some workers to spend more time at home.) In order to entertain such ideas, the traditional dichotomy between the family and the market must be relaxed. Business can sometimes be conducted from home; family responsibilities can sometimes be met from or at work. The division need not be as sharp as tradition has had it.

Second, some problems may be best addressed by state action or by cooperative endeavors between government and business. (For example, many elders have been greatly helped by Social Security

and Medicare, and such assistance could be expanded in cooperation with employers.) In order for innovative programs to be tried,
the dichotomy between private enterprise and public action also
needs to be eased. Not every social program is socialism.

Third and finally, traditional gender roles—the dichotomy between male and female, masculine and feminine stereotypes—
must be countered and, as Williams puts it, "deinstitutionalized."
The gendered structure of wage labor and domestic responsibility
needs to be dissolved, or at least not built into our institutions in a
way that marginalizes women and restricts everyone's freedom.

Reform will always be restricted by ideology. To cure the crisis
of caregiving, it must be recognized as a social responsibility, not a
personal problem. For that to happen, every woman, as well as
every man, must be recognized as a full-fledged human being with
both a career and a life.

Notes

1. The concern over the "barbarians at the gates" has been expressed for
centuries. For recent examples, see William Bennett, *The Death of Outrage: Bill
Clinton and the Assault on America* (New York: Doubleday, 1998); Robert H.
Bork, *Slouching Toward Gomorrah: Modern Liberalism and American Decline* (New
York: Harper, 1995); or D. Murphry, "America's Civilizational Crisis: The Rise
of Internal Barbarism," *Conservative Review*, October 1993.

2. See, for example, Stephanie Coontz, *The Way We Never Were: American
Families and the Nostalgia Trap* (New York: Basic Books, 1992), and Rosalind
Rosenberg, *Divided Lives: American Women in the Twentieth Century* (New York:
Hill and Wang, 1992).

3. See, for example, Sylvia A. Hewlett, *A Lesser Life: The Myth of Women's
Liberation in America* (New York: Warner, 1986).

4. The influx of women in the workplace was actually more gradual and
steady than this statement suggests. There was a continual increase in work-
force participation among women during the twentieth century, but it clearly
exploded numerically and changed qualitatively from roughly 1970 onward.
See Coontz, *American Families*, chap. 7, or Rosenberg, *Divided Lives*, chaps. 3–7.

5. By way of contrast, consider the oddity of describing a father as a
working father, a single father, an unwed father, or a welfare father, despite the
existence of all such categories.

6. Coontz, *American Families*, 182.

7. Bureau of Labor Statistics, 1998.

8. See, for example, David Popenoe, *Life Without Father: Compelling New
Evidence That Fatherhood and Marriage Are Indispensable for the Good of Children
and Society* (Cambridge: Harvard University Press, 1996).

9. Ibid.

10. But attitudes about divorce are ambivalent. In the abstract, people are

against it, but when asked about specific reasons — adultery, abuse, desertion, crime — most agree that divorce is justified. Thus, it is apparently assumed that most divorces are based on frivolous grounds.

11. See, for example, George Gilder, *Wealth and Poverty* (New York: Basic Books, 1981), or Hewlett, *Lesser Life*, 36.

12. For example, see Jean Bethke Elshtain, *Public Man, Private Woman: Women in Social and Political Thought* (Princeton: Princeton University Press, 1993); Carol Gilligan, *In a Different Voice: Psychological Theory and Women's Development* (Cambridge: Harvard University Press, 1982); or Martha Albertson Fineman, *The Neutered Mother, the Sexual Family, and Other Twentieth-Century Tragedies* (New York: Routledge, 1995).

13. Betty Friedan, *The Feminine Mystique* (New York: Norton, 1963).

14. Joan C. Williams, "Deconstructing Gender," *Michigan Law Review* 87 (1989): 797–845.

15. On this point, see also Frances E. Olson, "The Family and the Market: A Study of Ideology and Legal Reform," *Harvard Law Review* 96 (1983): 1497.

16. See, for example, Thorstein Veblin, "The Theory of the Leisure Class," in *Poverty and Wealth,* ed. K. Alrutz et al. (Washington, DC: University Press of America, 1982).

Chapter Fourteen

By Right and Not by Virtue: Rights of Retarded People in a Just Society

Sigal R. Benporath

Since Aristotle's day, it has been believed that a person must be a member of society if he or she is to thrive and fulfill his or her freedom. For a society to be just, it must allow all its members to flourish. Political theory today follows Rawls in maintaining that justice is the basic virtue of political institutions, thus claiming that the assessment of such institutions should be based on their commitment to principles of justice rather than on parameters such as efficiency or utility.

Theories of justice tend to exclude the weakest and most vulnerable groups while constructing principles for the distribution of resources, fostering rights that should be granted to all members of the just society. The exclusion of the mentally (and sometimes also physically) disabled from the data that are taken into account when principles of justice are formulated is in some cases undeclared. In other cases it is acknowledged, but justified (or dismissed) by the claim that considering the needs of retarded or sick people would cause the model to fail. The general scheme of justice would collapse, it is claimed, since these individuals require unlimited resources to achieve equality.[1]

Since the resources at the disposal of any society are limited, many theoreticians conclude that no society can be compelled to satisfy the needs of the retarded and the mentally ill (and sometimes other difficulties are mentioned, too). By trying to equate their situation with that of the rest of society, we risk the deterioration of other groups' positions as a result of the vast resources required for the empowerment of the worst-off groups. Thus, they remain in a state of inferiority and weakness: depending for the satisfaction of their needs not upon a claim of rights but on the good-will and generosity of society and its members.

Most theories, however, fail to acknowledge the absence of these groups from their discussion of a just society. To examine a theory's attitude about the rights of the weaker groups, one should pose the following questions: Should the talents, abilities, or needs of individuals in the society that the theory constitutes determine the quantity and quality of the resources placed at their disposal? On the other hand, do individuals have rights to material and other resources (such as opportunities) independent of their abilities, and are those rights an immanent part of their membership in society or their mere humanity?

This chapter examines contemporary political theory's main-stream conception of justice from the point of view of the weakest groups, namely, the retarded and mentally ill. Such groups are re-ferred to in these pages as the weakest or worst-off groups. In ac-tual society, these are marginal groups whose rights and needs can easily be disregarded, as they do not enjoy vast social recognition and in many countries have no strong advocates to speak for them. On the theoretical level, these groups are routinely ignored, as I will describe, for they distort the standard concept of human nature.

Can members of these groups be included in the definition of the members of a just society? What would be the status of retarded and mentally ill individuals in a just, utopian society established according to these theories? The answer to these questions sheds a new light on the desirability of such a society.

Justice and Disability

The social contract is a moral relation in which individuals are par-ticipants. As such, it is one of the elements that constitute the indi-vidual's identity.[2] This identity is shaped by the individual's contacts with society as well as by his or her relations with people close to him or her.

Modern philosophers understood the reasons for and purposes of the establishment of social unions in different ways. Locke, who considered property a major component of human life, described the state of nature as one in which people could not adequately protect and expand their property. It was for this purpose that they joined together and were prepared to yield some of their rights and property to the society they had established. According to this view, the major right that society must protect is the right to one's property. Libertarian theories based on Locke's view place this right at the center of the social order. The right to one's talents and their products is the original right of every member of the society.[3] Even this minimal sketch makes it clear that a libertarian society cannot be attractive to people with limited capacities, and therefore this chapter will not concentrate on libertarian theories.

Hobbes considered personal security to be a necessary condition for human existence, and so the original obligation of the society he describes as emerging from the state of nature is the safeguarding of the life and personal security of each of its members. The subjects give the ruler the power to protect their lives and make sure that no one either within or outside the society will harm them. Mill considered individual liberty the one value that the society must provide for its members, and his structure of a just society reflects the importance he endows to the rights and freedom of individuals.

However, these authors, among others, regard the very fact of belonging to a society and participating in its practices as one of the main purposes of the social union. Individuals cannot live absolutely autonomously; they cannot provide all their own physical needs or guarantee a variety of rights for themselves. In addition, as Rousseau insisted, life in a prepolitical state cannot provide the possibilities of development that exist in a social framework.

As political thinking has progressed and new political structures have evolved, the rights to one's life, property, and freedom have been taken as the basis for discussion and have been used to construct a complex system of protections and benefits that members of the political union would obtain. Theoreticians talk today about two "generations" of human rights. The first generation includes the basic civil and political rights, such as the right to life, freedom of expression, and freedom of religion. These rights are now generally endowed to all members of democratic societies (with some exceptions).

The second generation includes economic, social, and certain political rights, such as the right to work and to education, which have developed only in the past several decades. The just allocation of "second generation" rights is still a controversial issue in both political theory and praxis. Contemporary theories search for political and social arrangements that would allocate resources and rights justly and would offer a political structure that guarantees rights of the second generation for all members of society.

John Rawls's *A Theory of Justice* has been, ever since its publication, the point of origin for vast political and philosophical discussion.[4] It will serve here as a principal example for the way contemporary theories of justice exclude retarded and mentally ill persons, both from the theoretical process of establishing a just society and from the goods that such an ideal society provides for its members.

Through a critical analysis of some main ideas in Rawls's theory, a disturbing phenomenon will be exposed, namely, that political theory tends to define human nature in preclusive terms. The political definition of being human depends on certain qualities, among which rationality takes an important part, that (manifestly or unintentionally) exclude retarded persons from the just society and maybe even from being recognized as members of the human race. Through the discussion of Rawls's theory it will be made apparent that even in the realistic-utopian discussion of the just society, a discussion that is not burdened by pragmatic limitations, most retarded and mentally ill persons are excluded, neglected, or marginalized.

Rawls's theory aims at constructing a basic structure of a just society, in which one's quality of life will not be dependent upon his or her natural endowments. His intent was to guarantee a reasonable quality of life, as well as the right to take part in the distribution of basic goods, to all individuals, regardless of their capacities. Rawls emphasizes this point by stating that "there is no more reason to permit the distribution of income and wealth to be settled by the distribution of natural assets than by historical and social fortune."[5] To ensure the dissociation of assets and quality of life, Rawls sets the difference principle as a central part of the just basic structure. He defines the difference principle as follows:

Assuming the framework of institutions required by equal liberty and fair equality of opportunity, the higher expectations of those better situated are just if and only if they work as part of a scheme which improves the expectations of the least advantaged members of society. The intuitive idea is that the social order is not to establish and secure the more attractive prospects of those better off unless doing so is to the advantage of those less fortunate.[6]

Rawls considers society to be "a cooperative venture for mutual advantage." The purpose of the society is to obtain mutual benefits for its members. His aim in constructing the just society is to guarantee that the worst off will benefit as much as possible from their membership in society. In spite of his declared interest in the situation of the worst-off groups, Rawls insists that just institutions and procedures should be established for the mainstream in society, and only then broadened to include those on the fringes: "Since we wish to start from the idea of society as a fair system of co-operation, we assume that persons as citizens [are] . . . normal and fully co-operating members of society. . . . I leave aside permanent physical disabilities or mental disorders."[7]

Moreover, in discussing the range of the political arrangement his theory offers, Rawls says that he does not intend to consider the status of those who do not possess the physical or mental fitness required to take an active part in society. It seems that he thus attempts to avoid the difficulties posed by the extensive needs of the disabled (and anyone who requires expensive treatment). In addition to this declared rejection of the needs of retarded and other handicapped persons, the Rawlsian just society has two features that disregard the rights of the weakest groups. The first belongs to the theoretical process of establishing the just society and the second to the functions of the society itself.

First, Rawls claims that the right to equal treatment and respect is manifested in the fact that all individuals in the just society participate equally in selecting its basic structure, institutions, and characteristic procedures. To allow for this participation, Rawls suggests a thought-experiment, which he refers to as "the original position." In the original position, representative members of the future just society discuss and agree upon the principles of justice for their future society. These individuals are placed behind a "veil of ignorance" that withholds from them any information about their personal characteristics. In this sense, they allegedly represent any possible member of society, as they cannot take into consideration their own contingencies.[8] Dworkin claims that "Rawls's most basic assumption" is that all men have "a right to equal concern in the design of political institutions."[9] Rawls even claims that those present behind the veil of ignorance can be reduced to one person, who, unaware of the details that identify him or her, can represent all other members, with all their capacities, statuses, aspirations, and the like.

The individuals in the original position wish to enlarge as far as possible their share of "rights and liberties, powers and opportunities, income and wealth (later on . . . self respect has a central place)."[10] The way these benefits are to be obtained is one of the issues discussed by the representatives in the original position. They must decide on the principles according to which the institutions of their future society will be established and will function, principles constituted to safeguard the just distribution of the basic goods.

Rawls maintains that, in the institutions and principles of justice that they choose, the representative members will take care to secure the position of the weakest individuals in the society. This generosity stems from the definition of the original position—as a result of their ignorance of their own characteristics, their rationality and self-interestedness, they will assume that the weakest member may well turn out to be themselves after the veil of ignorance is lifted. Hence, their aim when constructing the principles of justice is to maximize the position of the worst off.

Despite the veil of ignorance, the individuals in the original position are aware of several of their personal features, which Rawls considers "general human characteristics." They are rational, capable of a sense of justice, and mutually disinterested. Each of them is trying to acquire the greatest possible quantity of basic goods so as to be able to use them to advance his or her own conception of the good when he or she finds out what it is. The rational individuals in the original position, much like the rational members of society, strive to obtain as many basic goods as they can.

Any person who corresponds to the description of the persons in the original position should be interested, and able, to use these basic goods. Rawls's conception of humanity, however, prevents people with certain cognitive or mental deficiencies from participating fully in society and thus, in a sense, limits their rights and their share of the basic goods. This exclusion is an outcome of the definition of rationality as a "general human characteristic." This trait, I would like to claim, cannot be regarded as definitive of humanity, as most retarded and mentally ill persons (as well as some other individuals) do not satisfy Rawls's criteria of rationality. Let us consider his description of a rational person:

> A rational person is thought to have a coherent set of preferences between the options open to him. He ranks these options according to how well they further his purposes; he follows the plan which will satisfy more of his desires rather than less, and which has the greater chance of being successfully executed . . . a rational individual does not suffer from envy.[11]

These components of rationality imply that most members of the worst-off groups, including retarded and mentally ill persons, cannot partake in the symbolic process of establishing the society in which they are to live. Thus, they are excluded from the central expression of equal treatment and respect to which all individuals in the society are entitled. Moreover, since the representative individuals in the original position are described as mutually disinterested, these differential capacities diminish their ability to faithfully represent all members of the just society, and specifically those members who are not characterized by (this type of) rationality. Hence, it is clearly to the benefit of the parties in the original position to avoid sharing the future social goods with anyone who cannot participate in the original position. Those who fail to demonstrate the "general human characteristics" of the parties in the original position are ignored when the principles of justice are chosen. Therefore, the basic structure of society formulated in the original position is destined to fail to take these groups' interests into account.

The rationality precondition for participation in the original position excludes retarded and mentally ill persons both from the theoretical process of the constitution of society and from the allocation of rights and goods in the established just society. Rawls mentions that full members of the society should possess the moral capacities, mental capabilities, and concepts of right and wrong that would allow them to take part in determining the society's future.[12] The conception of humanity underlying Rawls's theory of justice considers individuals to be moral, rational citizens with equal rights. The principles of justice chosen by the representative

Rawlsian individuals need not be applicable to individuals who are essentially different from them in talents, capacities, and needs. Those who decide on the principles of justice have no motivation to take into account the needs of these "other" individuals.[13]

Consequently, in the just society constituted on the principles accepted in the original position, no one would be concerned about the interests of those who were not permitted to take part in founding the society in the first place. The principles of justice, and the basic structure of society that Rawls derives from the original position, are actually embodied in the description of the original position.[14] Hence, they do not satisfy the needs of the weakest groups, although they are supposed to take their point of view into account.

In fact, the definition of "political players" does not allow many weak individuals to participate in the symbolic establishment of society. Retarded people are thus left out of the distribution scheme, at both its symbolic and pragmatic levels, and hold the status of nonmembers (or, at best, partial members) of society. True, the Rawlsian principles of justice are designed to address the needs of the worst-off members of society. The theory is not oblivious to the existence of weak individuals, and Rawls even acknowledges and tries to justify his lack of treatment of the needs of the handicapped. Moreover, the representative individuals in the original position should consider the possibility that they themselves may suffer an illness or injury, which would disable them physically or mentally. However, the exclusion of retarded persons is an inherent part of Rawls's theory of justice, which derives from his description of human nature.

Rawls's exclusive definition of humanity is not unique to his theory of justice. Many other modern liberal theories exclude or ignore retarded and mentally ill members of society through a restrictive definition of what it means to be a human being. In addition to this discriminatory component in Rawls's theory of justice, a structural element that contributes to the marginalization of retarded persons will be described in the next section.

Principles Versus Procedures of Justice

Rawls's principles of justice disregard the weakest members of society, although these principles are proclaimed to answer the needs of the worst-off groups. How can this incongruity between Rawls's intention and the practical implication of his principles of justice be accounted for? One explanation can be his exclusive definition of humanity, as described in the previous section. Another elucidation will be offered now, namely, that the very reliance on principles of justice constitutes the unjust perspective on retarded members of society. Some authors suggest that even the principles of justice should be examined in reflective equilibrium, which means that if undesirable social consequences result from those principles, they should be corrected or the definition of the original position should be amended.[15] Under this description, it is hard to defend the stable or constitutional nature of these principles.

Generally, it is hard to offer a definite, detailed description of the social functioning of a just society. Rights, needs, and reasonable living conditions are concepts stemming from the view of humanity that underlies Western thinking, but their range is changing rapidly. An analytic derivation of rigid principles of justice will be hard to adapt to the political structure of a real society. Rawls's explicit intention is to derive principles of this sort, but it is difficult to achieve this goal for dynamic societies with the analytical tools he uses.[16] Today, the variety of rights that are available to individuals in Western societies continues to expand with rapid technological and political developments, which influence concepts of human rights and needs. Thus, rigid principles of justice become detached from the social reality they were supposed to arrange and amend.

As Michael Walzer points out, decisions that are made behind the veil of ignorance are not sufficient to determine all modes of social activity for rational individuals from the moment that they know their own personal characteristics.[17] When the veil of ignorance is removed, and individuals are aware of their own status, traits, and ambitions as well as the characteristics of the society in which they live, they will probably develop additional expectations and present new demands to the social system. It is also unlikely that all these demands will be derived from the principles of justice that were chosen in the original situation, yet they may nevertheless be justified and even rational.

The needs of both strong and weak individuals in the society change in accordance with changes in the social structure, interpersonal relationships, technological and medical progress, and the information at the society's disposal. If we were to point out the social development most destructive for retarded and mentally ill members of society, it would probably be social fragmentation. In the past, it might have been possible to assure the well-being of these people—as socially and politically weak as they are—through the goodwill of their family and community. Today, the disempowerment of these institutions often renders this solution irrelevant.

In past times, it seemed plausible to base the welfare systems on charity, but at present the numbers of poor and needy people are too great, the family is too weak, and the growth of individualism has decreased many people's feelings of social obligation. These factors have made it necessary to transfer the responsibility for the welfare of the needy to the state. Charles Taylor puts it this way: "Fragmentation arises when people come to see themselves more and more atomistically, otherwise put, as less and less bound to their fellow citizens. . . . This fragmentation comes about partly through a weakening of the bonds of sympathy, partly in a self-feeding way."[18]

We are now living in an age that is characterized, perhaps more than anything else, by the collective belief in individual human rights. That is, since the middle of the twentieth century humanity has been permeated with the feeling that every person, by virtue of being human, is entitled to personal freedoms that underlie the relationship between the individual and the society to which he or she belongs. The individual's self-actualization and the fulfillment of his or her needs and aspirations are the focus of contemporary Western social thought.

This change in the focus of discussion about the relationship between the individual and the society—from the society to the individual—is analyzed in different ways. Allan Bloom, Daniel Bell, and other writers claim that the present period is "narcissistic" or "hedonistic." Charles Taylor sees the shift in a more positive light, as heralding a period in which individuals are able to actualize themselves, since there is a wide range of opportunities for leading an authentic life. Whereas the course of the individual's life used to be restricted (or determined) by his or her status and family membership, and the opportunities available to him or her were known in advance, nowadays each individual must define himself or herself, choose his or her own goals, and try to actualize them on his or her own.

This shift in the center of gravity of social discourse about the individual creates a need for a redefinition of various aspects of the relationship between the individual and the society. In this situation, the range of opportunities available to the individual is enhanced but so is the danger of detachment and alienation. This danger is particularly threatening for the weaker members of society, who find it difficult to construct a meaningful life plan or act to bring it about. These are the individuals whose degree of social belonging is insufficient, and who find it difficult to create a network of relationships that would strengthen it. The opportunities provided by an individualistic society cannot compensate the weakest people for the harm done by the loss of the communal membership, which was a given in past generations. Not only the weakest members are hurt by this state of affairs; the details of their situation shed light on the problems facing everyone in the new structure of relationships between the individual and the society.

Let me offer a quick look at my culture's history to exemplify the consequences of these changes. The traditional Jewish community in the Diaspora regarded the care for the needy as a personal obligation of each of its members as well as of the community's official institutions. At least at the declaratory level, and often also in reality, the needs of the poor, the ill, and the socially disempowered (like widows and orphans) were to be accommodated by the goodwill of their fellow members as well as by semiformal social arrangements of donation and charity.

By contrast, in the Jewish State of Israel, the well-being of the weak members of society is placed in the hands of governmental institutions. Where they fail to provide for the needs of individuals or groups, there are instances of private people or organizations that come forward to help. In other cases, the needs are left unanswered.[19] As in many other Western countries, the dissolution of the welfare state and the rise of individualistic capitalism are evident at both the political and the social level. The dangers stemming from changes of this sort loom primarily over the weakest individuals, but they may affect everyone's quality of life.

This short description illustrates the difficulties in applying principles of justice to an ever-changing sociopolitical reality. The constant changes in society's structure render absolute principles of justice obsolete at a rapid pace; perhaps they were always too gen-

eral to provide clear rules for social action. Society should, therefore, be founded on a more flexible code. Guiding rules, rather than
rigid principles, should be derived from this code, as the latter cannot provide for people's needs or help them actualize their rights in
a modern (or postmodern) society over the long term.

Society must, therefore, encourage extensive discussion of the
way in which its guiding principles are to be realized in practical
plans. The advantage of a constant discussion of the implementation of justice over a given set of principles of justice is twofold.
First, a continual debate is more likely to remain relevant to the circumstances and needs of individuals and groups in a changing society. Second, participation in the discussion on the just
arrangements can promote a sense of solidarity and belonging in
members of society.

The significant consequence of this argument is that the demand to change the "entrance conditions" for a just society (Rawls's
precondition of rationality, which is required for participation in establishing the society's institutions and principles of justice and for
enjoying its basic goods) must be replaced by a new criterion for
participation in the sociopolitical activity, namely, the willingness to
contribute to society. Moreover, the symbolic self-respect endowed
to individuals by their hypothetical participation in the selection of
the principles of justice should be replaced by the more realistic self-
respect that comes with actual participation in structuring society's
procedures and attitudes.

Generally, the main compensation that a society can offer for
the loss of a sense of group or class belonging, as well as the loneliness and identity crises that this loss creates, is the construction of
a new sort of relationship between the individual and society.
These new relations should permit a new sense of belonging and an
opportunity for the individual to base his or her identity on the
self-respect that will develop out of the new mutual relations
within the society.

Since rights in a just society are supposed to apply to all individuals, the threshold of rationality creates a situation of unfairness
in the just society. The allocation of rights and goods, "among
which self-respect has a central place," to full members prevents the
weakest members from sharing this basic good from which they
can benefit as much as anyone else. As the rationality precondition

mainly affects the availability of the "most important basic good"—self-respect—a different interpretation of this good and a just method for its distribution, namely, the principle of belonging, will be offered in the next section. It will be described not as an alternative principle of justice but as a general guideline from which specific policies can be derived.

Conclusion: Dignity and Belonging

Human dignity stems from an awareness of the individual's abstract humanity, unrelated to any specific role or social characteristic, whether it involves belonging or achievement. The self-respect of all the individuals in a society is a goal of the ethical-social enterprise that attempts to provide each individual with the opportunity to create a favorable self-identity and fulfill his or her authenticity. Meaningful "equal citizenship" can be established only in a social setting that permits the ongoing actualization of the self-respect of all the individuals in the society.

Setting the grounds for the realization of such enterprise requires the abandonment of strong concepts of respect, "for respect . . . requires seeing that the respected person has personal standards or ideals and believing that he lives by them. But, unfortunately, not everyone seems to have such standards, and, even more obviously, not everyone lives by the standards he has."[20] If this is the case, then the concept of respect should be replaced with a more basic one, one that could broaden the range of individuals who can benefit from it. Later in the same discussion Hill offers an alternative concept of respect, saying, "The respect in question need not be merited by special talent, achievement, or even ambition." Here Hill attempts, in a sense, to promote the same objective that Rawls sets for his theory, namely, the detachment between talents and quality of life.

Enhancing retarded individuals' ability to understand the opportunities for action that the social setting allows them and strengthening their sense of belonging to the society should develop their sense of self-esteem and self-respect and contribute to their ability to live a good life. If these prior conditions are satisfied, then the weakest individuals, such as the retarded, will be able to enjoy the freedoms that a just society is supposed to accord them as well as the resources devoted to their advancement. This assistance will enable them to participate in social activities, which, in turn, will enhance their self-respect and their sense of belonging to the society. Participation and a sense of belonging are necessary for the actualization of membership in a society.

The mutual cooperation of all the individuals in society can result from an extended discussion about the varied needs of these individuals, the goods that the society must provide to them, and the principles of distributing these goods. Such cooperation should create a sense of belonging, which should make it possible for many more individuals to develop a sense of self-respect. The basis of the connection between the individual and the society and the development of the individual's identity as a member of society is this discussion about the nature of the relationship between the individual and the society, and the commitments it establishes for both sides.

The participation of various individuals in the processes of shaping this relationship can be adapted to their particular capacities. Functioning on the social and economic levels—working, forming social ties, and performing a variety of activities suited to the capacity of the individual—can also be a form of participation in shaping the social fabric. The ability of all individuals to take part in such activity depends on the conditions provided to them by society's institutions. Since this process of helping form the society through participating in it is the foundation for enjoying the basic goods, the society has the obligation to give all the individuals a real opportunity to participate. In other words, the preconditions for receiving one's share of the basic goods are not defined in terms of "general human characteristics," which tend to exclude the weakest groups and especially retarded persons. On the contrary, these are practical preconditions that society itself is in charge of providing to all its members.

Social recognition and esteem permit the individual to value his or her own choices by continuing to hold and apply them. The connection between the two is dialectical, as the individual's ability to choose stems from his or her mutual relationship with the society, an awareness of the variety of opportunities available to him or her, and the sense of self-esteem he or she is able to develop on the basis of the esteem accorded by the society. Hence, in order for the individual to fulfill the Rawlsian criteria—to be a moral person who is worthy of enjoying the basic good of self-respect—he or she must exist within a social framework. He or she must know what the important and meaningful issues are in the social sphere and must be capable of evaluating his or her choices with regard to these issues. Such acts must, as mentioned, take place in a continuous interaction between the individual and the society.

Allowing individuals to participate in the systems of social welfare and justice constitutes a twofold recognition of them—a recognition of their needs as well as of their belonging to the group.[21] When society's basic structure is aimed at paving the way for social participation, then the basic goods should be distributed in a way that treats all individuals equally, as far as possible. This equality should be actualized not only in the results of the distribution but also in the way it is carried out: by allowing those who need it most to participate in making and realizing decisions.[22]

Rawls considers the sense of belonging to the society an important element in the actualization of the principles of justice.[23] He claims that proper social relations are a vital basis for founding a just basic social structure. In his discussion of equality, he puts forth the principle of fraternity as an essential component of the principles of justice, explaining that fraternity means the quality of social relations. In a just society, fraternity is manifested in the actualization of the principle of difference—the aspiration to achieve advantages on the condition that these advantages will also benefit the weaker individuals. This principle seems to consider the needs of weaker members of society. However, it can be said to have been satisfied by libertarian practices—such as trickle-down economics—which (in their ideal form) disregard the special needs of weak groups or individuals. Hence, it does not constitute a satisfactory social arrangement that allows for the equity of retarded and other deprived members of society.

It is suggested here that a society that wants to give all its members the opportunity to achieve self-respect should not be content with the principle of fraternity. Rather, it should define a broader obligation to all its members' well-being and means of achieving self-respect. This more extensive obligation can be titled "the principle of belonging." From this principle, society should derive practical obligations on the part of its social and political institutions toward the weaker groups.

Work, for example, is one of the most important areas for developing a sense of belonging to a society and shaping one's personal identity. A person who feels that his or her work is meaningful often feels satisfied with his or her social status and connection to the society, thus developing a favorable sense of identity. Rawls deals with this issue in his discussion of the necessity for making all positions available to all members of the society, according to the principle of "fair equality of opportunity." He explains why people who are not permitted to apply for a job that is open only to those who have some specific capabilities are justified in feeling hurt by this exclusion. Rawls asserts that even if filling the position by employing the most capable person actually advances the society as a whole, including those who were denied the right to apply for it, this advance is not worth the damage to the rights of those who were not permitted to apply:

> They would be justified in their complaint not only because they were excluded from certain external rewards of office such as wealth and privilege, but because they were debarred from experiencing the realization of self which comes from a skillful and devoted exercise of social duties. They would be deprived of one of the main forms of human good.[24]

Rawls is aware that mere distribution of resources is not enough to fulfill all members' aspirations or to guarantee a proper attitude toward the varied life plans of individual members. If people's freedom to choose an occupation is restricted by decisions of the government or the structure of the social system, then money is insufficient to compensate for the harm done to them. If a high salary is the only compensation for work that is done without the opportunity to choose, it is not necessarily an appropriate compensation.

In order to allow for a sense of belonging to society to develop, all members must be permitted to take part in what Rawls himself calls "one of the main forms of human good": taking responsibility, participating in a human society that they belong to, and contributing their share. Rawls therefore gives equal opportunity employment pride of place among his principles of justice. He proposes free competition for social positions with guarantees of fairness.

There are, however, people who cannot succeed in free competition for positions, even if the competition accords with Rawls's fairness conditions. The weakest people, such as the retarded, will fail in most of the free competitions for desired positions, and since self-realization through assuming social responsibility is of major importance in the development of self-respect, the principle of belonging must be applied here, too. The society has the obligation to develop special positions to fit the abilities of the weakest people (even if these abilities are limited), thus allowing them a sense of participation and belonging in the society. The distribution principle Walzer supports can be used to justify this demand: "From each according to his ability, to each according to his socially recognized needs." The social recognition of a broader variety of needs, of as many members as possible, is the main aim of the principle of belonging.

Social recognition of various groups is another important means of creating a sense of belonging. Disabled people as well as members of minorities, women, and people with different sexual orientations demand recognition of their status as equals as well as representation and other related requirements. As Taylor puts it, "On the social level, the crucial principle is that of fairness, which demands equal chances for everyone to develop their own identity, which include . . . the universal recognition of difference, in whatever mode this is relevant to identity."[25]

Retarded people, who are weak and often rejected (personally and as a group), could benefit much from recognition of their common needs and group rights. This recognition does not entail that they have the right to be represented in positions that require activities they are unable to perform, but they should be allowed to fill positions that suit their abilities, enabling them to form models for identification and develop a sense of participation in social activities and the everyday functioning of social institutions. They could thus form a positive identity and a sense of belonging and, consequently, self-respect.

An important path to realizing this goal is to include members of these groups in the processes of decision-making about ways they can participate in society. Allowing retarded people to participate in shaping the ways in which they will become a more central part of society advances the aim of these processes.

The principle of belonging is dependent on an attitude of respect for all people, which leads to a sense of openness in accepting others in any social position they are capable of achieving and a willingness to interact with them on various levels. If weak people are defined as passive and treated as helpless and in need of protection, if they are regarded as persons who have nothing to contribute to society, then they cannot enjoy the devoted fulfillment of their social obligations, one of the basic human social goods. Giving such an opportunity for self-actualization to all the individuals in a society requires some investment, but it also provides the society with some recompense. The society is obligated to provide all its members with the basic preconditions of participation if it aspires to function as a just society.

An example of how this suggestion is being actualized in Israel today is the opportunity given to young retarded people (among them individuals with Down's syndrome) to serve as volunteers in the army.[26] Through their military service these young people realize their right to feel (and to be) part of Israeli society, in which army service constitutes a fundamental experience for forming young citizens' identity. This enterprise would be socially justified even if it were not economically worthwhile (and it may even be economically justified).

The moral justification for investing in enterprises of this sort stems from society's obligation to provide all its citizens with the opportunity to share social responsibility and to grant them equal citizenship—in short, it is derivative of the principle of belonging. Extending these sorts of activities and defining them not as charitable acts but as part of society's commitment to all its members can lead to the development of a sense of self-respect for most individuals in a society, including those with mental and cognitive deficiencies. This opportunity will help them develop a sense of belonging to the society and expand their participation in it, and consequently allow them to develop dignity and self-respect.

This sort of "mainstreaming" should be applied to philosophical theories dealing with justice. The range of abilities and disabilities of all the individuals in the society should be taken into account when the social structure and the just rules that arrange its activities are constituted. This attitude should replace the common failure to acknowledge retarded people as part of the human race and as part of every normal society. It should replace approaches such as Rawls's, which constructs a theory of justice within the mainstream with the intention of applying it later to those on the margins of society. And it should take the place of justifications for disregarding the needs of retarded and mentally ill members of society on the basis of lack of resources.

Treating disabled individuals as belonging fully to the society, and including them within the definition of moral persons and as full members of society, is the first political step that should be taken. This effort will allow for the second step: actualizing the moral obligations that stem from this theoretical standpoint in order to act fairly and justly toward all members of society, whatever their natural endowments might be.

Notes

1. See, for example, Christopher Jencks, "Whom Must We Treat Equally for Educational Opportunity to Be Equal?" *Ethics* 98 (1988): 518–533, and Ronald Dworkin, "What Is Equality?" *Philosophy and Public Affairs* 3 (1981): 185–246.

2. Michael Walzer, *Spheres of Justice* (New York: Basic Books, 1983), 82.

3. See Robert Nozick, *Anarchy, State, and Utopia* (New York: Basic Books, 1974), and John Griffin, *Well-Being* (Oxford: Clarendon Press, 1986).

4. John Rawls, *A Theory of Justice* (Cambridge: Harvard University Press, 1971).

5. Ibid., 74.

6. Ibid., 75.

7. John Rawls, "Justice As Fairness: Political Not Metaphysical," in *Equality and Liberty*, ed. Kai Nielsen (Rowman and Allanheld, 1985), 153.

8. Ibid., 141.

9. Ronald Dworkin, *Taking Rights Seriously* (Cambridge: Harvard University Press, 1977), 182.

10. Rawls, *Theory of Justice*, 72.

11. Ibid., 143.

12. Rawls, "Justice as Fairness," 154.

13. A strong criticism of the description of the "representative" individuals as such can be found in Michael Sandel, *Liberalism and the Limits of Justice* (Cambridge: Cambridge University Press, 1982).

14. For a detailed analysis of the claim that the conditions of the well-ordered society can be revealed in the definition of the original position, see K. Baynes, *The Normative Grounds of Social Criticism: Kant, Rawls, Habermas* (New York: State University of New York Press, 1992), chap. 2.

15. C. Kukathas and P. Pettit, *Rawls: A Theory of Justice and Its Critics* (Stanford: Stanford University Press, 1990).

16. Rawls, "Justice as Fairness," 146.

17. Walzer, *Spheres of Justice*, 79.

18. Charles Taylor, *The Ethics of Authenticity* (Cambridge: Harvard University Press, 1991), 112–113.

19. The transition from communal to national arrangements has its effects on the sense of mutual obligation as well. The issue is too broad to discuss in detail here; however, I believe that the diminishing of social commitment can be largely attributed to the general social changes described above.

20. Thomas E. Hill, *Autonomy and Self-Respect* (Cambridge: Cambridge University Press, 1991), 24.

21. For an elaborated account of this point, see Walzer, *Spheres of Justice,* 78.

22. For an interpretation of Rawls's theory as offering practical tools to improve the sociopolitical reality in terms of the processes that produce justice, see Thomas W. Pogge, *Realizing Rawls* (Ithaca, NY: Cornell University Press, 1989).

23. Rawls, *Theory of Justice,* 105.

24. Ibid., 84.

25. Taylor, *Ethics of Authenticity,* 50.

26. Like other volunteers (as differentiated from regular soldiers), retarded soldiers are not recruited to combat positions. They serve as armorers, supply managers, cooks, and in other service positions.

Bibliography

Abel, Elizabeth. "Race, Class, and Psychoanalysis? Opening Questions." In *Conflicts in Feminism*, ed. Marianne Hirsch and Evelyn Fox Keller. New York: Routledge, 1990.

Adler, Sy, and Johanna Brenner. "Gender and Space: Lesbians and Gay Men in the City." *International Journal of Urban and Regional Research* 16 (1992): 24–34.

Alcoff, Linda. "Cultural Feminism Versus Post-Structuralism: The Identity Crisis in Feminist Theory." *Signs* 13 (1988): 405–436. Reprinted in *Culture/Power/History: A Reader in Contemporary Social Theory*, ed. Nicholas Dirks, Geoffrey Eley, and Sherry Ortner. Princeton: Princeton University Press, 1994.

Allen, Anita. "Legal Rights for Poor Blacks." In *The Underclass Question*, ed. Bill Lawson. Philadelphia: Temple University Press, 1992.

Allen, Prudence. "Sex or Gender? Some Philosophical Implications." Paper presented at the annual meeting of the Canadian Philosophical Association, Queen's University, Kingston, Ontario, May 1991.

Almgren, Hans. "Community With/Out Pro-Pink-Unity." In *The Margins of the City: Gay Men's Urban Lives*, ed. Stephen Whittle. Aldershot, England: Ashgate Publishing, 1994.

Anaya, James. "The Native Hawaiian People and International Human Rights Law: Toward a Remedy for the Past and Continuing Wrongs." *Georgia Law Review* 28 (1994): 309–364.

Appiah, Anthony K., and Amy Gutman. *Color Consciousness: The Political Morality of Race*. Princeton: Princeton University Press, 1996.

Ashley, Lynda. "A Case for Feminism with Femininity." *Globe and Mail*, 23 February 1993.

Atkinson, Ti-Grace. *Amazon Odyssey*. New York: Links Books, 1974.

Austin, J. L. *How to Do Things with Words*. Ed. J. O. Urmson and Marina Sbisa. Cambridge: Harvard University Press, 1962.

Baker, Robert, and Frederick Elliston. *Philosophy and Sex*. Rev. ed. New York: Prometheus Books, 1984.

Barthes, Roland. *A Lover's Discourse: Fragments*. Trans. Richard Howard. New York: Hill and Wang, 1978.

Bartky, Sandra Lee. *Femininity and Domination: Studies in the Phenomenology of Oppression*. New York: Routledge, 1990.

Baynes, K. *The Normative Grounds of Social Criticism: Kant, Rawls, Habermas.* New York: State University of New York Press, 1992.

Benjamin, Stuart Minor. "Equal Protection and the Special Relationship: The Case of Native Hawaiians." *Yale Law Journal* 106 (1996): 537–612.

Bennett, William. *The Death of Outrage: Bill Clinton and the Assault on America.* New York: Doubleday, 1998.

Berger, John. *Ways of Seeing.* New York: Viking Press, 1995.

Berlin, Isaiah. "Two Concepts of Freedom." In *Collected Essays.* London: Oxford University Press, 1978.

Bordo, Susan R. "The Body and the Reproduction of Femininity: A Feminist Appropriation of Foucault." In *Gender/Body/Knowledge: Feminist Reconstructions of Being and Knowledge,* ed. Alison M. Jaggar and Susan R. Bordo. New Brunswick, NJ: Rutgers University Press, 1989.

———. *Unbearable Weight.* Berkeley: University of California Press, 1995.

Bork, Robert H. *Slouching Toward Gomorrah: Modern Liberalism and American Decline.* New York: Harper, 1995.

Bouthillette, Anne-Marie. "Queer and Gendered Housing: A Tale of Two Neighbourhoods in Vancouver." In *Queers in Space: Communities/Public Spaces/Sites of Resistance,* ed. Gordon Brent Ingram, Anne-Marie Bouthillette, and Yolanda Retter. Seattle: Bay Press, 1997.

Bradshaw, Howard. "The Bottom Line." *axiom news,* 20 May 1999.

Brodeur, Paul. *Restitution: The Land Claims of the Mashpee, Passamaquoddy, and Penobscot Indians of New England.* Boston: Northeastern University Press, 1985.

Brosman, Catherine Savage. *Simone De Beauvoir Revisited.* Boston: Twayne, 1991.

Burnette, Robert, and John Koster. *The Road to Wounded Knee.* New York: Bantam Books, 1974.

Butler, Judith. *Excitable Speech: A Politics of the Performative.* New York: Routledge, 1997.

———. "Gendering the Body: Beauvoir's Philosophical Contribution." In *Women, Knowledge, and Reality: Explorations in Feminist Philosophy,* ed. Ann Garry and Marilyn Pearsall. Boston: Unwin Hyman, 1990.

———. *Gender Trouble: Feminism and the Subversion of Identity.* New York: Routledge, 1990.

———. *The Psychic Life of Power: Theories in Subjection.* Stanford: Stanford University Press, 1997.

Canguilhem, Georges. *The Normal and the Pathological.* Trans. Caroline R. Faucet. New York: Zone Books, 1989.

Caputi, Jane, and Gordene O. MacKenzie. "Pumping Iron John." In *Women Respond to the Men's Movement,* ed. Kay Leigh Hagan. San Francisco: Harper Collins, 1992.

Castoriadis, Cornelius. *The Imaginary Institution of Society.* Trans. Kathleen Blamey. Cambridge: MIT Press, 1987.

Chancer, Lynn S. *Reconcilable Differences: Confronting Beauty, Pornography, and the Future of Feminism.* Berkeley: University of California Press, 1998.

Chauncey, George, Jr. *Gay New York: Gender, Urban Culture, and the Making of the Gay Male World, 1890–1940.* New York: Basic Books, 1994.

Chesler, Phyllis. "The Men's Auxiliary: Protecting the Rule of Fathers." In *Women Respond to the Men's Movement,* ed. Kay Leigh Hagan. San Francisco: Harper Collins, 1992.

Chodorow, Nancy J. "Gender As Personal and Cultural Construction." *Signs* 20 (1995): 516–544.
——. *The Reproduction of Mothering: Psychoanalysis and the Sociology of Gender.* Berkeley: University of California Press, 1978.
Clews, Wayne. "As Not Seen on TV." *Gay Times*, June 1999.
Clifford, William K. "The Ethics of Belief." In *Lectures and Essays*, 2d ed., ed. Leslie Stephen and Frederick Pollock. New York: Macmillan, 1986.
Cohen, Felix S. *Handbook of Federal Indian Law.* Charlottesville, VA: Michie, 1982.
Coontz, Stephanie. *The Way We Never Were: American Families and the Nostalgia Trap.* New York: Basic Books, 1992.
Dallery, Arleen B. "The Politics of Writing (the) Body: Écriture Feminine." In *Gender/Body/Knowledge: Feminist Reconstructions of Being and Knowledge*, ed. Alison M. Jaggar and Susan R. Bordo. New Brunswick, NJ: Rutgers University Press, 1989.
Daly, Mary. *Gyn/Ecology: The Metaethics of Radical Feminism.* Boston: Beacon Press, 1978.
De Beauvoir, Simone. *The Second Sex.* Trans. H. M. Parshley. New York: Vintage, 1989.
——. *She Came to Stay.* New York: Norton, 1954.
De Lauretis, Theresa. *Technologies of Gender: Essays on Theory, Film, and Fiction.* Bloomington: Indiana University Press, 1987.
Deleuze, Gilles, and Félix Guattari. *Anti-Oedipus.* Vol. 1 of *Capitalism and Schizophrenia.* Trans. Robert Hurley, Mark Seem, and Helen R. Lane. Minneapolis: University of Minnesota Press, 1993.
——. *A Thousand Plateaus.* Vol. 2 of *Capitalism and Schizophrenia.* Trans. Brian Massumi. Minneapolis: University of Minnesota Press, 1993.
Deloria, Vine Jr., and Clifford Lytle. *American Indians, American Justice.* Austin: University of Texas Press, 1983.
D'Emilio, John. "Capitalism and the Gay Identity." In *The Lesbian and Gay Studies Reader*, ed. Henry Abelove, Michèle Aina Barale, and David M. Halperin. London: Routledge, 1993.
De Quincey, Thomas. *Confessions of an English Opium Eater.* London: Penguin Classics, 1986.
——. "Levana and Our Ladies of Sorrow." In *English Essays from Sir William Philip Sidney to Macaulay*, ed. Charles W. Eliot. New York: P. F. Collier and Son, 1937.
Di Stefano, Christine. "Dilemmas of Difference: Feminism, Modernity, and Postmodernism." In *Feminism/Postmodernism*, ed. Linda J. Nicholson. New York: Routledge, 1990.
Dworkin, Ronald. *Taking Rights Seriously.* Cambridge: Harvard University Press, 1977.
——. "What Is Equality?" *Philosophy and Public Affairs* 3 (1981): 185–246.
Echols, Alice. *Daring to Be Bad: Radical Feminism in America, 1967–1975.* Minneapolis: University of Minnesota Press, 1989.
Eisenstein, Hester. *Contemporary Feminist Thought.* Boston: G. K. Hall, 1983.
Elliott, Patricia. "More Thinking About Gender: A Response to Julie A. Nelson." *Hypatia* 9 (1994): 195–198.
Elshtain, Jean Bethke. *Public Man, Private Woman: Women in Social and Political Thought.* Princeton: Princeton University Press, 1993.
Escoffier, Jeffrey. "The Political Economy of the Closet: Notes Toward an Economic History of Gay and Lesbian Life Before Stonewall." In *Homo Eco-*

nomics: Capitalism, Community, and Lesbian and Gay Life, ed. Amy Gluckman and Betsy Reed. London: Routledge, 1997.

Featherstone, Mike. "The Body in Consumer Culture." In *The Body: Social Process and Cultural Theory*, ed. Mike Featherstone, Mike Hepworth, and Bryan S. Turner. London: Sage Publications, 1991.

Ferguson, Ann. "A Feminist Aspect Theory of the Self." In *Women, Knowledge, and Reality: Explorations in Feminist Philosophy*, ed. Ann Garry and Marilyn Pearsall. Boston: Unwin Hyman, 1989.

———. *Sexual Democracy: Women, Oppression, and Revolution*. Boulder, CO: Westview Press, 1991.

Findlay, J. N. *Hegel: A Re-Examination*. New York: Collier Macmillan, 1958.

Fineman, Martha Albertson. *The Neutered Mother, the Sexual Family, and Other Twentieth-Century Tragedies*. New York: Routledge, 1995.

Firestone, Shulamith. *The Dialectic of Sex: The Case for Feminist Revolution*. New York: Bantam Books, 1970.

Flax, Jane. "Postmodernism and Gender Relations in Feminist Theory." *Signs* 12 (1987): 621–643.

Foucault, Michel. *Birth of the Clinic: An Archaeology of Medical Perception*. New York: Vintage Books, 1994.

———. *The Care of the Self*. Vol. 3 of *The History of Sexuality*. Trans. Robert Hurley. New York: Vintage Books, 1986.

———. *An Introduction*. Vol. 1 of *The History of Sexuality*. Trans. Robert Hurley. New York: Vintage Books, 1980.

———. *The Use of Pleasure*. Vol. 2 of *The History of Sexuality*. Trans. Robert Hurley. New York: Penguin Books, 1985.

Friedan, Betty. *The Feminine Mystique*. New York: Norton, 1963.

Frye, Marilyn. *The Politics of Reality: Essays in Feminist Theory*. Freedom, CA: Crossing Press, 1983.

———. "The Possibility of a Feminist Theory." In *Theoretical Perspectives on Sexual Difference*, ed. Deborah L. Rhode. New Haven: Yale University Press, 1990.

Garland-Thomson, Rosemarie. "Narratives of Deviance and Delight: Staring at Julia Pastrana, the 'Extraordinary Lady.'" In *Beyond the Binary: American Identity and Multiculturalism*, ed. Timothy Powell. New Brunswick, NJ: Rutgers University Press, 1999.

Gilder, George. *Wealth and Poverty*. New York: Basic Books, 1981.

Gilligan, Carol. *In a Different Voice: Psychological Theory and Women's Development*. Cambridge: Harvard University Press, 1982.

Ginzberg, Ruth. "Audre Lorde's (nonessentialist) Lesbian Eros." *Hypatia* 7 (1992): 73–90.

Goffman, Erving. *Stigma: Notes on the Management of a Spoiled Identity*. New York: Simon and Schuster, 1986.

Grealy, Lucy. *Autobiography of a Face*. New York: Harperperennial Library, 1995.

Griffin, John. *Well-Being*. Oxford: Clarendon Press, 1986.

Grimshaw, Jean. "Autonomy and Identity in Feminist Thinking." In *Feminist Perspectives in Philosophy*, ed. Morwenna Griffiths and Margaret Whitford. Bloomington: Indiana University Press, 1988.

Grobsmith, Elizabeth. *Lakota of the Rosebud: A Contemporary Ethnography*. New York: Holt, Rinehart, and Winston, 1981.

Harvey, David. *The Conditions of Postmodernity: An Enquiry in the Origins of Cultural Change*. Oxford: Basil Blackwell, 1989.

Heilbrun, Carolyn G. *Towards a Recognition of Androgyny*. New York: Harper and Row, 1973.

Hewlett, Sylvia A. *A Lesser Life: The Myth of Women's Liberation in America*. New York: Warner, 1986.

Hill, Thomas E. *Autonomy and Self-Respect*. Cambridge: Cambridge University Press, 1991.

hooks, bell. *Yearning: Race, Gender, and Cultural Politics*. Boston: South End Press, 1990.

Hopkins, Patrick D. "How Feminism Made a Man of Me: The Proper Subject of Feminism and the Problem of Men." In *Men Doing Feminism*, ed. Tom Digby. New York: Routledge, 1998.

Jackson, John. "Sympathetic Soundbites Are Not Enough." *Gay Times*, June 1999.

Jaggar, Alison M. *Feminist Politics and Human Nature*. Totowa, NJ: Rowman and Allanheld, 1983.

———. "Human Biology in Feminist Theory: Sexual Equality." In *Beyond Domination: New Perspectives on Women and Philosophy*, ed. Carol C. Gould. Totowa, NJ: Rowman and Allanheld, 1983.

———. "Sexual Difference and Sexual Equality." In *Theoretical Perspectives on Sexual Difference*, ed. Deborah L. Rhode. New Haven: Yale University Press, 1990.

James, William. "The Will to Believe." In *The Will to Believe and Other Essays in Popular Philosophy*. Reading, PA: Longmans, Green, 1987.

Jencks, Christopher. "Who Must We Treat Equally for Educational Opportunity to Be Equal?" *Ethics* 98 (1988): 518–533.

Kates, Steven Maxwell. *Twenty Million New Customers! Understanding Gay Men's Consumer Behavior*. London: Haworth Press, 1998.

Keith, Michael. "Angry Writing: (Re)presenting the Unethical World of the Ethnographer." *Environment and Planning D: Society and Space* 10 (1992): 551–568.

Kirk, G. S., J. E. Raven, and N. Schofeld. *The Pre-Socratic Philosophers*. Cambridge: Cambridge University Press, 1983.

Knopp, Lawrence. "Sexuality and the Spatial Dynamics of Capitalism." *Environment and Planning D: Society and Space* 10 (1992): 651–669.

Kukathas, C., and P. Pettit. *Rawls: A Theory of Justice and Its Critics*. Stanford: Stanford University Press, 1990.

Levine, Judith. *My Enemy, My Love: Women, Men, and the Dilemmas of Gender*. New York: Doubleday, 1992.

Lorde, Audre. "The Uses of the Erotic." In *Sister Outsider: Essays and Speeches*. Freedom, CA: Crossing Press, 1984.

Lugones, María C. "Playfulness, 'World'-Traveling, and Loving Perception." In *Feminist Social Thought: A Reader*, ed. Diana Tietjens Meyers. New York: Routledge, 1997. Originally published in *Women, Knowledge, and Reality: Explorations in Feminist Philosophy*, ed. Ann Garry and Marilyn Pearsall. Boston: Unwin Hyman, 1989.

Lutholtz, William M. *Grand Dragon: D. C. Stephenson and the Ku Klux Klan in Indiana*. West Lafayette, IN: Purdue University Press, 1991.

Mann, Patricia. "Glancing at Pornography: Recognizing Men." In *Feminist Social Thought: A Reader*, ed. Diana Tietjens Meyers. New York: Routledge, 1997.

Mason, Angela, and Anya Palmer. *Queer Bashing: A National Survey of Hate Crimes Against Lesbians and Gay Men*. London: Stonewall, 1996.

Meyers, Diana Tietjens. "Intersectional Identity and the Authentic Self? Opposites Attract!" In *Relational Autonomy*, ed. Catriona MacKenzie and Natalie Stoljar. New York: Oxford University Press, forthcoming.

———. *Self, Society, and Personal Choice*. New York: Columbia University Press, 1989.

———. *Subjection and Subjectivity: Psychoanalytic Feminism and Moral Philosophy*. New York: Routledge, 1994.

Minow, Martha. *Making All the Difference: Inclusion, Exclusion, and American Law*. Ithaca, NY: Cornell University Press, 1990.

Mitchell, Don. "The End of Public Space? People's Park, Definitions of the Public, and Democracy." *Annals of the Association of American Geographers* 1, no. 85 (1995): 108–133.

Morrison, Toni. *Beloved*. New York: Plume, 1998.

Mort, Frank. *Cultures of Consumption: Masculinities and Social Space in Late Twentieth Century Britain*. London: Routledge, 1996.

Murphry, D. "America's Civilizational Crisis: The Rise of Internal Barbarism." *Conservative Review*, October 1993.

Murphy, Robert. *The Body Silent*. New York: W. W. Norton, 1990.

Myslik, Wayne D. "Renegotiating the Social/Sexual Identities of Places: Gay Communities As Safe Havens or Sites of Resistance?" In *Bodyspace: Destabilizing Geographies of Gender and Sexuality*, ed. Nancy Duncan. London: Routledge, 1996.

Neihardt, John G. *Black Elk Speaks*. New York: Pocket Books, 1972.

Nelson, Julie A. "More Thinking About Gender: Reply." *Hypatia* 9 (1994): 199–205.

Nicholson, Linda J., ed. *Feminism/Postmodernism*. New York: Routledge, 1990.

Nietzsche, Friedrich. *The Birth of Tragedy Out of the Spirit of Music*. Trans. Walter Kaufmann. New York: Vintage, 1967.

Noddings, Nel. *Caring: A Feminine Approach to Ethics and Moral Education*. Berkeley: University of California Press, 1984.

Northmore, David. "Flower Power in the Heart of Soho." *Pink Paper*, 21 May 1999.

Nozick, Robert. *Anarchy, State, and Utopia*. New York: Basic Books, 1974.

O'Brien, Mary. *The Politics of Reproduction*. Boston: Routledge and Kegan Paul, 1981.

Olson, Frances E. "The Family and the Market: A Study of Ideology and Legal Reform." *Harvard Law Review* 96 (1983): 1497–1578.

Ostling, Richard N. "Man Trouble: Broken Promises?" *Time*, 13 July 1998.

Pascal, Blaise. *Pensées and Other Writings*. Trans. Honor Levi. Oxford: Oxford University Press, 1995.

Passover Haggadah with Music. New York: Hebrew Publishing, 1912.

Penelope, Julia. *Call Me Lesbian: Lesbian Lives, Lesbian Theory*. Freedom, CA: Crossing Press, 1992.

Pielke, Robert G. "Are Androgyny and Sexuality Compatible?" In *"Femininity," "Masculinity," and "Androgyny": A Modern Philosophical Discussion*, ed. Mary Vetterling-Braggin. Totowa, NJ: Littlefield Adams, 1982.

Pogge, Thomas W. *Realizing Rawls*. Ithaca, NY: Cornell University Press, 1989.

Polchin, James. "Having Something to Wear: The Landscape of Identity on Christopher Street." In *Queers in Space: Communities/Public Spaces/Sites of Resistance*, ed. Gordon Brent Ingram, Anne-Marie Bouthillette, and Yolanda Retter. Seattle: Bay Press, 1997.

Popenoe, David. *Life Without Father: Compelling New Evidence That Fatherhood and Marriage Are Indispensable for the Good of Children and Society.* Cambridge: Harvard University Press, 1996.

Quilley, Stephen. "Constructing Manchester's 'New Urban Village': Gay Space in the Entrepreneurial City." In *Queers in Space: Communities/Public Spaces/Sites of Resistance,* ed. Gordon Brent Ingram, Anne-Marie Bouthillette, and Yolanda Retter. Seattle: Bay Press, 1997.

Quinn, Philip. *Divine Commands and Moral Requirements.* Oxford: Clarendon, 1987.

Rawls, John. "Justice As Fairness: Political Not Metaphysical." In *Equality and Liberty,* ed. Kai Nielsen. Totowa, NJ: Rowman and Allanheld, 1985.

———. *A Theory of Justice.* Cambridge: Harvard University Press, 1971.

Raymond, Janice. *The Transsexual Empire.* London: Women's Press, 1979.

Rhode, Deborah L. *Justice and Gender.* Cambridge: Harvard University Press, 1989.

———. *Theoretical Perspectives on Sexual Difference.* New Haven: Yale University Press, 1990.

Richards, Janet Radcliffe. *The Sceptical Feminist: A Philosophical Inquiry.* Harmondsworth, England: Penguin Books, 1980.

———. "Separate Spheres." In *Applied Ethics,* ed. Peter Singer. Oxford: Oxford University Press, 1986.

Richardson, Colin. "Police Hate." *Gay Times,* May 1999.

———. "Police Under Pressure to Review Michael Booth Murder." *Gay Times,* June 1999.

Ricouer, Paul. *Time and Narrative.* Vol. 1. Trans. Kathleen McLaughlin and David Pellauer. Chicago: University of Chicago Press, 1984.

Rosenberg, Rosalind. *Divided Lives: American Women in the Twentieth Century.* New York: Hill and Wang, 1992.

Roseneil, Sasha. "Greenham Revisited: Researching Myself and My Sisters." In *Interpreting the Field: Accounts of Ethnography,* ed. Dick Hobbs and Tim May. Oxford: Oxford University Press, 1993.

Rothenburg, Tamar. "'And She Told Two Friends': Lesbians Creating Urban Social Space." In *Mapping Desire: Geographies of Sexualities,* ed. David Bell and Gill Valentine. London: Routledge, 1995.

Rubin, Gayle. "The Traffic in Women: Notes on the 'Political Economy' of Sex." In *Toward an Anthropology of Women,* ed. Rayna R. Rapp. New York: Monthly Review Press, 1975.

Sandel, Michael. *Liberalism and the Limits of Justice.* Cambridge: Cambridge University Press, 1982.

Sanderson, Terry. "Mediawatch." *Gay Times,* June 1999.

Sartre, Jean-Paul. *Being and Nothingness.* Trans. Hazel E. Barnes. New York: Simon and Schuster, 1956.

Scott, Joan Wallach. *Gender and the Politics of History.* New York: Columbia University Press, 1988.

Serlin, David. "The Twilight (Zone) of Commercial Sex." In *Policing Public Sex,* ed. Dangerous Bedfellows. Boston: South End Press, 1996.

Sloterdijk, Peter. *Critique of Cynical Reason.* Trans. Michael Eldred. Minneapolis: University of Minnesota Press, 1987.

Soble, Alan. *The Philosophy of Sex: Contemporary Readings.* 2d ed. Savage, MD: Rowman and Littlefield, 1991.

Sommers, Christina. "Philosophers Against the Family." In *Vice and Virtue in*

Everyday Life: Introductory Readings in Ethics, ed. Christina Sommers and Fred Sommers. Fort Worth, TX: Harcourt Brace Jovanovich, 1993.

Spinoza, Baruch. *The Ethics*. Trans. R. H. M. Elwes. New York: Dover, 1955.

Stambaugh, Joan. *The Formless Self*. Albany: State University of New York Press, 1999.

Sterba, James P. "Understanding Evil: American Slavery, the Holocaust, and the Conquest of the American Indians." *Ethics* 106 (1996): 424–448.

Stoltenberg, John. *Refusing to Be a Man: Essays on Sex and Justice*. New York: Penguin Books, 1989.

Taylor, Charles. *The Ethics of Authenticity*. Cambridge: Harvard University Press, 1991.

Torres, Gerald, and Kathryn Milun. "Translating Yonnondio by Precedent and Evidence: The Mashpee Indian Case." *Duke Law Journal* 4 (1990): 625–659.

Trask, Haunani-Kay. *From a Native Daughter: Colonialism and Sovereignty in Hawai'i*. Honolulu: University of Hawaii Press, 1993.

———. "Politics in the Pacific Islands: Imperialism and Native Self-Determination." In *Hawaii: Return to Nationhood*, ed. Ulla Hasager and Jonathan Friedman. Copenhagen: International Work Group for Indigenous People, 1994.

Trebilcot, Joyce. "Two Forms of Androgynism." In *"Femininity," "Masculinity," and "Androgyny": A Modern Philosophical Discussion*, ed. Mary Vetterling-Braggin. Totowa, NJ: Littlefield Adams, 1982.

Valentine, Gill. "Out and About: Geographies of Lesbian Landscapes." *International Journal of Urban and Regional Research* 19 (1995): 96–111.

———. "(Re)negotiating the 'Heterosexual Street': Lesbian Production of Space." In *Bodyspace*, ed. Nancy Duncan. London: Routledge, 1996.

Veblin, Thorstein. "The Theory of the Leisure Class." In *Poverty and Wealth*, ed. K. Alrutz et al. Washington, D.C.: University Press of America, 1982.

Vetterling-Braggin, Mary. "Introduction to Notions of Sex and Gender." In *"Femininity," "Masculinity," and "Androgyny": A Modern Philosophical Discussion*. Totowa, NJ: Littlefield Adams, 1982.

Walzer, Michael. *Spheres of Justice*. New York: Basic Books, 1983.

Warren, Mary Anne. "Is Androgyny the Answer to Sexual Stereotyping?" In *"Femininity," "Masculinity," and "Androgyny": A Modern Philosophical Discussion*, ed. Mary Vetterling-Braggin. Totowa, NJ: Littlefield Adams, 1982.

Wasserstrom, Richard. "Sex Roles and the Ideal Society." In *Vice and Virtue in Everyday Life: Introductory Readings in Ethics*, ed. Christina Sommers and Fred Sommers. Fort Worth, TX: Harcourt Brace Jovanovich, 1993.

Watson, Justin. *The Christian Coalition: Dreams of Restoration, Demands for Recognition*. New York: St. Martin's Press, 1997.

Weston, Kath. "Get Thee to a Big City: Sexual Imaginary and the Great Gay Migration." *GLQ: A Journal of Lesbian and Gay Studies* 2 (1995): 253–277.

Whitman, Walt. *Leaves of Grass*. New York: Bantam Classics and Loveswept, 1983.

Whittle, Stephen. "Consuming Differences: The Collaboration of the Gay Body with the Cultural State." In *The Margins of the City: Gay Men's Urban Lives*. ed. S. Whittle. Aldershot, England: Ashgate Publishing, 1994.

Williams, Joan C. "Deconstructing Gender." *Michigan Law Review* 87 (1989): 797–845. Reprinted in *Feminist Legal Theory: Readings in Law and Gender*, ed. Katherine T. Bartlett and Rosanne Kennedy. Boulder, CO: Westview Press, 1991.

Williams, Patricia. *The Alchemy of Race and Rights*. Cambridge: Harvard University Press, 1991.

Williams, Robert A., Jr. "Documents of Barbarism: The Contemporary Legacy of European Racism and Colonialism in the Narrative Traditions of Federal Indian Law." *Arizona Law Review* 31 (1999): 237–278.

Wittig, Monique. *The Straight Mind and Other Essays*. New York: Harvester, 1992.

Woolf, Virginia. *A Room of One's Own*. Harmondsworth, England: Penguin Books, 1928.

Young, Iris Marion. "Gender As Seriality: Thinking About Women As a Social Collective." *Signs* 19 (1994): 713–738.

———. *Justice and the Politics of Difference*. Princeton: Princeton University Press, 1990.

Zita, Jacquelyn N. "Male Lesbians and the Postmodernist Body." *Hypatia* 7 (1992): 106–127.

Editors and Contributors

Sandra Bartky is professor of philosophy at the University of Illinois at Chicago Circle and an active member of the University of Illinois women's studies program. She writes essays on phenomenology, feminism, and Marxism. The essays collected in her book *Femininity and Domination: Studies in the Phenomenology of Oppression* have been widely influential in feminist philosophy.

Sigal R. Benporath is lecturer of philosophy at the School of Education, Tel Aviv University, Israel. She recently received her doctoral degree in philosophy. She specializes in political philosophy, philosophy of education, and feminist philosophy. Her publications include "Rights of Worst-Off Groups in a Just Society" (in Hebrew) in *Journal of Welfare* and "Sophie's Choice: Feminist Moral Education" (written with Yael Tamir in Hebrew) in *Moral Education*.

Gavin Brown is a professional administrator at the University of East London, where he is also a graduate research student in the Department of Sociology and Anthropology. He originally trained as an artist and has been active in the antiracist, trade union, and other progressive campaigns for more than fifteen years. His current research focuses on the queer spaces of East London, where he lives. His publications include "The Queer Spaces of Tower Hamlets: Gay Men and the Regeneration of an East London Borough" in *Rising East: The Journal of East London Studies*.

Jeffrey Bussolini is a lecturer of sociology at Baruch College, City University of New York. He is completing a doctorate in sociology at the CUNY Graduate School, and his dissertation examines the history and culture of Los Alamos, New Mexico, emphasizing the ontology of nuclear physics and molecular biology.

Yolanda Estes is assistant professor of philosophy at Mississippi State University, specializing in German idealism (particularly the philosophy of Fichte) and feminist ethical philosophy. She is a participant in the women's studies program. Her publications include "The Myth of the Happy Hooker" (written with Clelia Smyth) in *Violence Against Women: Legal, Medical, and Philosophical Dimensions*.

Arnold Lorenzo Farr is assistant professor of philosophy at Saint Joseph's University in Philadelphia, specializing in nineteenth-century philosophy, social theory, and philosophy of race. He is the author of articles on Kant, Fichte, and the philosophy of race and is currently completing *Reading Farrakhan, Reading America: An Essay on Racialized Consciousness and the Obstruction of Understanding.*

Rosemarie Garland-Thomson is associate professor of English literature at Howard University, specializing in literary criticism and Afro-American literature. She writes about the cultural manifestations of illness and disability. Her recent work in this area includes *Extraordinary Bodies: Figuring Physical Disability in American Culture* and *Literature and Freakery: Cultural Spectacles of the Extraordinary Body.*

Patrick D. Hopkins is assistant professor of philosophy at Ripon College in Wisconsin, specializing in ethics, biomedical ethics, philosophy of technology, and social philosophy. He has published essays on euthanasia, masculinity, and medical technology. Most recently, he coedited *Rethinking Masculinity: Philosophical Explorations in Light of Feminism.*

Diana Tietjens Meyers is professor of philosophy at the University of Connecticut, where she specializes in social and political philosophy and feminist philosophy. On these topics she has written numerous articles, edited six volumes, and written four books, among these *Inalienable Rights: A Defense, Self, Society, and Personal Choice* and *Subjection and Subjectivity.*

Wallace A. Murphree is professor of philosophy and religion at Mississippi State University, where he has taught for more than thirty years. While his early work was on Whitehead and the philosophy of mind, his recent emphases have been in logic and the philosophy of religion. In the latter area, he has published "Natural Theology: Theism or Atheism?" and "Faith for Atheists and Agnostics" in *Sophia.*

Christine Overall is professor of philosophy and an associate dean for the faculty of arts and sciences at Queen's University, Kingston, Ontario, Canada. She is the author of *A Feminist I: Reflections from Academia, Human Reproduction: Principles, Practices, and Policies,* and *Ethics and Human Reproduction: A Feminist Analysis.* She writes a weekly feminist column for the *Kingston Whig Standard* and is the mother of two children.

Patricia Smith is professor of philosophy at Baruch College, City University of New York, specializing in legal, social, and feminist philosophy. She is the author of articles on legal, social, and feminist philosophy and on reproduction as well as of two recent books, *Feminist Jurisprudence* and *Liberalism and Affirmative Obligation.* She is presently completing *The Reproductive Revolution,* which considers the impact of sexual changes on fundamental social values.

Clelia Smyth is an educational adviser for the University of Kentucky Dental School and a member of the ethics board at the University of Kentucky Medical Center. She specializes in feminist ontology, sexuality, and phenomenology of the body. Her publications include "The Myth of the Happy Hooker" (written with Yolanda Estes) in *Violence Against Women: Legal, Medical, and Philosophical Dimensions.*

Rebecca Tsosie is associate professor of law and executive director of the Indian legal program at Arizona State University. A Native American, she specializes in federal Indian law, cultural property, and Indian environmental issues. She focuses her writing on the political identity of indigenous peoples and indigenous rights, especially as related to environmental and cultural issues.

Jami Weinstein is a lecturer of philosophy at Baruch College, City University of New York. She is pursuing a doctorate in the history of technology at L'École des Hautes Études en Sciences Sociales in Paris. She is completing her dissertation, entitled "Technobody," on the phenomenology and ontology of the body as it relates to technology. Her publications include "On the Leveling of the Genre Distinction Between Theory and Fiction" in *Conference: A Journal of Philosophy and Theory.*

Index

www.ingramcontent.com/pod-product-compliance
Lightning Source LLC
Chambersburg PA
CBHW050646270326
41927CB00012B/2888